FACTORY-ORIGINAL
MG T-SERIES

FACTORY-ORIGINAL
MG T-SERIES

The originality guide to MG TA, TB, TC, TD & TF, including special bodies

BY ANDERS DITLEV CLAUSAGER
PHOTOGRAPHY BY SIMON CLAY

Herridge & Sons

Published in 2019 by
Herridge & Sons Ltd
Lower Forda, Shebbear
Beaworthy, Devon EX21 5SY

Reprinted 2023

© Copyright Anders Ditlev Clausager 2019

Design: Muse Fine Art & Design

All rights reserved. No part of this publication may be reproduced in any form or by any means without the prior written permission of the publisher and the copyright holder.

ISBN 978-1-906133-80-1
Printed in China

CONTENTS

ACKNOWLEDGEMENTS 6

T-SERIES PAST AND PRESENT 8

THE TA, TB AND TC MODELS 28

THE TD AND TF MODELS. 84

SPECIALS AND SPECIAL-BODIED CARS. 130

BUYING GUIDE. 155

ACKNOWLEDGEMENTS

It was in 1989 that Charles Herridge first asked me to write a book on the MG T-series, and I am a little amazed that thirty years later, I now find myself doing an updated version of that book, still working with Charles, as well as Ed Herridge. Even if you already possess a copy of my *Original MG T-Series* (which has been kept in print for most of the years in between) we hope that you will find some additional and new information in the present volume.

Much of the information has remained more or less as it was, but I have taken the opportunity in many cases to revisit the original source material, or have followed up amendments and corrections which have appeared elsewhere in the still-growing canon of MG T-series literature – a selection of suggested further reading appears below.

Compared to 1989, we now have that remarkable resource the internet, and there is a lot of information available from many websites. Obviously one has to treat some of this with a degree of circumspection, since errors and misunderstandings are only too easily enshrined through the relentless copying which seems to be the norm in the digital world, perhaps more so than in the days when we simply had printed media. However, there is no doubt that the internet means that a lot of material, which might otherwise have languished in limited-circulation specialised club publications, has become available to a wider public. I have used many websites as well as books and magazines, and primary archive sources, for the research for the present volume.

To enhance the previous volume, there is now an extended back story to the T-series in the sections headed "Past and Present", and somewhat in contradiction to the title *Factory-Original* there is also a substantial section devoted to specials and special-bodied cars, which have sometimes been rather neglected in MG histories.

Most of the modern photography of the cars featured in this book was shot by Simon Clay, who also provided some photos from his existing portfolio of MG cars, but we are very grateful that Frank Langridge in New Zealand owner of TB0498 and Tim Jackson owner of TC0999 both volunteered to help us out with their own photos of their cars, in Tim's case especially as he had documented his restoration in detail, which yielded many informative shots of parts which are otherwise hard to photograph. The full list of owners who kindly permitted their cars to be featured in the book is as follows:

Kevin and Melanie Howe	white TA, BDF 315
Andy and Angie King	TA prototype, CJO 617, and black TA, MG 6317
Martin Curren	green TA Tickford drophead coupé, DOR 33
Frank Langridge	black TB, "MG TB"
Georg Cummin	black TB, DRY 70
Tim Jackson	black TC, RSU 772
Jim Pielow	Clipper Blue TC, KYL 878
John Hinds	MG Red TD, KVU 27
Barry Lomas	black TD Mark II, 762 UYS
Malcolm Reid,	Almond Green TF 1250, HHS 138
Mike Coope	Birch Grey TF 1500, 745 UYH

Our thanks to all of you. Other images came from Andrea and Malcolm Green, Stewart Penfound, Hagen Nyncke, Roly Alcock, Dr Stefan Dierkes, Dansk Veteranbil Klub, the BMIHT archive, the publisher's archive, and my own collection.

As well as supplying illustrations, Andrea and Malcolm Green, Stewart Penfound, and Dr Stefan Dierkes, were also most helpful when I researched the various special-bodied cars. We'd also like to thank the archive team of the BMIHT at Gaydon, especially Charlotte Gallant and Richard Bacchus; Ian Ferguson and colleagues in the library of the VSCC at Chipping Norton; Peter Neal in the archive of the MG Car Club at Abingdon; Terry Sanders of the Arnolt Register in the USA; Ian Palmer, Sally Silcock, and Barrie Jones of the MG Car Club's T register; Roy Miller, Roger Muir, and Brian Rainbow of the MG Octagon Car Club.

For the reader in search of further information on MG T-series cars, the following bibliography may be useful, but bear in mind that many of these titles are now out of print:

Anon *MG Car Club T-Register Yearbook* (various years from 1987 to 2003-2004 but sadly not published since)
Blower, WE *The MG Workshop Manual* (Motor Racing Publications ca. 1952, and numerous editions since; still in print!)
Clausager, Anders Ditlev *Essential MG T Series and Pre-War Midgets* (Bay View Books, 1995)
Edwards, Jonathan (pseud.) *MG TF Super Profile* (Haynes, 1984)
Green, Andrea *M.G.s on Patrol* (Magna Press, 1999)
Green, Malcolm *MG T Series Restoration Guide* (Brooklands Books, 1993-2011)
Harvey, Chris *MG The Immortal T Series* (Oxford Illustrated Press, 1977)
Jacobs, Dick *An MG Experience* (Transport Bookman Publications, 1976)
Knowles, David *MG The Untold Story* (Windrow & Greene, 1997)
Knudson, Richard L and Old, F E *The T-series Handbook* (The New England MG T Register, 1981)
Knudson, Richard L *M.G.: The Sports Car America Loved First* (Motorcars Unlimited, 1975)
Nyncke, Hagen und Schrader, Halwart *MG Aus Liebe zum Sportwagen* (Copress Verlag & Rover Deutschland, 1999)
Penfound, Stewart *Harry Lester His Cars & The Monkey Stable* (BR Books, 2015)
Robson, Graham *MG T-Series The Complete Story* (Crowood Press, 1998-2014)
Robson, Graham *The T-series MG: A Collector's Guide* (Motor Racing Publications, 1980, and later editions)
Schach, Horst *The Complete M.G. TD Restoration Manual* (The New England MG T Register, 1996)
Sherrell, Michael *TCs Forever!* (Mike's Garages, 1991)
Thomas, Roger *M.G. Trials Cars* (Magna Press, 1995)
Willmer, Paddy *MG T Series In Detail* (Herridge & Sons, 2005)
Wilson, Roger *History of the MPJG XPAG and XPEG Engines and Transmissions* (MG Car Club T Register, 2012, 2014)

The list is probably incomplete. Not included are the general MG histories, of which *MG by McComb* originally by F Wilson McComb (Dent, 1972) and later updated by Jonathan Wood (Osprey, 1978-98), must still be considered as the best. In addition, there are now reprints of many original factory publications for T-series cars, e.g sales brochures, handbooks, parts lists, and the TD/TF workshop manual, some in downloadable pdf form from various websites. Of contemporary magazines, *The Autocar, Autosport, Light Car, The Motor, Motor Racing, Motor Sport, Motor Trader, Practical Motorist, Road & Track*, and the Nuffield Exports publication *News Exchange* have yielded material. Many of these original articles have been reproduced in the handy compendiums published by Brooklands Books.

Anders Ditlev Clausager Birmingham June 2019

T-SERIES PAST AND PRESENT

The M-type was MG's first Midget, introduced in 1928, with a boat-tailed two-seater body, originally fabric covered. It was based on the chassis of the Morris Minor, complete with overhead camshaft engine of 847cc. (Photo copyright BMIHT)

When the first MG cars were made in 1924, the small affordable sports car for the less wealthy enthusiast was already a well-established idea. The pioneers had been the cyclecars which had begun to appear from 1910 onwards, at first in France but soon also in Britain, and in other countries, although more rarely. Intended as cheap transport for the motorist of moderate means, the cyclecars were usually mechanically simple, even crude, with air-cooled single- or twin-cylinder motorcycle-type engines, often with belt drive, and sometimes with three wheels.

In 1912, the international federation of motorcycle clubs agreed to classify cyclecars in two categories by weight and engine size, small up to 300kg (661lb) and 750cc, and large up to 350kg (771lb) and 1100cc. The latter category spilled over into the light car class proper, which also gained rapidly in popularity between 1910 and 1914.

There were in round figures about 100 makes of cyclecar in France but no fewer than 150 in Britain, which were the two most important producing countries. Soon there were clubs, magazines and races for cyclecars. Among the more sporting types were the French Bédélia, and in Britain the GN. The Bédélia had been the pioneer of its type in 1910. Among the later entrants to the cyclecar group were the French Amilcar and Salmson, both from about 1920. Salmson began by making a GN under licence but, like Amilcar, soon offered more conventional small cars.

Around the same time, the Rover Eight with an air-cooled two-cylinder engine enjoyed commercial success in Britain. Then the Austin Seven was introduced in 1922. With its miniature water-cooled four-cylinder engine and two-plus-two seating, it offered a degree of refinement and practicality that no cyclecar could match. Its French equivalents were the Citroën 5CV and the Peugeot Quadrilette.

These "proper" light cars quickly replaced most of the cyclecars, except in France where small cyclecars attracted lower road tax (as three-wheelers did in Britain) and some had performance enough to appeal to sporting drivers. This was the case for the Amilcar and Salmson, and for the Derby, Rally and BNC which followed. These small French sports cars most likely influenced developments also in Britain, where racing versions of the Austin Seven appeared in 1923 and sporting models were added to the catalogued Austin range for 1924.

MG: THE BEGINNINGS

This was around the time that an enterprising young garage manager began to realise his ambition of making cars. This was Cecil Kimber (1888-1945), and the company where he worked was The Morris Garages of Oxford. This business had been founded by William Morris (later Lord Nuffield, 1877-1963) in 1910, and when Morris began to make cars at Cowley out-

A charming if impractical alternative to the M-type two-seater was this Sportsman's coupé. (Photo copyright BMIHT)

*With the C-type of 1931, MG had a powerful entrant in the small-capacity racing classes. These C-types did outstandingly well in the Double-Twelve race at Brooklands.
(Photo copyright BMIHT)*

side Oxford in 1912 his original garage business became the Oxfordshire distributorship for the cars. As William Morris now spent his time running the car manufacturing company he employed a manager to look after the garage business, and Kimber, who had joined as sales manager in 1921, succeeded to this position in 1922.

Kimber later expressed his philosophy as making a car which was 10 per cent better than standard, and charging 50 per cent more for it – perhaps a rather cynical approach, but I suspect it is a business model which will be well recognised by the motor industry today! His cars had to be based on components from the Morris "Bullnose" cars which were the bread-and-butter of the garage business. Kimber's talent as a body designer was clear almost from the start, but it seems unlikely that he set out specifically to make sports cars; his early products were better described as "fast tourers".

Kimber's cars were at first called "MG Super Sports Morris", or soon just MG, from the initial letters of the garage business. They were special-bodied cars based on little-modified chassis and mechanical components of the Morris Oxford, with a four-cylinder 1800cc side-valve engine rated at 14 RAC hp. The MG range from the start included open two- and four-seaters as well as saloons – even a landaulette! There was also a very special sporting one-off built for Kimber to use in the Land's End Trial in 1925: the famed "Old Number One" which despite its name was not the first MG.

Gradually over the period from 1923/24 to 1927, Kimber's MGs evolved their own special character and features, and acquired an image and status increasingly different from the Morris models on which they were based. They were sufficiently successful for Kimber to persuade his boss, William Morris, to set up a proper factory to make MG cars, and in 1927 production moved to Edmund Road at Cowley.

Morris Motors had now become Britain's largest car manufacturer and spread its wings by introducing several new models from 1926 onwards. These included, in 1927, the company's first six-cylinder car, with a 2468cc single overhead camshaft engine, and in 1928 the first Morris Minor, also with an ohc engine, of four cylinders and 847cc. This gave Morris a rival to the popular Austin Seven.

The Minor had been designed by the Wolseley company in Birmingham, which William Morris had bought after it went bankrupt in 1926. Under his direction, Wolseley introduced a new range of cars. These all had overhead-camshaft engines with a vertical shaft driving the camshaft, a feature which Wolseley had originally adopted in 1919; this design had been inspired by the Hispano-Suiza aero engines which they had made under licence during World War One.

An unusual feature of the Minor engine was that the drive shaft was also the armature shaft of a vertically-mounted dynamo. This idea had come from an engine designed by EG Wrigley of Birmingham, a company which Morris had bought in 1923 and which had become Morris Commercial Cars; incidentally, Kimber had worked for Wrigley before joining Morris. Wolseley made these engines for the Morris Minors until the ohc-engined model was discontinued in 1932, and they continued to make ohc engines for MG, as well as for their own cars, until 1936.

The new chassis developed for the C-type was quickly adopted for road-going production cars, starting with the D-type Midget, which was only available in four-seater open or closed form. (Photo copyright BMIHT)

BIRTH OF THE MIDGET

Both the new Morris cars attracted Kimber's attention in turn. The Morris Six engine was fitted in a redesigned chassis and this car became the MG Six or 18/80, a fast tourer somewhat in the mould of the Bentley or Lagonda 3 litre. Launched in August 1928, the 18/80 became reasonably successful and would remain in production until 1933.

Kimber also got his hands on the Morris Minor. He took the standard Minor chassis, which with a few modifications became an MG: a mildly-tuned engine, a new radiator, and a boat-tailed two-seater body of the cheap, and therefore popular, lightweight fabric construction. This car was launched as the MG Midget M-type at the Olympia Motor Show in October 1928, with a price of £175, which was £50, or 40 per cent more than a Morris Minor tourer. It has been described as "Britain's first really cheap and practical sports car… it was more an MG and less a Morris than any of Kimber's earlier cars."

At first, the engine and chassis were barely changed from the Morris Minor. With a single SU 1 1/8in carburettor and a compression ratio of 5.4:1, the 847cc engine of 57mm by 83mm bore and stroke developed 20bhp at 4000rpm, which was later improved to 27bhp at 4500rpm thanks to a new camshaft with improved valve timing. The gearbox had three speeds but on later cars a four-speed box became optional.

Morris made much of the fact that, unlike the primitive Austin Seven, the Minor had a proper chassis, semi-elliptic leaf springs front and rear, and coupled four-wheel brakes. These features were inherited by the Midget. On the early cars the brakes were rod-operated and the hand brake worked on the transmission, while later cars acquired cable-operated brakes with the handbrake working on all four wheels. The bolt-on wire wheels were fixed to three studs. The wheelbase was 6ft 6in (1981mm) and track 3ft 6in (1067mm). The fabric-bodied car weighed 1134lb (515kg), and would do about 65mph (105km/h). Later on, MG offered an alternative metal-panelled two-seater weighing 128 lb (582kg), and there was also a charming but impractical sportsman's coupé, MG's first small closed car, which cost a not inconsiderable £245.

The M-type became not only a commercial success, with over 3200 made up to 1932, but also scored MG's first important success in serious motor racing, when three of these cars won the team prize in the Double-Twelve race at Brooklands in May 1930. As night-time racing was not allowed at Brooklands, this race was held over two days, in two twelve-hour sessions, hence the name. By then, MG had moved again, this time to a factory at Abingdon-on-Thames south of Oxford which would be the company's home until 1980.

The MG Car Company had been set up in 1928 as a subsidiary of The Morris Garages but it now became an independent limited company, with a share capital of £19,000 held by Morris Industries Limited, William Morris's personal holding company, except for five £1 shares which were allocated to Morris personally, to his secretary, his solicitor, his accountant, and to Cecil Kimber, who became managing director.

MG now began to grow and expand the model range. Somehow, the company got hold of an example of the French Rally sports car, and the chassis of this served as the pattern for a new MG chassis which was underslung at the rear, i.e. the frame side members passed below the rear axle. Other ideas added by MG's chief engineer Hubert Noel Charles were tubular cross members, and road springs whose rear ends were fitted in sliding bronze trunnions rather than shackles.

The first prototype to use the new chassis design was EX.120 (EX for Experimental), which was subsequently much modified by Ernest Eldridge and George Eyston for record breaking. It went on to set a number of Class H (750cc) speed records. Eyston reached over 103mph (166km/h) at Montlhéry in France in February 1931, with a 743cc supercharged engine based on the M-type unit. This was the first time a 750cc car had run at over 100mph and was a new class world record: the first of many for MG.

Within a few months, MG had produced a batch of racing Midgets, the C-types or Montlhéry models, with a new 746cc engine featuring a shorter 73mm stroke. It was at first

In 1932, the Midget range was completely renewed, with the M-, C-, and D-types, being replaced by the J models. The J2 two-seater was the biggest seller. This was the factory demonstrator road-tested by The Autocar.

unsupercharged, and with a compression ratio of 8.5:1 and a carburettor of 1¼in developed 37.4bhp at 6000rpm. A Powerplus supercharger soon became available, and later cars had a cross-flow cylinder head, so power eventually went up to 52.5bhp. With the supercharger, top speed was 88mph (142km/h), but the price in this form was no less than £575.

Thirteen C-types took part in the 1931 Double-Twelve race. Seven of them finished, including taking first to fifth places, and C-types also took the team award. Further successes followed during the 1931 season, and MG built a new record car based on the C-type, EX.127, which became famous as the "Magic Midget". This car broke the 120mph barrier, and later when sold to German driver Bobby Kohlrausch even covered a flying mile at just over 140mph.

FROM C VIA D AND J TO P

At that autumn's Motor Show MG introduced two new road cars which both used the basic chassis design from the C-type. The D-type Midget was a miniature four-seater with the up-rated 27bhp version of the M-type engine and a longer wheelbase of at first 7ft (2134mm) and later 7ft 2in (2184mm). Improvements included a remote control for the gear change, centre-lock wire wheels, and a rear-mounted petrol tank. It was offered as an open car or a closed "salonette". The D-type was heavier, weighing 1484lb (674kg) for the open car, which cost £210, and top speed is estimated as 55-60mph (88-97km/h).

The F-type Magna was a new departure: a small six-cylinder car with a 1271cc engine which was basically a Midget engine with two extra cylinders. This engine was also made by Wolseley, and had been borrowed from their Hornet model. The M/C/D/F models only lasted for about another year, as in 1932 the entire MG range was overhauled and the existing models were replaced by the new J-type Midgets and the K-type Magnette.

The J-type range included the J1 four-seater, J2 two-seater, both with 847cc engines, and the J3 and J4 which were supercharged 746cc racing models; all were now built on the wheelbase of 7ft 2in (2184mm). The K-type range was rather more complicated, although at first all models shared a new short-stroke 1087cc version of the Magna engine. The K1 had a longer wheelbase for four-seater tourer and saloon bodywork. The K2 and K3 had a shorter wheelbase, but the K2 was a road-going two-seater while the K3 was a supercharged racing version. It went on to become the most successful MG racing car, with notable successes in the Mille Miglia and the Tourist Trophy.

An important improvement was that the engines in both of the new MGs featured cross-flow cylinder heads, a feature also now adopted for Wolseley's own engines. On the other hand, the MGs kept the vertical dynamo shaft drive for the camshaft, whereas the new Wolseleys had the camshaft driven by chain. The J-type engines still had the original crankshaft with just

The most formidable version of the J-types was the supercharged J4 racer, of which only a handful were made. (Photo copyright BMIHT)

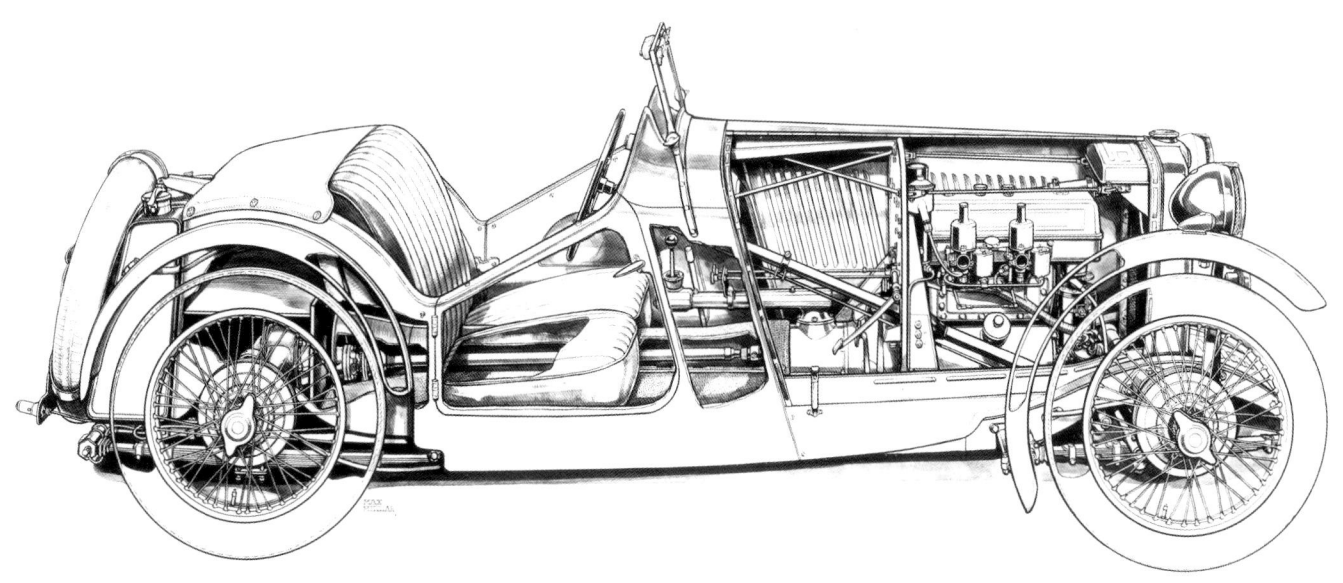

The J2 set the pattern for the following Midgets, through the TC model to 1950. Among its characteristic features were the chassis underslung at the rear, the elbow cut-outs in the doors, and the external rear-mounted petrol tank. We can just see the sliding trunnions at the rear of the rear springs.

In 1933, the J-types adopted the long flowing front wings combined with running boards, and the MG Midget had found its classic look.

The P-types of 1934 featured a much-improved engine with a three-bearing crankshaft for greater reliability and smoother running. Like the J-types, they were offered in both two- and four-seater forms. (Photos copyright BMIHT)

two main bearings. On the J1 and J2, there were now two carburettors, and power was improved to 36bhp at 5500rpm. The three-speed gearbox of the M and D was replaced by a four-speed unit

It was with the J and K-types that MG introduced what became the classic MG "look": the scuttle with two cowls or humps to carry the airflow over the heads of driver and passenger when the windscreen was folded flat, the doors with deep elbow cut-aways, and the slab fuel tank at the rear, with the spare wheel mounted behind it. On the K-types from the start, but only in 1933 on the J-types, there were also long sweeping front wings continuing into running boards. This style continued on MGs until 1955 and set the pattern for most other British sports cars.

With a combined production total of nearly 2500 cars, the J-types continued to be commercially successful – little wonder as the most popular model, the J2 two-seater, cost just £199 10s, and according to the road test in *The Autocar* offered a top speed of 82mph (132km/h) – though in practice it was more like 75mph (121km/h).

After a two-year production run the J-types were in turn replaced by the P-type Midget in early 1934. On this car the engine for the first time had a crankshaft with three main bearings, which made for smoother running and greater reliability. Power was 35-39bhp depending on the compression ratio. The chassis was improved in a number of ways and had a slightly longer wheelbase; however the price was increased to £222 for the two-seater. Performance was about the same, with a 76mph top speed (122 km/h). There was also a four-seater, and the charming and elegant Airline Coupé, a streamlined "art deco" fastback design.

In the meantime the F-type Magna had been replaced by the L-type Magna, with an engine of 1087cc or the same size as the K Magnette, while the K-type itself was giving way to the N-type Magnette, with the 1271cc engine! Furthermore, to replace the J4 racing model, MG introduced an even more specialised racing Midget, the Q-type, which was not actually a great success: its 746cc engine with a Zoller supercharger developed more than 100bhp, making the car simply too fast for its still-conventional chassis.

The final versions of the original family of single ohc MG

T-SERIES PAST AND PRESENT

A delightful addition to the P-type range was this elegant Airline coupé, so typical of the fashionable streamlined shapes of the 1930s.

Also in 1935, MG made a handful of the very special racing R-type, with this backbone chassis and all-independent suspension with torsion bars. The design was not adopted for road cars.

Midgets came in 1935. The R-type racing car, introduced in April 1935, was a very different car from any other MG. It inherited the Q-type engine but had a revolutionary new chassis with all-independent suspension by torsion bars designed by chief engineer HN Charles assisted by Syd Enever and Reg Jackson. It was MG's only single-seater and looked somewhat like the new Mercedes-Benz Grand Prix racing car.

A few months later, to counter competition from the 972cc Singer Nine Le Mans, which had been faster than the P-type at Le Mans in 1935, the P or PA-type became the PB, with the engine bored out from 57mm to 60mm and 939cc, which made it a 9hp car but gave a useful boost to the power output to 43bhp. Between them, the two P-types reached a total production of about 2500 cars.

A NEW ERA FOR MG

The R-type barely had time to make an impression, as in July 1935 MG pulled out of racing. The MG Car Company

In 1935, the PB featured a slightly larger engine of 939cc, and for the first time had painted slats to the radiator. It was to be the last of the overhead camshaft Midgets.

Instead of a car derived from the R-type, the next road-going Midget was the TA. The car photographed here in 1936 still exists, and has been photographed for this book in its current unrestored state, owned by Andy and Angie King. (Photo copyright BMIHT)

Limited, hitherto in the personal ownership of William Morris or Lord Nuffield as he had become in 1934, was sold to Morris Motors Limited, which had been a public company since 1926. At the same time, the Wolseley company was also sold to Morris Motors. Both brands, together with Morris, were now controlled by the managing director of Morris Motors, Leonard Lord, who believed in rationalising the product range and using similar components in cars of different makes; in a sense, he introduced what became known as "badge engineering". Lord also disapproved of motor racing.

The upshot for MG was that the racing and experimental workshops at Abingdon were closed down, together with the design office. Future models would be designed in the Morris Drawing Office at Cowley. HN Charles moved to Cowley but left Morris in 1938 to join Rotol Airscrews and subsequently worked at Austin from 1941-46, where he designed the A40 engine which was the foundation for the later BMC B-series. Also working on new MG cars at Cowley was the young draughtsman Jack Daniels, who later became famous as Alec Issigonis's closest collaborator. Syd Enever, and Bill Renwick formerly of Aston Martin, were allowed to stay at Abingdon to look after design liaison. Kimber was initially demoted, with the title of general manager, but eventually resumed the title of managing director after Leonard Lord had fallen out with Lord Nuffield and resigned from Morris in 1936; he joined the rival Austin company two years later.

The first tangible result of the new Lord-inspired policy was the MG SA or Two-litre model, launched at the 1935 Motor Show. At the time the car horrified MG enthusiasts: it was a large six-cylinder four-door saloon, with several un-MG-like features, including a pushrod overhead-valve engine made by Morris Engines and shared with the new Wolseley Super Six. Matters were not helped by a long delay before the new model eventually reached customers in 1936, by which time the SA had already undergone many modifications, including fitting a 2.3-litre engine, and more changes were to follow.

Dispassionately assessed, the SA was in a sense a return to the kind of "fast tourer" which MG had made with the 18/80, and it was an admirable competitor for the new SS Jaguar which it strongly resembled. It was followed by two other similar models, the four-cylinder 1½-litre VA in October 1936, and the six-cylinder 2.6-litre WA in 1938. These "SVW" models together were actually produced in larger numbers than MG's sports car. All three were discontinued at the outbreak of World War Two, and did not make a comeback afterwards.

FIRST OF THE T-SERIES

With the SA just about in production, clearly time was running out for the remaining MG cars with ohc engines. Most importantly, MG needed a new small sports car, a new Midget. And so the first of the T-series, the TA, was introduced in June 1936. Although it was not reflected in contemporary magazine articles (which as always in those days were universally favourable) it is likely that the new model was greeted by contemporary enthusiasts with some dismay. It was a larger car than previous MG Midgets, in dimensions and engine capacity more on a par with the Magna or Magnette models, and was inevitably heavier. Furthermore, like the SA, the TA had a pushrod ohv engine of humble parentage, combined with a wet cork-lined clutch and a synchromesh gearbox.

Engine and transmission apart, there was still a good deal of true MG heritage in the TA. It incorporated distinct improvements such as the hydraulic brakes. It was rather more civilised and comfortable than most previous models, it was easier to drive and had a useful performance – and this time, a

SELECTED POPULAR BRITISH SPORTING CARS, 1936-39					
	BSA Scout	HRG 1100, 1 ½ litre	MG TA, TB	Morgan 4/4	SS Jaguar 100
Production period	1935-39	1935-39	1936-39	1936-39	1935-39
Engine size	1075cc, 9hp	1074cc, 9hp	1292cc, 10hp	1122cc, 10hp	2667cc, 20hp
	1203cc, 10hp	1496cc, 12hp	1250cc, 11hp		3485cc, 25hp
Price	£150-185	£289 (1100)	£222	£210-225	£395-445
		£395-425 (1 ½ litre)			
Top speed	65-70mph	78mph (1100)	80mph	78mph	95-100mph
		90-92mph (1 ½ litre)			
Production figure	3003	35	3382	820	309

true top speed of 80mph (129 km/h). All this for a mere £222! Although most of the design work was carried out at Cowley rather than at Abingdon, Cecil Kimber still kept a watchful eye on the development of the new car, ensuring that it measured up to his exacting standard for what an MG sports car should be, and perhaps especially, that it looked like a proper MG.

The TA went on to become one of the most popular pre-war MG cars. Just over 3000 TAs were made over a period of three years – only the M-type MG Midget of 1929-32 had reached a higher production figure. Apart from one or two cars fitted with the very pretty Airline coupé body as originally used on the P and N-type MGs, only the open two-seater was available until 1938, when the Tickford drophead coupé was introduced. Heavier and more expensive than the two-seater, it gave the Midget renewed appeal to customers less interested in out-and-out-sports cars and more inclined to prefer the additional comfort offered by the drophead coupé body.

On the other hand, the TA added little to MG's long list of successes in motor sport. It was never intended as a competition car and the engine was not suitable for tuning. In the strange and somewhat parochial world of British motor sport in the 1930s, trials had become very popular, and it was in this field that factory-supported teams such as the "Cream Crackers" and the "Three Musketeers" used specially developed TAs to good effect.

Odd though it may seem to modern classic car enthusiasts, in the late 1930s the British public seems to have turned away from sports cars. Companies which had previously made small sports cars, such as Austin, Riley, Singer, Triumph, and even Wolseley with the oft-maligned Hornet Special, by and large stopped making out-and-out sports cars and at best produced touring cars with a sporting flavour. I believe that one possible cause were the accidents which befell Singer sports cars in the 1935 Tourist Trophy race, and it seems that insurers were now demanding higher premiums for what they considered as "sports cars". The result was that between 1936 and 1939 there was but a handful of popularly-priced sports cars on the market, and the MG was the best-seller by far.

While clearly the SS 100 was in a different league from the T-series and the rest, it was the best-selling of the larger-engined cars, and more affordable than most. Other sports cars were either out of production (Rapier, Riley, Singer, Triumph), or out of reach for most people financially (Alta, Aston Martin, Atalanta), or both (Squire), and most of the other survivors were made in tiny numbers.

The TB, launched in 1939 a few months before war broke out, was a TA with the much improved XPAG engine, which was to prove immensely tolerant of tuning. But only 379 TBs were made before production was stopped and Abingdon was turned over to the manufacture of munitions. Disagreement over war-time production led to Cecil Kimber being sacked by his boss, the managing director of the Nuffield Organization, Miles Thomas, in 1941. Then, in

Apart from the Morris-derived pushrod overhead-valve engine, the TA chassis was still typical for MG.

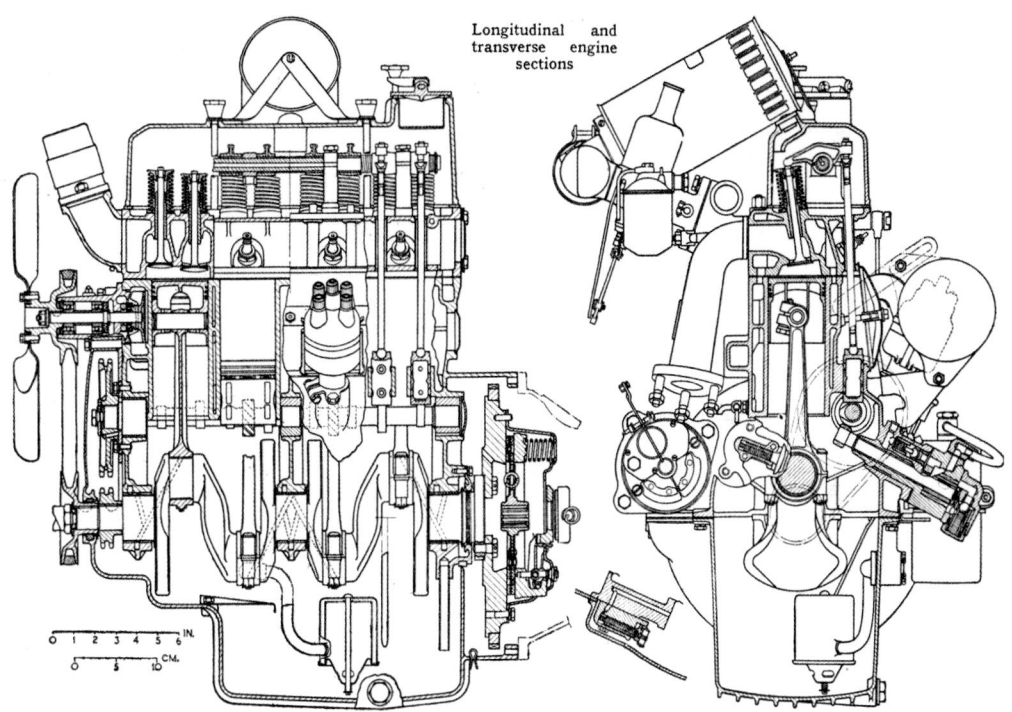

First introduced in 1939 in the TB, the XP engine became the power plant of all the MG Midgets until 1955, here in 1250cc XPAG form from the TC. It was both robust and very responsive to tuning.

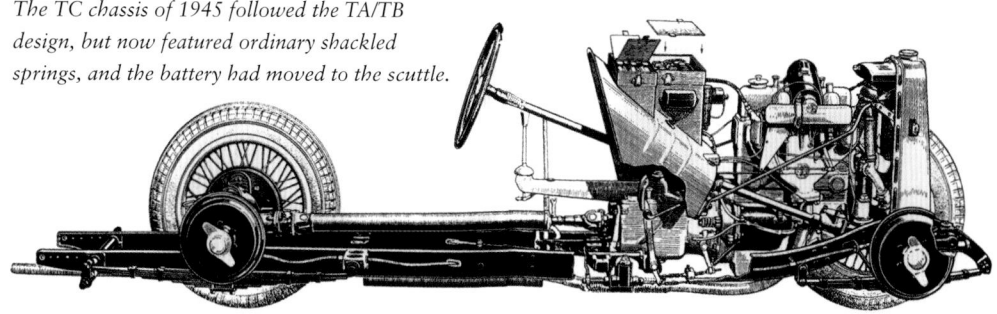

The TC chassis of 1945 followed the TA/TB design, but now featured ordinary shackled springs, and the battery had moved to the scuttle.

APPROXIMATE ANNUAL PRODUCTION OF MG CARS, 1935-39						
	Earlier	1935	1936	1937	1938	1939	Total
KN	64	137					201
N-types	349	248	137	3			737
PA/PB	1440	810	248				2498
RA		10					10
SA		2	1118	966	524	128	2738
TA/TB			765	1028	1017	572	3382
VA			3	912	1045	447	2407
WA					55	314	369
Total	1853	1207	2271	2909	2641	1461	

With the TD in 1950, the Midget got an all-new chassis with independent front suspension, rack-and-pinion steering, and the frame running above the rear axle. However, the looks stayed the same, except for the adoption of smaller disc wheels.

1945, Kimber was killed in a railway accident.

HA Ryder of Morris Radiators had taken over as managing director of MG after Kimber's dismissal, but he retired in 1947 and SV Smith, the Cowley plant director, assumed this title. In the Abingdon factory, George Propert had taken over as MG's general manager, and at the end of the war he had an enthusiastic team around him – including long-serving colleagues Cecil Cousins, Reg Jackson, Alec Hounslow and Syd Enever, soon re-joined by John Thornley when he returned from war service.

POST-WAR: NEW HORIZONS

Eager to get back to making sports cars as soon as possible, they got out the TB demonstrator and made a few improvements to it. With a wider body, and shackles in place of sliding trunnions for the spring-mounts, they launched it as the TC. By the end of 1945, 81 of the new model had been made. Abingdon never looked back from there; when the TC was discontinued in 1949, 10,000 had been made.

During the years of post-war austerity the Nuffield Organization, like other British car manufacturers, needed to export most of its output. Traditionally, the main export markets for British cars had been in the Empire, with smaller numbers to Europe. A handful of MGs had been exported to the USA before the war, followed by 20 TCs in 1946. Miles Thomas, vice-chairman of the Nuffield Organization until November 1947, toured the USA and Canada in 1946, and Donald Harrison of Nuffield Exports undertook a four-month tour of the USA in 1947, incidentally driving a Riley 1½-litre saloon.

A number of American distributors were signed up under the auspices of the Hambro Trading Company, and already in 1947 the USA had become MG's biggest export market. A novel idea was to sell the cars to US Service Personnel stationed in the UK through the US Forces Post Exchange, a programme which was established jointly with Nuffield Exports in 1949.

MG also extended a very cautious feeler towards factory participation in motor sport. Works-prepared but privately owned TCs were run in the sports cars race at Silverstone in August 1949 by Dick Jacobs, Ted Lund and George Phillips. Phillips had already raced his own much-modified special bodied TC at Le Mans in 1949, where the car was disqualified after his co-driver made a mistake, and ran again in 1950, when he came second in the 1½-litre class.

In the USA, the TC was the natural choice for the new generation of amateur sports car racers who got together in the recently-formed Sports Car Club of America. They included the Collier brothers, who were the MG importers before the war and until 1946, and Cameron Argetsinger, who founded the Watkins Glen Grand Prix – which was actually a road race for sports cars – in 1948, where TCs performed with honour. A TC was even fifth in the first endurance race at Sebring on New Year's Eve in 1950.

A MODERN MIDGET

It was the success of the TC in the USA which virtually dictated the design of its replacement. While the idea of a small British sports car had been accepted with enthusiasm by American customers, most of them would prefer left-hand drive, which was never offered on the TC. Independent front suspension would cope better with American roads, and bumpers (already fitted to North American specification TCs) were a necessity when parking in American cities. The wire wheels, although pretty, could be dispensed with in favour of more practical (and cheaper!) disc wheels, using 15-inch tyres which were probably more readily available.

Abingdon duly complied with all these requirements and introduced the TD in January 1950. Immediately recognisable as an MG Midget, it incorporated the independent front suspension, the rack-and-pinion steering and some of the chassis design from the contemporary MG saloon, the 1¼-litre Y-type.

With the TD, MG became a household name in the USA. Of

nearly 30,000 TDs made over a four-year period, more than 21,000 found buyers in North America. Although it, like the TC, was offered only as a two-seater, two variations on the theme were sponsored by American distributors. One was the lengthened four-seater made by the renowned house of Inskip in New York. The other was the Bertone-bodied "family and sports car" offered by MG's Chicago distributor, Arnolt. There was actually a surprising number of other special-bodied cars (discussed on page 130 onwards).

The drivers of the works-prepared TCs changed to the new model, and were rewarded by a 1-2-3 in class in the 1950 Tourist Trophy race, while in the USA, TDs took the team award in the 1952 Sebring 12-hour race. MG offered the slightly hotted-up Mark II or TD/C model, based on the car which Dick Jacobs had raced in 1950, and which in production form was mainly aimed at the American market. A streamlined TD-based racer had been built for George Phillips to run at Le Mans in 1951, and this car, EX.172, would in turn sire a new generation of MG sports cars.

In fact, the production version of the Le Mans car might have appeared rather earlier than 1955 (the year of the debut of the MGA), for John Thornley and Syd Enever, now general manager and chef engineer respectively, had a prototype ready in 1952, the EX.175. However, in that year the Nuffield Organization joined forces with Austin to form the British Motor Corporation. The boss of Austin and now BMC was Leonard Lord, who once before had swayed MG's destiny. When Lord was shown the prototype MG he had just committed the company to build a Healey-designed sports car with an Austin engine, and did not want internal competition from a very similar-looking MG, so he turned Abingdon's proposal down.

Ultimately Lord changed his mind, but for the time being all MG was allowed to go ahead with was a slightly modified TD, incorporating the tuned engine from the Mark II and a mild facelift. Sympathetically received in Britain, the new TF of 1953 was ridiculed in America. MG was now competing against much more modern-looking and more powerful sports cars such as the Austin-Healey 100 and the Triumph TR2. As an interim measure, after the first year the TF was given a bored-out 1466cc engine and was dubbed the TF 1500. But it was not surprising that only 9600 TFs were made over a two-year period before MG's new sports car generation began with the MGA in 1955.

These days, the TF is as revered as any of its forebears, and if anything even more sought-after – it certainly commands higher prices than any of the earlier models. After the passing of more than 60 years, the shape that was once described in the most unflattering terms has come into its own and it is considered by many to be one of the prettiest MGs ever made. Indeed, all the T-series models can be described as easy on the eye, which is surely one reason for their continued and increasing popularity. Another reason is the simplicity and robustness of their construction, which makes for straightforward restoration and enjoyable running. Finally, there is that ever-lasting bit of MG Magic!

The lasting legacy of the post-war MG Midgets is that they spearheaded the British sports car revolution and created the US market for sports and other imported cars. They were followed by numerous other cars of similar type, starting with the Jaguar XK120 in 1948, and were eventually imitated by many other car makers who all wanted a slice of the American pie, including some in other European countries. Most of these aimed to fill the gap in size, price, and performance, between the MG and the Jaguar. However, the most important MG competitors were those introduced by the other large mass-producers of cars in Britain, some of which by 1954 were snapping at MG's heels, despite being more expensive. The Austin-Healey and the Triumph went on to become long-term success stories, though the original Sunbeam Alpine was commercially a flop.

When the T-types were new or nearly new, and when they were often actively campaigned, no-one thought twice about modifying the cars – especially if it would make them go faster. There was always a good market for accessories, bolt-on goodies (some of which now seem to have acquired a certain status because of rarity!) and engine tuning, which was regulated by the factory in the famous "Stage" tuning booklets.

Inevitably, many T-types were treated more or less as bangers in the secondhand car market of the late 1950s and 1960s, but since the 1970s they have gained recognition as prime examples of what we now call classic cars. Many T-types are still used for racing, but generally speaking most owners are now concerned with keeping the cars in as original condition as possible for road use. The following chapters have been compiled with this in mind.

MG AND SELECTED OTHER BRITISH SPORTS CARS IN 1954

	Austin-Healey 100	Jaguar XK 120, XK 140	MG TF	Sunbeam Alpine	Triumph TR2
Production period	1953-56	1948-57	1953-55	1953-55	1953-55
Engine size, power	2660cc, 90bhp	3442cc, 160-190bhp	1250cc, 57bhp; 1466cc, 63bhp	2267cc, 80bhp	1991cc, 90bhp
Price	£1064	£1598 (XK 140)	£780	£1212	£887
Top speed	102-106mph	120-125mph	80-85mph	96mph	103-107mph
1954 production figure	5940	2496 (OTS only)	6516	235	4897

The early 1936 TA owned by Kevin and Melanie Howe.

Front view complete with MG registration of the later TA owned by Andy and Angie King.

The Tickford drophead coupé was a more luxurious alternative to the open two-seater; this TA is owned by Martin Curren.

T-SERIES PAST AND PRESENT

The TB was only made for a few short months in 1939. This car has been owned by Frank Langridge in New Zealand for over 40 years. (Courtesy Frank Langridge)

A second example of the TB, owned by George Cummin.

An early 1946 TC, originally a Police car, superbly restored by owner Tim Jackson. (Courtesy Tim Jackson)

This later TC owned by Jim Pielow is finished in the unusual colour of Clipper Blue.

Red is still the colour most associated with MG Midgets. This early TD owned by John Hinds has the solid disc wheels.

T-SERIES PAST AND PRESENT

A late TD to the Mark II specification, owned by Barry Lomas.

This TF 1250 in Almond Green with the standard disc wheels is owned by Malcolm Reid.

Wire wheels are fitted to this TF 1500 in Birch Grey, owned by Mike Coope.

THE TA, TB AND TC MODELS

This section of the book deals with these three models, made from 1936 to 1949, effectively under the same headings, with the important proviso that there are two sections dealing with the two different types of the engine, the MPJG type of the TA, and the XPAG type of the TB and TC models.

CHASSIS

In many ways, the TA model represented a sea-change from previous MG Midget models, but the chassis frame design at least followed MG's traditional practice, introduced with the C-type in 1931. Dimensions were however increased, as the wheelbase was now 7ft 10in (2388mm) and the track 3ft 9in (1143mm). These dimensions were the same as on the MG Midget Q-type racing car, but I expect this will have been a coincidence.

The frame was a simple and straight-forward ladder-type, with channel section side members, which were partially boxed in towards the front, alongside the engine and back to the third

This rolling chassis, more or less complete, is of a TC, specifically TC0999. It is similar to that of a TB, and except for the engine and transmission, to a TA chassis. (Courtesy Tim Jackson)

The bare chassis frame, again of TC0999; the front is at the top of the photo. The TA/TB frame would be similar, but had battery cradles in front of the rear axle. (Courtesy Tim Jackson)

THE TA, TB AND TC MODELS

This is one end of one of the tubular cross members and shows the way it is fitted in the inside of the chassis side member, together with the handbrake cable, the pipe to the rear brakes, and the wiring loom. (Courtesy Tim Jackson)

cross-member at the rear of the gearbox. The boxing-in plates, inside the chassis side members, continued a little further back on the later TCs. The side members were straight, parallel, and flat from the rear end forwards to the point where they swept up over the front axle. The chassis was underslung at the rear, meaning that it went under the rear axle. The side members were made from 10 gauge steel.

The cross-members were tubular, which was MG practice. At the very front of the chassis, the first cross-member held the dumb-irons together, while the second cross-member carried the radiator. On the pre-war cars, this cross-member had brackets for a canvas engine tie strap either side, they attached to the front engine plate via tie rods. The front engine mounts were just behind this cross-member. The third cross-member was at the rear of the gearbox, and incorporated the two rear mounting points for the power unit. Cross-members number four and five supported, respectively, the front and rear anchorage points for the rear springs.

On the TA and TB models, the chassis frame incorporated two battery cradles, fitted just in front of the rear axle on either side of the prop shaft, they held two six-volt batteries connected in series. On the TC, they were replaced by a single twelve-volt battery which was mounted under the bonnet, so the battery cradles were deleted. A shock absorber tie-bar was mounted across the chassis behind the rear axle.

The body was fitted to four main body mounting points, which were outriggers to the main frame: two on each side by the third and fourth cross-members. The body was also attached at the rear through a wooden cross-member which formed the bottom of the side screen box (see sections on bodywork and weather equipment). The chassis and all related parts attached to it were finished in black.

A centralised chassis lubrication system was fitted to TA models from chassis number TA 2253, and subsequently on the TB models. On each side of the car there was a small panel with three Tecalemit lubrication nipples, mounted on either side at the front of the scuttle under the bonnet. The panels had identification plates engraved with the description of the points they served, as follows: "rear [hand] brake cable", "rear spring shackle", and "front spring pin", notwithstanding the fact that it was actually the spring trunnions which were lubricated. After the war, when the sliding trunnions were replaced by spring shackles on the TC, the centralised system was deemed to be less necessary, and was deleted – which presumably also represented a cost saving. Furthermore, the system could give trouble, if the correct lubricant was not used: a heavy gear oil such as EP 140 is suitable, or lithium grease.

Before the grouped lubrication nipples were introduced, the early TAs had lubrication nipples on the hand brake cables, and these were introduced again on the TC, being fitted to the cables just in front of the rear wings on each side of the car. Similarly, the early TAs had lubrication nipples on the sliding trunnions. The front spring front swivel pins always had their own conventional lubrication nipples, while the similar swivel pins for the rear springs were mounted in Silentbloc bushes which required no lubrication.

It should be mentioned that in general, the nuts and bolts originally used on the chassis, body, and associated parts on the T-series cars have BSF threads and imperial dimensions including the Whitworth hexagon heads, except for the engines where the fixings have metric threads but still Whitworth heads.

FRONT AXLE AND SUSPENSION

The I-section (or, if you like, H-section) front axle beam had upswept ends of oval section, with an eye at each end for the king pin, and was mounted above the springs. The leaf springs were of the semi-elliptic type, and were fitted below the chassis side members (rather than outside the chassis). On the early TAs, the springs had five leaves, and an additional two rebound leaves were fitted above the main leaf. These springs were later replaced by springs with seven leaves and no rebound leaves, which were also found on the TB (see list of production changes p.76)). The TC had front springs with six leaves. The springs

Later TAs, and all TBs, like TB0415 seen here, had grouped nipples for chassis lubrication, mounted on either side in front of the scuttle. They were identified by these plates, this one from the right-hand side; the plate on the other side had the nipples to the left of the text. (Courtesy Frank Langridge)

The same type of front shock absorbers was fitted to all pre-war cars, here on TB0598.

29

On cars with centralised lubrication, individual pipes led to lubrication points, as in the example seen here, to the front sliding trunnions. (Courtesy Frank Langridge)

Taken from the front, this is the left-hand front wheel and brake drum, with part of the front axle, front spring, and track rod arm, of TC0999. (Courtesy Tim Jackson)

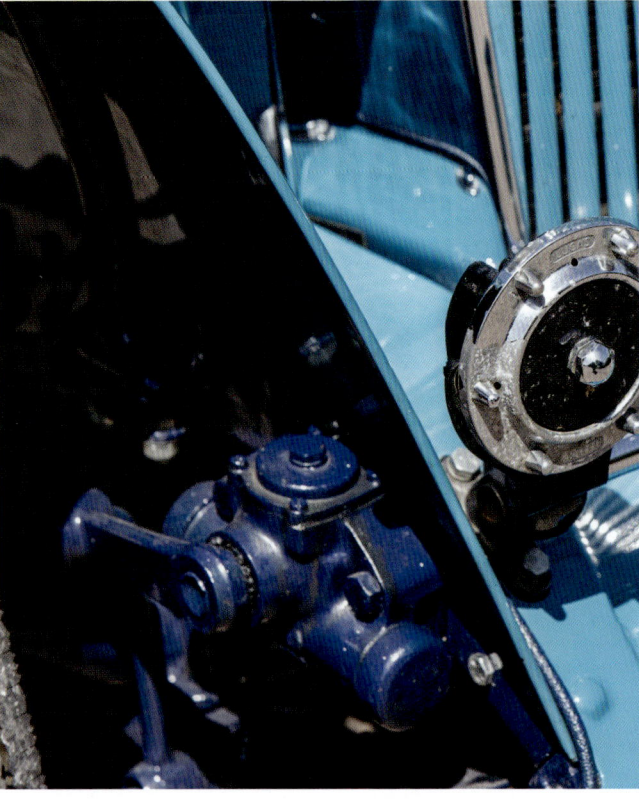

The post-war TC had this type of front shock absorber. The colour is not original, it should be black.

were 26¾ in long (between laden centres) and 1¼ in wide. They were mounted asymmetrically on the axle, with about 12¼ in of the spring length in front of the axle centre line, and 14½ in to the rear.

The front springs were pivoted at the front, with swivel pins fitted in the ends of the front cross-member. At the rear, on pre-war cars the master leaves of each spring passed through slots in bronze trunnions, fitted in the chassis side members and protected by moulded rubber covers; this was another inheritance from earlier MGs. On the TC, however, the sliding trunnions were replaced by ordinary spring shackles, mounted in rubber bushes.

Two different types of shock absorbers were found on the pre-war TA and TB models; first the Luvax vane-type AR adjustable shock absorbers, later the AC type. The TC had the latest improved Luvax-Girling double-acting type, with rather larger housings. Both types were mounted on the chassis side members in front of the axle, and had the vertical movement of the shock absorber arms in the fore-and-aft plane.

REAR SUSPENSION

The rear suspension was similar to the front suspension, in that the springs were pivoted with swivel pins at the front, and had sliding trunnions at the rear on the TA and TB – replaced by shackles on the TC. However, the rear springs had seven leaves with two rebound leaves. They were mounted outside the chassis side members. The rear shock absorbers, of similar Luvax type, were mounted behind the axle, and had the vertical movement of the shock absorber arms in the transverse plane.

At some time much later, I understand that some replacement rear springs were made to incorrect dimensions, which resulted in the rear wheels sitting too far forward, relative to the rear wings; however, it cannot have amounted to much, since there would have been a problem with the length of the prop shaft.

Some rear axle details, on the left-hand side of TC0999 taken from the rear, showing brake drum with brake pipes and hand brake cable, rear spring and shock absorber. (Courtesy Tim Jackson)

The later type of steering wheel, found on cars with the adjustable steering column from late TAs onwards, here on TC0999, featuring the chrome cover plate. (Courtesy Tim Jackson)

The original type of steering wheel, here seen on TA0375.

STEERING

The steering gear was of the conventional Bishop Cam type. The steering box was effectively mounted on its side, compared to other cars with a similar type of steering gear. The box contained a worm or helical cam at the bottom of the inner steering column. A peg or follower fitted to the top of a vertical rocker shaft rode in the groove of the cam. At the bottom, the rocker shaft was splined into the drop arm. Adjustment to the amount of play in the steering was by shims under the side plate (which in a T-type was on the top of the box) and the column end float was adjusted by shims at both ends of the worm. The steering box should be lubricated by EP 140 oil. The drag link and track rod were adjustable.

All cars were available only with right-hand drive. The steering column was at first not adjustable, but a telescopic column was introduced in 1938, from TA 2882. It should be found on all TA Tickford coupés, as well as on the TB and TC models. The original standard steering wheels of 17 inch (432mm) diameter had three solid spokes, with the longer outer sections of the spokes, and the rim, covered in a black plastic material.

On the early TAs with the non-adjustable column (to TA 2881), the inner ends of the spokes without plastic covering were silver, integral with the hub. The hub was in fact in two parts, and was held together by nine rivets; it had the MG logo engraved in the centre. On the later TA cars with adjustable steering column, as well as TBs and TCs, the wheel had a one-piece solid cast hub, finished in black, but with a chrome cover plate which again carried the MG logo, and which was fixed with three visible screws.

The alternative type of steering wheel which is very often seen on T-types, is the Brooklands (or Malcolm Campbell) type by Bluemels, which was quoted as an approved accessory. The Brooklands wheel has four sprung spokes at right angles, each spoke consisting of five "wires" held together by a tie-bar, and one of these four tie-bars carrying a light blue enamel badge with the words "Bluemel's Brooklands". Before the war, it usually had a black rim, but post-war Brooklands steering

Although this Brooklands steering wheel is on TA2864, it may well be of post-war manufacture, as it has the brown mottled rim. Note the Bluemels badge on the lower right.

By contrast this Brooklands wheel on a late TC has a black rim, but it may well be a reproduction, and it lacks the Bluemels badge.

wheels typically had mottled grey or mottled brown rims. MG also quoted an approved Ashby steering wheel, which looked very similar to the Bluemels wheel. Needless to say, reproductions (or interpretations) of both are widely available.

On the TC, the steering box bracket was mounted further forward on the chassis and the box itself was slightly higher up. This small change gave greater clearance for the starter motor. In the USA, TCs have often had the normal Bishop steering gear replaced by locally-made gears, which some American owners considered better. Nowadays, some cars have had the Bishop box replaced by steering gearboxes from VW Beetles or some earlier models of Nissans. Also popular are the Tompkins kits which allow finer adjustment of the steering gearbox.

The following are the settings for the front axle and steering: camber angle, 3°; castor angle, 6° on TA and TB; early TC, 8° (3° on beam and 5° on chassis); late TC fitted with 2½° taper plates, 5½°. Front wheel toe-in was 3/16in (4.8mm) on the TA and TB, ¼in (6.4mm) on the TC. To get the geometry right, care should be taken that the front axle faces the right way; it can be installed back to front. On a TA front axle which is lettered front and rear, the legend M5-1 should face forward. On the TC, there is lettering only on one face of the axle and this should face rearwards. The steering ratio was 8 to 1 until 1938, and was then changed to 11 to 1, probably at the same time that the telescopic column and new steering wheel were introduced, from TA 2882. By modern standards, all of these cars have very high-geared steering, requiring only about 1.5 turns on the wheel from lock to lock.

BRAKES

Allegedly, Cecil Kimber – like Ettore Bugatti – distrusted hydraulic brakes, so while Morris and Wolseley had introduced Lockheed brakes on some models as early as 1929, the first MG with hydraulic brakes only appeared in 1935: the SA 2-litre, followed by the TA-series in 1936. On the T-types, a combined fluid reservoir and master cylinder was mounted under the

The front brake drum on TB0415, with the flexible hose leading to it. (Courtesy Frank Langridge)

There is a flexible brake hose to the three-way union mounted on the rear axle, then a stretch of normal pipes, and finally another flexible hose to the brake cylinder. (Courtesy Tim Jackson)

floor, inside the right-hand chassis side member. The master cylinder was of 7/8in (22mm) diameter, and the combined unit was Lockheed number 8768 on the pre-war cars, number 14923 on the TC.

The brake pedal activated the master cylinder directly. Both brake and clutch pedals had vertical arms which rose from the floor through a joint moulded rubber dust excluder, except early TAs. The pads were slightly curved in side view, and were fitted with rectangular ribbed pedal rubbers, again except early TAs, see list of Production Changes (p.76).

The brake drums were the same size front and rear, 9in (229mm), and both had Ferodo MT linings of 8½in (216mm)

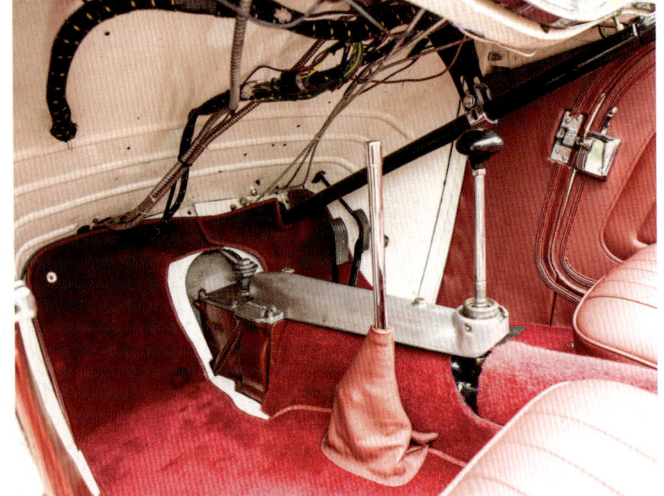

On all cars, the hand brake lever rises from the floor on the left-hand side of the gearbox tunnel, it is chrome-plated, and enclosed in a leather gaiter

THE TA, TB AND TC MODELS

The brake fluid reservoir combined with the master cylinder, sitting in its bracket inside the right-hand chassis side member on TC0999.

The brake fluid reservoir, together with front and rear brake wheel cylinders, new or reproductions and unrestored originals. I am a little surprised if the original brake fluid reservoir filler cap actually said Girling rather than Lockheed? (Courtesy Tim Jackson)

by 1½ in (38mm), however the front brakes had 1in (25mm) brake cylinders, on the rear brakes they were 7/8 in (22mm). Both the brake drums and the backing plates with attached fittings were painted black. From contemporary pictures it appears that some TCs had brake drums painted in body colours, probably mostly show cars, and cars exported to the USA could have had the drums re-painted by local distributors. One point to note is that pre-war cars originally had the brake hoses fitted with clamps, but this is now not considered to be safe.

The hand brake was mechanical. It was fitted on a rotating cross-shaft which was mounted in special bearings inside the chassis side members, just behind the gearbox. The hand brake cables were sheathed for protection, and ran back to the rear drums on each side of the car. The cables were lubricated, either from nipples fitted to the cables, or on cars with centralized lubrications, from nipples under the bonnet as previously described.

The vertical hand-brake lever rose from the cross-shaft, immediately on the left-hand side of the gearbox, a little in front of the gear lever. The lever was chrome-plated and was of course MG's traditional fly-off type. At floor level, the lever was protected by a black leather gaiter sown into the carpet. The gaiter was laced at the top, and could be unlaced to give access to a chrome-plated wing nut adjuster, fitted at the base of the brake lever.

REAR AXLE

This semi-floating rear axle incorporated spiral bevel final drive. The axle housing was of the "banjo" or one piece type, with a bolted-on differential carrier at the front. The TA had a rear axle ratio 4.875:7 (8/39), but since the TB model was fitted with the higher-revving XPAG engine, on this car the ratio was lowered to 5.125:1 (8/41) which improved acceleration without a reduction in top speed. On the TC, the ratio was also 5.125:1. The rear axle was painted black.

The rear axle on TC0999 from above, with the light-coloured filler plug showing prominently, also the brake pipe layout, rear shock absorbers, exhaust pipe, and rear universal joint in the prop shaft. (Courtesy Tim Jackson)

The side-laced wheel found on early TAs, the hub cap here reads "right side" and has the word "undo" twice.

WHEELS AND TYRES

The 19in wire wheels were made by Dunlop and were of the Rudge-Whitworth central locking pattern with splined hubs. The wheels had well-base rims and the rim size was 2.50-19. They were painted silver, but could be finished in other colours, as an extra-cost option (see Colour Schemes, p.83). Another optional extra were 16in wheels, which were sometimes required for competition purposes, such as trialling. The wheels were retained by two-eared knock-ons or hub caps, chrome-plated and with an engraved MG logo, as well as the words "right/offside" or "left/nearside" and "undo" with an arrow in the appropriate direction.

Early cars to chassis number TA 1769 in October 1937 had side-laced wheels meaning that the spokes were fitted towards the outside of the rim; all subsequent cars had spokes fitted in the centre of the rim, therefore called centre-laced wheels. In both types of wheels, there were 48 spokes, 16 outer longer spokes, 32 inner shorter spokes. Although the very typical fashionable 1930s extra, Ace wheel discs, was not quoted officially as an option, it was fitted on some cars, perhaps especially on Tickford drophead coupés, whose owners might have been less inclined to getting their hands dirty by cleaning wheel spokes!

Tyres were always Dunlop 90 as standard, with Dunlop Fort tyres as an option, typically fitted on export cars; both were size 4.50-19, and were fitted with inner tubes. Recommended tyre pressures were quoted as 24 lbs front, 26 lbs rear. The spare wheel was at the rear of the car, carried on a triangular body-colour bracket which was attached to the rear chassis cross member and side members. One spare wheel was standard, but pre-war cars could be ordered with two spare wheels, carried on a special bracket in the same location. The knock-on which retained the spare wheel was a special type, it had a brown and cream MG enamel badge, similar to the radiator badge, but mounted on a special spring key, so that the badge stayed upright, regardless of the position of the knock-on.

Other hub caps have just one "undo" but read "right(off)side" and "left(near)side". These are from TA3184 and TB0598, the latter with red wheels; coloured wheels could be specially ordered.

The later centre-laced wheel, introduced on the TA, and found on all cars thereafter. This is TB0415, and also shows the special hub cap retaining the spare wheel, with an MG medallion. (Courtesy Frank Langridge)

THE TA, TB AND TC MODELS

This is a restored engine in TA0375, showing 10G as well as 10W&M3 on the head. We can easily see details such as the external oil filter and pipework, the black dynamo with the rev counter drive, what are probably the correct plug caps, and the spacer for the plug leads.

TA ENGINE

MG enthusiasts in 1936 allegedly objected to the fact that the new TA-series Midget had an engine with push-rod operated overhead valves – never seen before on a Midget, and only introduced on an MG production model with the SA of the previous year – rather than the traditional single overhead camshaft. Furthermore, the TA engine was much bigger than any previous Midget engine, indeed the capacity of this four-cylinder engine was greater than the six-cylinder engines found in the Magna and Magnette models (of 1087 and 1271cc). For comparison with earlier Midgets, the data were:

MIDGET SPECIFICATIONS							
	M (early)	D, M (late)	J1, J2	PA	PB	TA	TB, TC
Cylinders	4	4	4	4	4	4	4
RAC tax hp	8	8	8	8	9	10	11
Bore	57	57	57	57	60	63.5	66.5
Stroke	83	83	83	83	83	102	90
Capacity	847cc	847cc	847cc	847cc	939cc	1292cc	1250cc
Bhp/rpm	20/4000	27/4500	36/5500	34.9/5500	43.3/5500	52.4/5000	54.4/5200
Bhp/litre	23.61	31.88	42.50	41.20	46.11	40.56	43.52
Piston speed m/s at max bhp	11.07	12.45	15.22	15.22	15.22	17.00	15.60
Car weight, kg From road tests	518kg		572kg		686kg	879kg	840kg
Bhp/ton	39		63		63	60	66
Top speed, mph	62-65		75-80		76	77-80	75-83

The TA in fact had performance similar to if not slightly better than its predecessors. The increase in size and weight, were largely offset by the larger and more powerful engine. The TA engine was less highly stressed than the preceding smaller engines, but its Achilles heel was the long stroke which led to higher piston speeds, and conceivably shortened engine life. The engine was less susceptible to tuning, and there was always the danger of over-revving. On the other hand, it was flexible and torquey, characteristics typical of long-stroke engines. Another problem area was that the cylinder block had very narrow waterways, and was prone to cracking from freezing in winter. Furthermore, many TAs were plagued by porous cylinder block and head castings. In consequence many TAs have been fitted with the much better XPAG engine from the TB and TC models.

Rather than made by Wolseley in Birmingham as the ohc engines had been, the new TA engine was made by the Morris Engines Branch (the old Hotchkiss company) in Coventry. As was common on Morris engines, and betraying the French ancestry of the original Hotchkiss company, the nuts, bolts, and studs had metric threads, but imperial Whitworth

This engine is in the as-yet unrestored prototype, TA0252, and is included to show the cylinder head with the cast-in marking of just 10W&M3. Some trace of the original dark red colour can be discerned, and the chrome-plating for the rocker cover, with the tappet clearance plate on the top at rear. The position of the guarantee plate on the lid of the tool box is unusual. Of course there are quite a few non-original features.

Even later, on TA2864, the head is simply marked 10G. This car has the centralised lubrication nipples. Note that on all of the TAs shown, the scuttle is painted black. However, the MG logo on the dipstick handle is not correct for a TA.

On the carburettor side of TA2864, we can see the octagonal brass plate on the side of the crankcase giving the engine number, in this case MPJG 2924. There is also the external water inlet pipe leading to the rear of the cylinder head, with a vertical by-pass to the thermostat housing in the header tank. Of course there was an MG logo cast into the exhaust manifold.

hexagons. Morris Engines designated the TA engine as the MPJG type, which was also the engine number prefix. This decoded as follows:

M – for the family of 10hp engines
P – for push-rod operated overhead valves
J – for the hp rating or size, 10 hp or 1292cc
G – for MG (M stood for Morris, and W for Wolseley)

The TA engine was based on the engine from the Wolseley 10/40 Series II of 1936-37, where it was known as the MPJW type and had a single downdraught carburettor. This in turn was an overhead valve version of the Morris Ten engine first introduced in 1932, and a similar ohv engine was subsequently used in the Morris Ten Series III of 1937-38, the MPJM type. It has been suggested that the TA owner, bereft of an original engine and in search of the closest similar alternative, should look for an engine from one of these cars. Good luck with that, there were only 2500 of the Wolseleys, and although there were 13,721 of the Morrises, this model is now much scarcer than the TA. The 1548cc versions of the ohv engine of the same family, from the MG VA, and Morris and Wolseley 12hp cars, may be slightly easier to find, and should fit straight into a TA, as it did in the trials cars.

The 102mm stroke, a fraction over 4 inches, was a very traditional dimension for Morris engines. The bore of 63.5mm or exactly 2.5 inches was the maximum dimension to fit into the 10hp class under the formula for calculating RAC or tax horsepower. The capacity was 1292cc, and standard compression ratio was 6.5:1. This could be increased to 7.3:1 by machining the cylinder head for competition work, as discussed in the section dealing with competition parts (p.80). To achieve this, the head was reduced in depth from the standard 3.386in (86.00mm) to 3.292in (83.62mm).

Both the cylinder head and the cylinder block were made from cast iron. The head was attached to eleven studs, six on the right-hand side between the valve ports and outside the rocker cover, five on the left-hand side hidden by the rocker cover. On the left-hand side of the head, in the centre between plugs numbers 2 and 3, there was a cast-in legend, of "10W&M3", or, lower down, of "10G", or of both together, indicating that it was a 10hp head, with W, M, and G for the three makes of car which used it. The rocker cover was made from chrome-plated pressed steel with the oil filler cap at the front. It was retained by two anodised metal finger nuts. Some cars have been fitted with the alternative of a cast aluminium "coffin" type rocker cover, with an octagonal quick-release hinged oil filler cap, similar to the cam covers seen on the earlier MG ohc engines. This was not however quoted in the Service Parts List for the MPJG engine of the TA, only for the XPAG engine of the TB (and later models).

The block was in one piece with the crankcase, which was carried well below the crankshaft centre line. At the bottom, it was closed off by a ribbed cast-aluminium sump. The block and head were finished in a bright red colour; some shade variation may be seen, from "pillar box red" to darker. The block carried a nice big MG logo cast in on the left-hand side below the tappet cover towards the rear. There were three main bearings of 52mm diameter for the crankshaft, they were steel shells lined with white metal, fitted in the block, and in loose bearing caps below. The big end bearings of 45mm diameter were also lined with white metal. From the basic engine architecture, it follows that the crankshaft was removed by taking off the sump.

The Aerolite split-skirt pistons on early engines had two compression rings and two scraper rings. From engine number MPJG 697, they were replaced by simpler pistons with only one scraper ring. The camshaft ran in three bearings, it was mounted on the left-hand side of the engine and was driven by duplex chain from the crankshaft. Valve timing was:

Inlet opens	11 degrees BTDC
	1³⁄₃₂ inches (27.8mm) BTDC on flywheel
Inlet closes:	59 degrees ABDC
	5⅞ inches (149.2mm) ABDC on flywheel
Exhaust opens	56 degrees BBDCl
	5³⁷⁄₆₄ inches (141.7mm) BBDC on flywheel
Exhaust closes	24 degrees ATDC
	2²⁵⁄₆₄ inches (35.3mm) ATDC on flywheel

The front right-hand engine mount of TA3184, below which we get a glimpse of the steering gearbox with the "side plate" on the top.

Valve timing was by marks on the sprockets, corresponding with (originally) white links on the timing chain, with the shorter length of chain with 13 black links between the two white links uppermost, but could also be measured on the flywheel as indicated. The tappets were mounted in two separate bearing blocks. There was a single tappet inspection cover with a fume extractor.

The push-rods and rockers operated valves which were in line and vertical. Originally there were double valve springs, but from engine number MPJG 1605 triple valve springs were employed. The valve diameter was 30.5mm for the inlet valves, 26mm for the exhaust valves, with a 10mm valve lift. Tappet clearance was 0.015in (0.38mm) hot for both exhaust and inlet but could be reduced to 0.010in (0.25mm) for inlet valves. Tappet clearances were quoted on a small oval plate fitted with two rivets on the left-hand side of the rocker cover.

The valve ports and manifolds were on the right-hand side of the engine. The inlet ports were siamesed for the front and rear pairs of cylinders respectively. There were three exhaust ports, one each for the front and rear cylinders, and a siamesed port for cylinders number two and three. The lubrication system was the conventional wet sump type, with a total capacity of 1½ imperial gallons (6.82 litres), but has also been quoted as 1⅜ gallons (6.25 litres). The oil pump was driven from a skew gear on the camshaft and was mounted on the left-hand side of the cylinder block, with a pick-up float and strainer in the sump, and an external Tecalemit oil filter. Normal oil pressure was 60-80 lbs/sq.in.

TB & TC ENGINE

In the autumn of 1938, Morris had introduced the new Series M Ten which featured an all-new power unit, the XPJM type. In basic design principles it differed little from the previous generation of Morris engines, but the really important change was that the stroke had been reduced to 90mm (as on the Morris Eight). The new Morris still had a 63.5mm bore to keep it in the 10hp bracket, and therefore a capacity of 1140cc. It is worth noting that the principal designer at Morris Engines behind the new engine was Claude Baily who later gained further fame as the designer of the Jaguar XK engine.

This engine formed the basis for the new MG Midget engine which was launched, rather quietly, in the TB model in April 1939. In MG form, the bore was increased to 66.5mm, giving the TB a capacity of 1250cc. It also meant that the new Midget was rated at 11hp for tax purposes. The compression ratio was increased to 7.25:1 and the power output was 54.4bhp at 5200rpm. Maximum torque was 64lb ft at 2600rpm. This engine was known as the XPAG type, and in largely unmodified form (except for the addition of a timing chain tensioner) was also used in the TC model after the war.

Much of what has been said about the general architecture

of the TA engine also applies to the TB/TC engine. Among the important differences was the fact that the crankshaft was now fully counter-balanced, and replaceable steel-backed thin-wall shell bearings were used for the mains and the big ends. The tappets were mounted directly in the cylinder block. The cylinder head had separate exhaust ports for all cylinders, while the inlet ports were still siamesed. The valves were set at an angle from vertical and were bigger than on the TA engine, with diameters increased to 33mm (inlet) and 31mm (exhaust). Valve lift was 0.315in (8mm), and tappet clearance 0.019in (0.48mm) hot. Valve timing was:

Inlet opens	11 degrees BTDC/28.3mm BTDC on flywheel
Inlet closes	57 degrees ABDC/119.5mm ABDC on flywheel
Exhaust opens	52 degrees BBDC/108.9mm BBDC on flywheel
Exhaust closes	24 degrees ATDC/50.3mm ATDC on flywheel

Alternative camshafts which can be fitted to XPAG engines are the AEG 122 (which is the later BMC part number) semi-racing camshaft from TF 1250 Stage 3 tuning with valve timing of 13°/59°/50°/22°, and 35° of overlap, and the even "hotter" race camshaft of 31°/58°/60°/30°, with a full 62° of overlap; see section on XPAG tuning on page 116.

The crankcase now extended downwards by only 1/8in (3.2mm) below the crankshaft centre-line. The sump was longer than on the TA, but with the adoption of a dry clutch (see the transmission section), total oil capacity was reduced to 1⅛ imperial gallons (5.1 litres). The oil filter was of an improved design. On the TB model, two types of rocker cover were quoted – either the chrome-plated pressed steel type (with ebonite or Bakelite nuts), or the cast aluminium type. Most TC engines had the pressed steel rocker cover, which was now painted a silver-grey-green rather than chrome-plated, but the cast aluminium

With the TB came the XPAG engine, but unlike post-war engines the tappet cover did not have a raised lip around the edge, and there was no timing chain tensioner. The oil filler cap was now at the rear of the rocker cover, and the tappet clearance plate here is now fitted in the standard position on the side of the rocker cover. Please disregard the green engine colour, it should be red. The spark plug carrier is an extra. (Courtesy Frank Langridge)

The early TC has another unusual engine colour, but in this case we can be confident that the engine actually was grey, as is the scuttle. The silver-painted rocker cover is correct. (Courtesy Tim Jackson)

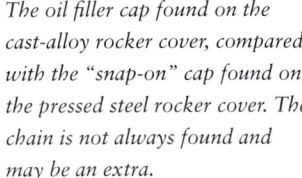

The oil filler cap found on the cast-alloy rocker cover, compared with the "snap-on" cap found on the pressed steel rocker cover. The chain is not always found and may be an extra.

This later TC has the cast-alloy rocker cover, which strictly speaking may not be original on chassis TC10215, and also a cast-alloy tappet cover, which is definitely not original. The dynamo and the fan should both be black.

type was fitted between engine numbers XPAG 2020 and XPAG 2966 in 1946-47, according to the parts list. On the TB and TC engines, the oil filler cap was at the rear of the rocker cover. The XPAG engine had a dipstick with an MG badge on the handle.

The XPAG engine was somewhat lighter than the MPJG unit, probably around 60 lbs or 30kg, so overall weight for the TB was down ¼cwt (about 13kg) compared to the TA. A small difference between the TB and the TC concerned the pressed steel engine-coloured tappet cover, which on the pre-war engines had a turned-in edge, lacking on post-war models. As originally fitted in the TB, the engine was painted red, but a darker, more maroon shade than the TA engine. After the war, TC engines were at first a mid-grey or even grey-green colour, before the red engine colour was re-introduced around chassis number TC 5000 in March 1948. However, I believe that there is still some dissension among the experts on the correct sequence and shades of TC engine colours!

The early and late TA for comparison, with wide tank (the white car) and narrow tank (the black car) respectively. The early narrow wings did not have the central rib found on the later wide wings. On the white car, we can make out the triangular spare wheel bracket, also body colour.

IGNITION SYSTEM

The distributor on the TA was type DK4AA35, on the TB and TC type DKY4A. Both types had automatic centrifugal advance and retard, and a manual micrometer adjustment. The ignition coil was type Q12 8LO, attached to the toolbox on the bulkhead (the battery box on the TC), horizontal on the TA, upside down on the later models. The plugs on the TA were Champion L.10 (14mm) with ½in reach (modern equivalent: L.874) and push-on plug caps were fitted. Champion L.10S plugs were quoted for the TB and TC. The firing order for both the MPJG and the XPAG engines was 1,3,4,2, and the ignition timing was TDC also for both engines, with a contact breaker points gap of .010-.012in.

CARBURETTORS AND FUEL SYSTEM

All the TA, TB and TC models used two SU carburettors, size 1¼in (32mm), of the semi-downdraught type (which meant that they were mounted at a slight angle). On the TA they were type HV3, with brass pistons, while the TB and TC had H2 carburettors. The main jet was 0.090in (2.3mm) for both carburettors. These were the original carburettor needles:

	Standard needle	Rich needle	Weak needle
TA	AC	M1	S
TB, TC	ES	EM	AP

The carburettors had round brass tops, with "penny" slots. There was a single SU low-pressure (L-type, L for low pressure) electric fuel pump mounted to the right of the front of the toolbox, or to the left of the front of the battery box on the TC. A cylindrical AC air cleaner painted black and

This is the prototype TA, with a side-hinged petrol filler cap. This was fitted only to the early cars with the wide tank.

The later front-hinged filler cap is more common. We can see the details of the petrol tank end plate, with the chrome visible on the edge, but otherwise painted over in body colour. The tank retaining strap should be body colour, not chrome plated.

The TC filler cap is basically the same. From this angle, we can see the body colour on the end plate and tank straps. (Courtesy Tim Jackson)

The TA had a carburettor silencer and air cleaner mounted horizontally at the rear of a simple air manifold. The rear (or, if you like, top) of the air cleaner was filled with oil-wetted mesh. It is worth noting the two-way petrol tap mounted on the outside of the toolbox, with the rod to the control on the dashboard.

On the XPAG engine of the TB and later models, the air cleaner was mounted at an angle above the rocker cover, between the two carburettors, and fed air downwards into a split manifold. As the air filter is out of the way, we can better see the petrol pump mounted on the front of the toolbox. (Courtesy Frank Langridge)

containing oil-wetted woven steel mesh was used. On the TA it was situated at the back of the engine compartment, with a tubular air inlet manifold running forward to the carburettors. On the TB and TC, a larger air cleaner was mounted at an angle above the rocker cover, between the carburettors, and secured with a bracket to the rocker cover nuts. The air manifold was in natural aluminium on all cars, and on the TB and TC had the MG logo cast in.

The fuel tank was strapped to the rear chassis cross-member and to the rear of the body. The original wide TA tank (see Production Changes) held 16 imperial gallons (approximately 72 litres) of which 3 gallons (13.6 litres) were held in reserve. The later TAs, and all TB and TC models, had a narrower tank holding 13½ gallons (61 litres) still with a reserve, on the pre-war cars, of 3 gallons. The pre-war cars had a petrol tap on the dashboard, and had two outlet pipes at the bottom of the petrol tank, the main pipe finishing at a higher level inside the tank than the reserve pipe. On the TC, the petrol tap was replaced by a warning lamp for low petrol level so there was only one outlet pipe to the tank, but a sender unit for the warning lamp was added.

The tank and its retaining straps were painted body colour. The end plates were chrome-plated but the chrome was painted over, except for the raised edges of the end plates which were

THE TA, TB AND TC MODELS

On the TC, the petrol tap was done away with, as the reserve facility was replaced by a warning lamp. Two points to make here are, firstly, the wider than standard battery box found on this ex-Police car, and secondly, the NOL oil can held in a bracket on the front of the battery box. (Courtesy Tim Jackson)

This later TC is a standard car, and therefore has a narrower battery box than the car seen above. It also has the body-coloured scuttle and the red engine.

left in polished chrome. The nuts retaining the end plates were chrome-plated. The fuel filler cap was on the left-hand side; it was made by Westwood from chrome-plated brass and was of the quick-release type. Two different types were found on the TA – the early cars with the narrow tank at first had the filler cap hinged on the right with the release button on the left. On later cars, as well as TBs and TCs, the cap was turned through 90 degrees and was hinged at the front, with a release lever with the word "PRESS" towards the rear.

EXHAUST SYSTEM

With the exhaust ports from cylinders number two and three siamesed, the TA had an aluminized three-branch exhaust manifold, inevitably with the MG logo cast in. A triangulated three-bolt flange led to a single down pipe running back on the right-hand side of the car. The down pipe incorporated a flexible section to compensate for the fact that the exhaust system was rigidly mounted to the chassis. A two-bolt flange linked the pipe to a single Burgess straight-through tubular silencer mounted to the chassis under the floorboards. There was a single tailpipe. The exhaust pipe and silencer were painted black. On the TB and TC, which had separate exhaust ports for all cylinders, the exhaust manifold had four branches; otherwise the exhaust system was not changed.

Common to all the cars under discussion is the brown-and-cream enamel MG badge on what is called the false nose piece, and the octagonal radiator filler cap. (Courtesy Frank Langridge)

Clearly radiators were manufactured in-house, by Morris Motors Radiators Branch, and often bore a plate such as this from a TC. I doubt that it is possible to make sense of the numbers found here. (Courtesy Tim Jackson)

COOLING SYSTEM

Previous MG Midgets had relied on simple thermo-siphon cooling, but the TA had a water pump (which was very prone to leakage) bolted to the front of the cylinder head and a four-bladed fan, while the temperature was regulated by a thermostat. The water pump and fan were driven from the crankshaft by belt, the same belt also driving the dynamo. The circulation was unusual, as the cold water inlet pipe went to the rear of the cylinder head, and the pump actually pumped hot water out of the cylinder head to the radiator header tank, while there was no direct forced circulation in the cylinder block at all. Coolant capacity was 1 7/8 imperial gallons (8.5 litres) on the TA, 8 pints (one gallon) in the radiator and 7 pints in the engine.

The radiator and header tank were black. The TA had a red fan, while the TB and TC had a black fan. The radiator cowl was chrome-plated and had an enamel MG badge on the false nosepiece, with the border and letters in brown and a cream background. The external filler cap was octagonal and chrome-plated.

The TB had a new type of radiator core, and the top water hose from the engine outlet was central in the header tank. On the XPAG engine, the water pump was mounted lower down, on the cylinder block, and pumped cold water through an external water gallery on the right-hand side of the cylinder block to the rear of the block. With less water in the engine, overall coolant capacity was reduced to 1¾ gallons (8 litres). There were no further changes on the TC model.

As there was no means of monitoring the coolant temperature – except for obvious distress symptoms, if the worst should happen – an external Moto-Meter thermometer (or similar: the UK equivalent was the Wilmot-Breeden Calormeter) fitted to the radiator cap was, and remains, a popular accessory amongst American T-type owners. In fact, a more sensible alternative available as an option was a dashboard-fitted Jaeger temperature gauge of a design matching the other instruments, and often fitted to the right of the rev counter in front of the driver.

The radiator slats were usually painted to match the upholstery colour. On the TA and TB, for many colour schemes, the upholstery and body colours matched (compare the colour section) so evidently the radiator slats were painted body colour, but contrast colour upholstery was found on cream, black, and some green cars, and these would then have the radiator slats in the upholstery colour. On TCs (and, presumably, TDs), if a car was green with green upholstery, or red with red upholstery, the slats were painted body colour; but on a black or cream car with red or green upholstery, the radiator slats were finished in shades of red or green which were apparently rather brighter than the normal MG Red or Shires Green paint colours used for the bodywork on cars in these colours.

THE TA, TB AND TC MODELS

The remote control and gearbox on the early TA0375, together with the clutch and brake pedals. Please ignore red carpet and incorrect heel mat. This car is missing the domed dust cap at the bottom of the gear lever, and also the rubber cover over the remote control. In common with many T-series cars, this TA has lost its under-scuttle masking board, so we get to see some details of the under-scuttle wiring, apart from the steering column.

TRANSMISSION

Together with its Morris-inspired engine, the TA inherited another Morris characteristic, a cork-lined clutch running in oil which was fed through from the engine lubrication system. The clutch driven plate had 46 cork inserts (according to the parts list, but another picture allegedly of a TA clutch shows 56 cork inserts) and a pressure plate with 12 springs, and the clutch was mechanically operated. The gearbox was of a design common to several Morris, Wolseley and MG cars of the period, but initially the gearbox lacked synchromesh. This was added, on top and third gears only, from engine number MPJG 684.

The internal gearbox ratios were unique to the TA, being rather closer than on other Nuffield cars of the period. There were two different sets, for the non-synchromesh and for the synchromesh gearbox respectively. The following table lists the internal and the overall gear ratios, in conjunction with the standard final drive ratio of 4.875:1:

The mushroom-shaped gear lever knob on the TA had this engraved diagram showing a "gate" for the gear positions. There should not be carpeting over the remote control.

GEARBOX RATIOS						
	NON-SYNCHROMESH BOX			SYNCHROMESH BOX		
	Internal ratios	Overall ratios	Mph/1000rpm	Internal ratios	Overall ratios	Mph/1000rpm
First	3.715:1	18.11:1	4.49mph	3.454:1	16.838:1	4.84mph
Second	2.2:1	10.725:1	7.58mph	2.04:1	9.95:1	8.17mph
Third	1.421:1	6.928:1	11.73mph	1.32:1	6.435:1	12.62mph
Top	1.00:1	4.875:1	16.67mph	1.00:1	4.875:1	16.67mph
Reverse	4.77:1	23.26:1		4.44:1	21.645:1	

FACTORY-ORIGINAL MG T-SERIES

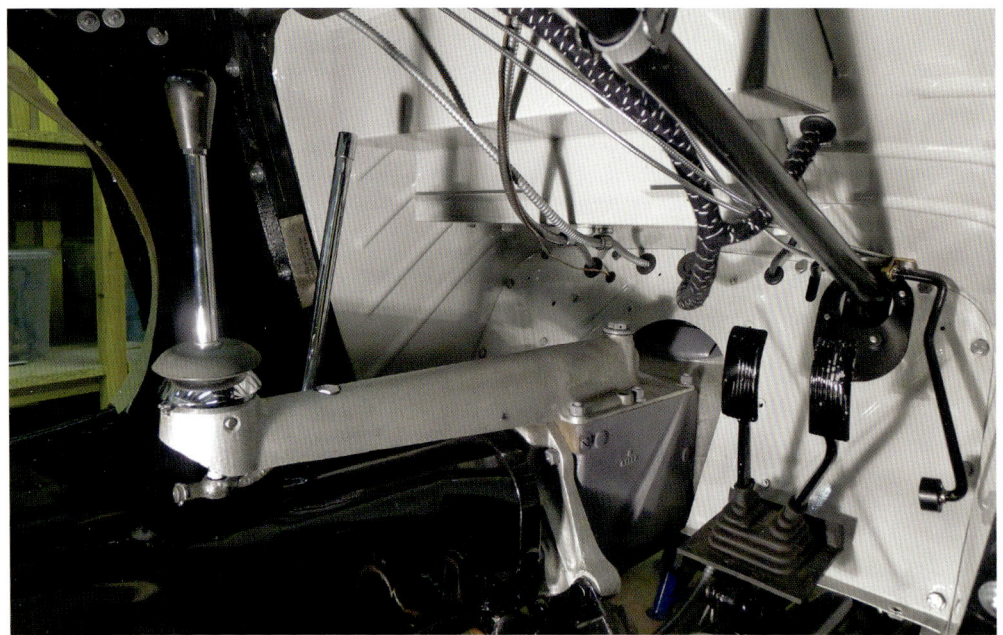

The remote control and gearbox on TC0999, broadly similar to the TA, but with some different details. For instance, the toolbox and battery box intrude on the underside of the scuttle. On this car we can also see the accelerator pedal. (Courtesy Tim Jackson)

The lid of the gearbox was fitted with a cast aluminium remote control extension for the gear lever, which was chrome-plated. Originally the TA had a flat-topped, mushroom-shaped gear lever knob with an engraved gate. Later on (but it is not certain whether during the TA or the TB production run) this was replaced by the more usual pear-shaped knob, also found on the TC and later models. This had single lines engraved between the gear positions. The shift pattern was the normal H, with reverse to the right of top gear. At the bottom of the gear lever was a chrome-plated, domed pressed steel dust cover (with an oiling hole) which sat under the gearbox rubber cover.

There was an open, one-piece balanced Hardy-Spicer propshaft with two universal joints; this was painted black. The gearbox and the bell housing were finished in engine colour, but the gearbox lid and the remote control were left in natural aluminium.

A major change occurred on the TB model with the new XPAG engine. On this model, a dry Borg & Beck single plate clutch of 7¼in (184mm) diameter was fitted, and the gearbox now had synchromesh also on second gear. Gearbox ratios were revised, and the TB and TC ratios were as follows (with the standard final drive of 5.125:1 which equalled 15.82mph/1000rpm in top gear):

	Internal ratios	Overall ratios
First	3.38:1	17.32:1
Second	1.95:1	9.99:1
Third	1.35:1	6.92:1
Top	1.00:1	5.125:1
Reverse	3.38:1	17.32:1

Apart from an improved type of clutch facing, here were no changes to the transmission on the TC, or during the production run of this model.

The underside of the gearbox and bell housing on TC0999, looking forward towards the engine sump and front axle. (Courtesy Tim Jackson)

THE TA, TB AND TC MODELS

The white car is TA0375 and the black car is TC0999. On the white car we clearly see the headlamp bracket in body colour. Both cars have the headlamp glasses with a horseshoe pattern, but the headlamp rims are of different section. The side lamps are the same, and both have the red translucent Lucas medallion. (Black TC, courtesy Tim Jackson)

ELECTRICAL EQUIPMENT AND LAMPS

The electrical equipment was supplied by Lucas. The two six volt batteries on TA and TB models, mounted in cradles in front of the rear axle, were type STLW 1lE with lids. The TC 12 volt battery mounted in a lidded box on the bulkhead was type STXW 9A. Battery capacity was 50 AH. The electrical system was wired positive to earth. The wiring had rubber insulation and cotton cover, black on the pre-war cars, colour-coded on the TC.

The TA and TB had a three-brush dynamo, type C45NV2. The TC dynamo was type C45YV, and the TC was fitted with a compensated voltage control regulator. The starter motor was type M418A84 on the TA and TB, and type M418G LO on the TC. Both the starter motor and the dynamo were painted black.

The cut-out and resistance on the TA and TB models was type CJR3L35. This and the fuse box containing six fuses were mounted on the left hand end of the toolbox. The TC had a type RF91 voltage regulator, mounted on the right-hand end of the battery box. TCs had only two fuses, originally found inside the cover of the voltage regulator. They controlled, respectively, circuits that could be operated with the ignition switched off (e.g. the lights), and circuits that could only be operated when the ignition was switched on (e.g. the wipers and horn). From chassis number TC 3414 in August 1947, an RF95/2 voltage regulator with exposed fuses was fitted.

The headlamps were mounted on body-colour brackets between ears on the radiator cowl and the front wings. The lamps had chrome-plated shells and rims. A Lucas medallion on the lamp shell was raised above the surface on pre-war lamps, and countersunk after the war. Before the war the rim was fixed with a screw, after the war with a clip. The early TA headlamps had a flat rim; later TAs and TBs had headlamp rims which curled inwards and formed a raised lip around the glass. The glasses were slightly convex and usually had the horse-shoe (U-shaped) pattern, but later TCs from TC 1850

A detail of the side lamp, clearly showing the red medallion. (Courtesy Tim Jackson)

had more domed headlamp glasses typically with the diamond or cat's eye pattern. Home market cars had headlamps type LBD 140EDS (TAs with solenoid dipping), M140 (later TAs and TB) or MBD140 (TC), all of 8in diameter (203mm).

On cars supplied in the home market, the now illegal "dip-and-switch" system was used. The left hand (nearside) lamp was dipped, and the right hand (offside) lamp was switched off. On the TA the left-hand lamp had a dipping reflector controlled by a solenoid, while on the TB this lamp had a special bulb with a flat-topped beam, so it was permanently dipped; hence the Service Parts List (helpfully!) describes the TB headlamps as "non dipping". The TC had a double filament bulb in the left-hand lamp, and these should now be fitted to both headlamps to achieve double-dipping lamps to comply with present-day regulations. Double vertical dipping lamps, Lucas Graves type LBG150 or LD140EF, were normally fitted to export cars at the time, and were optional

On TC10215, the headlamps have these much more domed glasses, with the cat's eye or diamond pattern. If you compare the photo taken from the front with the similar shot of the black TC, you can see that the "swan's neck line" or front edge of the wing is not cut as far back into the wing as on the earlier car.

Generally speaking, all headlamps should have this Lucas medallion inset in the shell. (Courtesy Tim Jackson)

These round tail lamps are both from TAs, either – or both – may be modern reproductions; there are detail differences. On the black car, the number plate backing plate with the small ear seems to be more correct, and this is a sensible way to mount reflectors.

These two cars both have the D-shaped lamp. On TB0598 with registration DR... the number plate backing plate has a slightly clumsy extension for mounting a flashing indicator, but what a nice period GB plate! The TC has a better shaped backing plate and a separately mounted indicator. (Black TC, courtesy Tim Jackson)

in the home market, being recommended on cars sold "for continental touring" (I should think so, too!).

The side lamps were type 1130 with round (not octagonal) bodies. They were chrome-plated, with chrome-plated rims and frosted glass lenses without any lettering. The earliest TAs may have had chrome-plated Lucas medallions set in the lamp bodies, otherwise a red translucent plastic "King of the Road" lens was fitted in the top of the lamp. A single combined stop and tail lamp with two separate bulbs was fitted to one side of the rear number plate, and through a clear window in the side of the lamp housing it also served as number plate illumination. Some very early TAs may have had a very small round lamp, seen in a contemporary factory

photo of the prototype CJO 617 – but not alas found on that car any more. Generally, however, on the TA it was a round, single lens lamp, type ST38, either black with a chrome-plated rim or all chrome-plated, or possibly all-black. It had a Lucas medallion and ribbed glass. It was seen already on the 1936 launch press cars, JB 9446 and JB 9447.

From body number 1790 (towards the end of the TA run, or from the start of the TB) a D-shaped ST51 lamp was fitted. This had a vertically split two-piece glass, and a chrome-plated housing. It was also found on the TC. Originally cars for the home market or for export to countries driving on the left, had the single tail lamp on the right-hand side of the number plate, but it moved to the left-hand side on cars for export to countries driving on the right. To comply with modern rules, cars should have two stop and tail lamps. The nicest way of doing this is to fit another lamp of the same type on the other side of the rear number plate.

Trafficators were quoted as an optional extra on TA and TB two-seaters and were fitted as standard on the Tickford coupé. The oft-seen photo of a TA two-seater with trafficators built into the scuttle sides is again of CJO 617, one of the two 1936 prototypes, which still has them. The TC did not have any signalling devices except on the 1948-49 North American cars (see pages 72-73) – MG's motto might have been, "It's what your right arm is for".

For reasons of safety as well as legality, it is obviously desirable to add flashing indicators on these cars now. They can be built into the front side lamps, and small orange flashers can be discreetly added on brackets outboard of the tail lamps at the back. The alternative is to make the stop lamp bulbs do the flashing, but this is likely to confuse most drivers following behind.

Rear reflectors were not fitted originally but have been a legal requirement since 1954 and are also a desirable addition, in the interest of safety. The rear lighting arrangements of any T-type are barely adequate for modern driving conditions, and more drastic modifications may

The wiper motor is a standard Lucas design, typically finished in crackle black paint, mounted in front of the passenger.

The wipers and their connection are chrome plated and very simple.

become increasingly common, including high-level lighting with LED bulbs.

On the badge bar at the front was fitted a chrome-plated fog lamp at one end, originally type FT27, changed in 1948 from TC 4739 to type SFT462. On the other end of the badge bar was an Altette horn, type HF 934/2 or, on the TC, type HF1234. The diaphragm was painted crackle black, the rim was chrome-plated and the housing and bracket were black. The nuts on the pre-war horns were of a scalloped pyramid design, the TC horns had domed nuts; all were chrome-plated.

It should be noted that on cars sold in the home market and in other countries which drove on the left, the horn was mounted on the right-hand side of the car, and the fog lamp on the left. These positions were reversed on cars sold in countries driving on the right, including the USA. In other words, the horn was always on the "off-side" and the fog lamp on the "near-side", regardless of the rule of the road.

The two-seater had a wiper motor type CW/3/4 DA14, or SW4 on the TC. It was painted crackle black, with a chrome-plated switch on the motor housing. It was fitted to the left on the top of the windscreen frame, in just the right spot to brain a hapless passenger in an accident! There were two wipers, with chrome-plated arms and a cross bar which was kinked to clear the bonnet hinge when the screen was folded flat. The Tickford coupé had a remote wiper motor and wipers below the windscreen.

TA BULBS		
Application	Lucas number	Wattage
Head lamps	54	36 watt
Head lamp, export double vertical dip		
	81	36 watt / 24 watt
Head lamp, export France	52	36 watt / 36 watt
Side lamps	207	6 watt
Stop and tail lamp	207	6 watt
Fog lamp	2	36 watt
Dash lamps	1224 MES	2.4 watt
Map lamp	207	6 watt
30mph warning light	207	6 watt
Ignition warning light	252 MES	0.5 watt; NB: 2.5 volts, 0.2 ampere
Trafficators festoon bulb	254	6 watt

TC BULBS		
Application	Lucas number	Wattage
Head lamp, off-side	54	36 watt
Head lamp, near-side	171	36 watt / 36 watt
Side lamps	207	6 watt
Stop and tail lamp	207	6 watt
Fog lamp, type FT 27	2	36 watt
Fog lamp, type SFT 462	162	36 watt
Dash lamps	207	6 watt
30mph warning light	207	6 watt
Ignition warning light	970	0.5 watt; NB: 2.5 volts, 0.2 ampere
Panel illumination	986 or 987	2.2 watt

Charts from the handbooks quoting the types of bulbs originally fitted

FACTORY-ORIGINAL MG T-SERIES

SUMMARY OF TA AND TB LUCAS ELECTRICAL EQUIPMENT

	Lucas type, TA	Lucas type, TB
Battery 6 volt, two of, with lid	SLTW 11 E	Same
Coil	Q.12.8	Q.12.8 type L-O
Cut-out	C.J.R.3 L.35	Same
Distributor	DK.4.AA35	DA32 or DK4 A with micrometer adjustment
Dynamo	C.45 N.V.2	C.45 NV 3
Starter motor	M.418 A.84	M.418 G type L-O
Starter switch	ST.9	ST.10
Stop lamp switch	54 C	Same
Stop & tail lamp (chrome plated)	ST 38 later ST 51	ST 51
Headlamp (chrome plated)	LBD 140 EDS	Same or MB 140 EDS
Side lamp (chrome plated)	1130	Same
Fog lamp (chrome plated)	FT 27	Same
Horn	HF 934/2	Same or H 1234
Driving mirror two-seater (chrome plated)	160 CAB; arm type DA	Same
Driving mirror coupé	Barnacle suction curved type	Same
Windscreen wiper two-seater	CW 3/4 DA 14/0	CW 3 DA 21
Windscreen wiper coupé	SW 4	SW 4 DA 31

SUMMARY OF TC LUCAS ELECTRICAL EQUIPMENT

	Lucas type	Lucas part number
Battery 12 volt one of	STXW 9A	
Ignition coil	Q 12 type L	45020 A
Distributor	DKY 4A type DA 34	40048 B or D
Dynamo	C 45 YV3 type GC 24	228334
Dynamo shaft extension	DA 31/1	228331
Starter motor	M 418 G type L-O	255378
Starter switch	ST 10	764251
Control box, to TC 3413	RF 91	
Control box, from TC 3414	RF 95/2 type L	37057 E
Instrument panel	DA 2148	30132 A
Stop lamp switch	54 C	315725
Stop & tail lamp (chrome plated)	ST 51	524754
Headlamp (chrome plated) dipping w. deep domed diamond glass	MBD 140	055232 or 50291 A
Headlamp (chrome plated) non-dipping w. deep domed horseshoe glass	MBD 140	055279 or 50102 A
Side lamp (chrome plated)	1130	523529
Fog lamp (chrome plated), to TC 4738	FT 27	532622
Fog lamp, from TC 4739	SFT 462	053143 or 55063 A
Horn	HF 1234	069212 A or 70083 A
Driving mirror	160 CAB; arm type DA	580435
Windscreen wiper motor	CWT DA 34	072545
Windscreen wiper arm, 5.5in (7in blade)		732928

The original pre-war type regulator and fuse box, here on TA0375, were mounted on the left-hand side of the toolbox.

On the TC, the regulator moved to the right-hand side and was mounted on the battery box. The early TC regulator had fuses concealed inside. (Courtesy Tim Jackson)

On later TCs, this type of regulator was fitted, with two external fuses below the cover, we can just see the end of one of the fuses.

THE TA, TB AND TC MODELS

BODY AND BODY TRIM

The body was constructed on classic coach building principles, with an ash frame reinforced by a steel framework and incorporating some plywood panelling; it was covered in steel panels. The bodies were made by Morris Motors Bodies Branch in Coventry (not as has been suggested by Carbodies in Coventry), although the front bulkhead was added by MG at Abingdon. This was the reason why the bulkhead was not originally painted in body colour. On the TA and TB it was black, on the TC it was at first light grey, but a change was made to a body-coloured bulkhead in 1948. Most experts agree that the engine colour was changed back to red at about the same time that the bulkhead was changed to body colour.

Being prone to attack from rot as well as rust, the body was by far the weakest area on any T-type. Fortunately, all body parts are available, even to the extent that complete replacement body kits are manufactured, and indeed have been since the 1980s. The basis for the body ash frame were the two bottom rails under the doors; these were reinforced by the steel "body chassis frame" members which also incorporated vertical extensions, joined to the front side pillar and the door hinge pillar at the back. The front side pillar and the front door (locking) pillar were joined at the top by cross-members to which the scuttle top panel was attached. The doors had two hinges which were painted body colour. The hinge pillars were quite substantial, and joined the rather intricate rear wheel arch top members. A back panel completed the basic wooden frame. A detachable plywood panel fitted into a wooden frame at the bottom of the tonneau; this gave access to the rear axle and shock absorbers, and to the batteries on the TA and TB models. The floorboards were made from seven-ply plywood, in one piece on either side of the prop shaft tunnel, and were originally left untreated. They were attached to the tunnel, to the front toeboard and side pillars, and with brackets to the heelboard. The prop shaft tunnel was a steel pressing, painted black and fixed to the chassis cross members. The toeboard at the front of the bulkhead was another steel pressing, usually painted black, but on the TC may also be grey or body colour to match the bulkhead.

The body tub from TC0999 while undergoing restoration gives some idea of the simplicity of the design. The rear panel is actually plywood. (Courtesy Tim Jackson)

The external panels were mostly extremely simple, only the double-humped top scuttle panel and the wings having any pronounced curvature. Where the wings met the bodywork or valances, there was body-colour beading made from Rexine wrapped round a cord centre. The wing stays and the underside of the wings were painted body colour. The running boards were separate pressings, bolted to the front wings with a beading, and did not quite butt up to the rear wings. It is debated exactly how much of a gap there should be here – about 1¼in (32mm) seems to be right! At the front end of the

These two photos show the new plywood floorboards and inner panels of the body of TC0999. We can also see the runners for the seat cushion slides, and the black-painted prop shaft tunnel. It can just be spotted that the centre panel at the rear of the tonneau is separate and opens out as the side screen storage compartment is behind it. (Courtesy Tim Jackson)

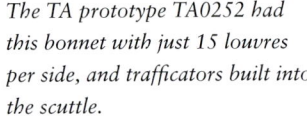

The TA prototype TA0252 had this bonnet with just 15 louvres per side, and trafficators built into the scuttle.

All the other cars from TA to TC have 21 louvres in each bonnet side. This photo of TC10215 also shows the position of the rear bonnet handle. On the post-war TCs, the foot of the windscreen pillar often seems to be above, rather than on, the feature line.

The TA prototype, showing the large bulge in the bonnet side to provide clearance to the dynamo, about half-way up the louvres.

The dynamo bulge was different on the XPAG-engined cars. The white car is TA0375 with the bulge higher up in relation to the louvres, the blue car is TC10215 with the bulge lining up with the bottom of the louvres, and the front bonnet handle was moved rearwards.

car was a valance or apron in the area between the chassis dumb-irons, with six louvres of increasing width from front to rear forming a triangular pattern. It was secured by body-coloured bolts, which on restored cars often end up being chrome-plated.

Some confusion has arisen because MG had the infuriating habit of handing out publicity pictures of a prototype TA (registered CJO 617) well into the TA's career. This car, which on occasion has even had to pose as a TB or TC, had only 15 bonnet louvres and trafficators built into the sides of the scuttle. In fact all production TA, TB and TC models had 21 bonnet louvres, and trafficators were not fitted on two-seaters as standard. The central bonnet hinge was made from chrome-plated brass and had chrome-plated end caps. Rubber protectors were fitted with rivets to the bottom corners of the bonnet side panels.

All of these cars had a pear-shaped bulge on the left-hand bonnet side panel to clear the dynamo. On the TA it was situated about halfway up the louvres, on the TB and TC it

THE TA, TB AND TC MODELS

The front apron, here on TA2864, is similar on all cars, as is the badge bar with the bracket for guiding the staring handle. This photo shows the front number plate backing plate with the raised lip and round corners, and the horn and fog lamp, which again were found on all cars. Late TCs had a different fog lamp.

On the pre-war cars, TA and TB, which had the slightly narrower body tub, there were three tread strips on each running board. (Courtesy Frank Langridge)

was lower down, towards the bottom of the louvres.

Although they are nearly indistinguishable to the casual observer, there were in fact three different types of open two-seater bodies fitted to these cars. The original TA body was body type number B.269. This can be distinguished by its narrow rear wings without a central stiffening rib, and the wide petrol tank. In 1937, it was replaced by body type number B.270 with wider rear wings incorporating a central rib, and a narrower petrol tank. This body was continued on the TB. The TC had body type number B.280, the main difference being that it was allegedly 4in (102mm) wider between the rear door pillars – I understand the actual width difference has been found to be more like 2in (51mm). A quick way of telling a TC from a pre-war car is by looking at the running boards: on the TA and TB they had three tread strips each, while the TC only had two. These strips were of rubber set in aluminium. The scuttle area remained the same width so the windscreen was the same on all three models, and the bonnet was the same width also.

The bright body trim parts were chrome-plated. These included the bonnet handles and the door handles which were of similar design, shaped like a very elongated diamond with the MG octagon towards the front. The two bonnet handles on either side should appear horizontal - if not, the locks are

The TC with the wider body had only two tread strips on the running board. (Courtesy Tim Jackson)

The door handles are the same design on all cars, with the MG octagon and a stretched octagon as escutcheon, and should sit at this angle.

53

The bonnet handles are of a design very similar to the door handles. This handle should perhaps be closer to horizontal.

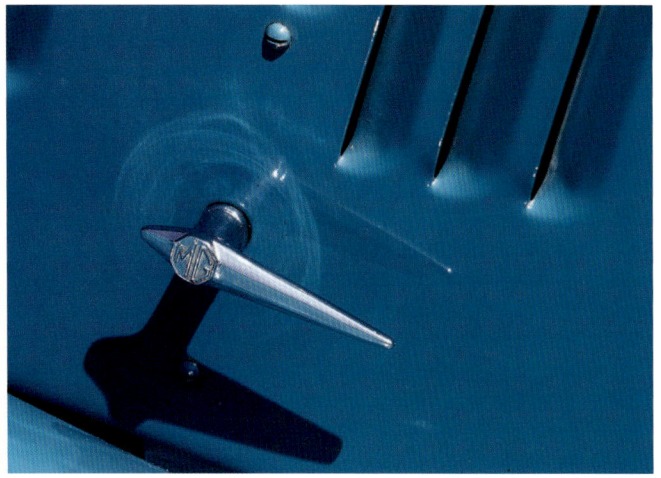

The pre-war mirror had a Lucas medallion. We can see the wing nut for tightening in the quadrant for either the upright or folded position for the windscreen. The foot of the windscreen pillar should probably be more closely aligned with the feature line on the pre-war TA and TB cars.

worn! The door handles were aligned parallel with the sloping, cut-away part of the door top. The door handle escutcheons were vertically elongated octagons, and should be at the same angle as that of the MG badge in the handle itself. The two-seater did not have external key-operated locks.

The windscreen was made by Auster and was fitted with toughened Triplex glass (except for some export TCs which had laminated glass). A small Auster badge appeared on the inside of the bottom frame. The frame and pillars were chrome-plated. By loosening a wing nut on either side, the windscreen could be folded flat over the bonnet. A rubber apron provided a seal between the windscreen frame and the scuttle, and rubber gaskets were interposed between the pillars and the bodywork. The pillars should be flush to the curvature of the scuttle panel, and they should stop above the panel break line on the side of the scuttle. On the inside of the windscreen there was often a suction-type tax disc holder with a small MG badge, but I am not certain whether this was supplied by the factory as standard equipment, and it would have been omitted on most export cars. It is not quoted in the TA/TB Service Parts List.

A rear view mirror, Lucas type 160 in chrome-plated finish, was mounted on an arm on the right hand windscreen pillar, so it could be used also when the screen was folded flat. The mirror was rectangular in shape and could be turned

The windscreen was the same on all cars, with a rubber apron providing a seal to the scuttle. This is the early TA, TA0375.

The Auster badge found on the inside of the lower windscreen frame. This car, by the way, would appear to have a full-length tonneau cover, hence the two lift-the-dot fixings.

THE TA, TB AND TC MODELS

for vertical or horizontal position. Pre-war mirrors had a Lucas medallion which was discontinued on the post-war version. Later Tickford coupés had an internal mirror with a suction type fitting. Post-war, export TCs were often fitted with a centrally-mounted internal mirror, typically fitted on the scuttle. A chrome-plated badge bar was fitted above the front dumb-iron apron. In addition to the horn and fog lamp previously mentioned, it carried a centrally mounted bracket for the starting handle.

Black-painted backing plates for front and rear number plates were fitted to all home market cars, but that on the front was deleted on some export cars. The rear one also carried the stop and tail lamp and was included on the export cars, except the late model North American specification TCs. The front plate had a raised lip round the edge, and should correctly be hung so that the top is level with the front of the front apron. There were different types of rear backing plates. On the TA, there was an "ear" for the round tail lamp at one end of the plate and the other end was square. On the TB and TC, the plate had both ends squared off. Some reproduction rear backing plates have two rounded-off ends which suits present-day installation of two D-shape lamps and looks very neat.

TOOL KIT

Opening the bonnet revealed a bulkhead-mounted toolbox, accessible from either side, with lids hinged in the centre, fastened by clips, and painted in the colour of the bulkhead. TA and TB toolbox lids were from nine-ply plywood. Early TAs had felt-lined toolboxes, with the small tools stored in a canvas roll. Later TAs and TBs had inserted moulded rubber tool trays

There are different opinions as to which tool tray goes which side of the toolbox, and even which way round the trays should fit... These are both from the same car, TB0415. The TA tool kit is similar. The spark plug holder is an extra. (Courtesy Frank Langridge)

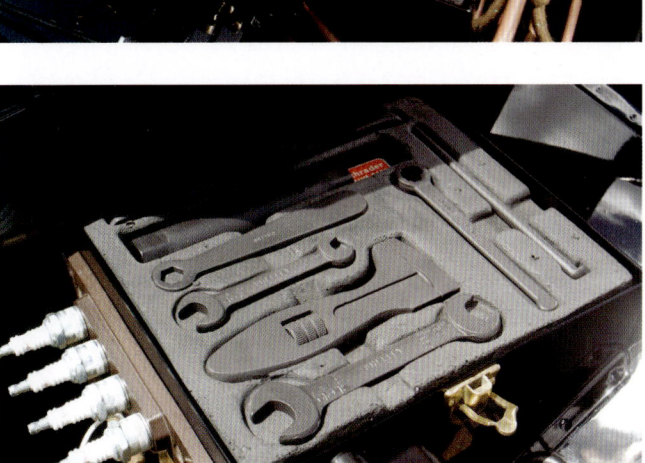

The pump, the jack with handle, and as a bonus, a contemporary style of hand-held inspection lamp which was plugged into the power point on the instrument panel. On the left of the picture, you may spot the lubrication nipple for the rear spring sliding trunnion on this early TA.

55

SUMMARY OF TOOL KIT (here listed in the order of the TC Service Parts List)

	TA/TB	TC	
Tappet spanner ring type	S 78/2	S 78/2	
Jack, with handle	A 1075	A 1075	Shelley double lift type
	Later A 1337		with separate handle
Cylinder head nut spanner ring type	2368	2368	
Lockheed bleeder screw wrench	S 78/13		TA and TB
Drain tube for Lockheed system	S 78/15	S 78/25	Or in container: Lockheed 3919/4
Lockheed bleeder screw wrench small, TC		S 78/26	Lockheed 8112
Lockheed bleeder screw wrench large, TC		S 78/27	Lockheed 13836
Hammer	P 330/130	P 330/130	¾ lb ball pein Hammer no. 89
Pliers	P 330/104	P 330/104	6in combination pliers no. 81
Grease gun, TA early	A 884		Enots; to TA 2517
Grease gun, TA late, and TB	A 1121		Tecalemit; from TA 2518
Grease gun, TC early		S 78/28	Tecalemit GB 2750
Grease gun, TC late		A 1135	
Tool roll, on early TA two-seaters	P 330/100		
Tool tray off-side (right-hand)	S 68/23		Late TAs and all TBs
Tool tray near side (left hand)	S 68/24		Late TAs and all TBs
Tool roll, TC, no. 1 canvas		S 78/29	
Adjustable spanner	P 330/103	S 78/30	TA and TB: 6in King Dick
			TC: 7in Shelley
Copper head hammer	P 330/117	P 330/117	
Tyre levers, 2 of	P 330/126	P 330/126	
Tyre valve spanner	S 78/11	S 78/11	
Distributor screwdriver and feeler gauge	S 78/12	S 78/12	Lucas 400174 E
Tyre pump	S 78/22	S 78/22	Shelley 14in black, stirrup type
Three box spanners			
3/16in by 1/4in by 4in	P 330/141	S 330/141	
5/16in by 3/8in by 4.75in	P 330/140	S 330/140	
7/16in by 1/2in by 8in	S 78/5	S 78/5	
Tommy bar	P 330/110	S 330/110	
Three pressed double ended spanners			
3/16in by 1/4in	S 78/6	S 78/6	
5/16in by 3/8in	S 78/7	S 78/7	
7/16in by 1/2in	S 78/8	S 78/8	
Screwdriver	S 78/9	S 78/9	10in Perfect Pattern
Tappet feeler gauge 0.015in TA and TB	S 78/3		
Tappet feeler gauge 0.019in; TC		S 78/31	
Starting handle	MG 706/378	MG 862/106	
Clip for ditto	S 52/9		

for the smaller tools. Below these trays the larger tools were held in place by clips. The jack was clipped to the front panel of the toolbox, and rested on a wedge-shaped block of wood. Clips on the sloping bulkhead panel held the jack handle shaft, the wheel hammer, the grease gun, and the tyre pump.

The TC had a lidded battery box in front of the toolbox, which was therefore considerably narrower. No tool trays were fitted, and tools were simply stored in a canvas roll. The TC toolbox was lined with cream or off-white felt (not very practical!), and the toolbox lids were metal. All cars, at least in the home market, were supplied with a spare quart-tin of oil, typically Duckham's N.O.L., but only on the TC was there a special holder for it on the front of the battery box. Opinions differ as to whether export cars had this oil can, I think some of them did. The grade of oil originally supplied was NP3 in winter, and NP5 in summer.

THE TA, TB AND TC MODELS

The pre-war seat had a squab with 20 flutes, here on TA0375, apart from the two end pieces. The two seat cushions had eight flutes each.

The TB seat is basically the same, and the door trim panels should be identical on all cars; this map pocket is not quite correct.

The TA and TB have the quadrants for squab adjustment fitted on the inside of the rear wheel arches.

INTERIOR TRIM

The seat had a one-piece squab but there were two separate seat cushions, individually adjustable on slides on the floorboards. The early TA model with body type B.269 had a rather tiresome squab adjustment where you had to re-position the squab manually, with dowels on the bottom of the squab fitting into different holes in two racks on the floor. On body type B.270 and on all later cars, the squab was hinged to the cushions. At the top, the squab was attached to the body with a quadrant on either side, adjustable by wing nuts. On the TA and TB, the quadrants were mounted on the inner sides of the rear wheel arches; on the TC, they were on top of the wheel arches.

The seat back and the bottoms were of five-ply plywood. TA and TB seats were constructed with horsehair padding over a spring base for both cushion and squab. On some cars, the cushions also incorporated Moseley "Float-on-Air" inflatable rubber cushions, which you pumped up with a bicycle pump. They are likely to have perished on most cars. The TC had a similar squab, but cushions of solid sponge rubber or Dunlopillo. The seat was upholstered in Connolly's Vaumol leather on the TA and TB, and Celstra leather on the TC. The extra width of the TC was revealed in the seat squab, which had 22 flutes, apart from a narrower flute at each end. The TA and TB only had 20 flutes and the end flutes. The seat cushions always had eight flutes each.

On early TCs, the seat cushions simply butted up to the squab. On later cars, the rears of the cushions were recessed into the bottom of the squab. The earlier TCs had leather all round on the inner sides and the back edges of the seat cushions, this was replaced by Rexine on later cars. There were some unspecified changes to the seat squab after 1300 bodies, and to the seat bases and cushions after first 1800 bodies. It is not clear whether this refers to the rearrangement of the cushion and squab, or to the change from leather to Rexine for some of the trim. The back of the seat squab was covered in Rexine leather cloth, supposedly black on the pre-war cars, but matching the upholstery colour on the TC.

The door panels and side trim panels were in thin plywood. Originally the door panels were trimmed in leather, but some time during the TC's career Rexine was substituted. Rexine was used on the other trim panels on all cars. For the restorer who craves absolute originality, Rexine is likely to be a bit of a headache – there is no comparably awful quality vinyl on the market now! The door panels each had a map pocket following the shape of the door, and the top edge of the pocket was always in leather, even on Rexine-trimmed door panels. Around the edge of the door was a stitched beading, hiding the panel pins, commonly called "Hidem Banding".

Like the pre-war cars, the early TCs had seat cushions which butted up to the bottom of the seat squabs. The squab now had 22 flutes. It is worth noting that this car was restored without tread plates, as these may have been missing on early TCs. (Courtesy Tim Jackson)

The later TCs had seat cushions which were recessed into the bottom of the seat squab. This car has the typical sill tread plates with the legend "The MG Car Company Ltd"…

… as can be seen in this photo.

I suspect that at least one of these door trim panels is a reproduction, but broadly speaking both have the correct pattern for the map pocket, and the correct Silent Travel door lock. The pre-war cars had this small round plate for the forward side screen mounting point, but the TC had the much bigger rectangular plate.

Chrome-plated Wilmot Breeden Silent Travel door locks were fitted on the door trims, with a release lever on top of the lock. Each door had two sidescreen mounting points, at the rear in a socket within the thickness of the door, at the front on the door trims. The front mounting points were chrome-plated with a one-winged fastening nut. Their backing plates were round on pre-war cars, rectangular on the TC. At the bottom of each door opening was an aluminium sill tread plate, originally neatly lettered with the legend "The M.G. Car Company Ltd." – at least on the pre-war cars. It has been suggested that early TCs did not have any sill tread plates,

THE TA, TB AND TC MODELS

The quadrants for adjusting the seat squab on the TC were mounted on top of the rear wheel arches. (Black TC courtesy Tim Jackson)

leaving the wood of the body frame exposed. I do not think this is likely, and the TC Service Parts List does indicate that the first 4836 bodies had sill tread plates of the pre-war type, part numbers B.269/120 (right-hand side) and B.269/121 (left-hand side). On later TCs there were plain sill tread plates without lettering, part numbers B.280/134 (right-hand side) and B.280/135 (left-hand side).

The floor covering was short-pile black carpet, Courtauld's Karvel, with a rubberized hessian or jute back. The edges were not originally bound, except the area immediately behind the gear lever. The prop shaft tunnel was carpeted, but the gearbox tunnel was only carpeted on early TAs; other cars had a moulded rubber cover over the gearbox and remote control. On the driver's side was a rubber heel mat with an outward-facing MG octagon. The carpet was secured with lift-the-dot fasteners and press studs and was laid over a felt underlay which did not extend to the toeboard or prop shaft tunnel. The heel board (the vertical panel just behind the seat) was not carpeted but was painted black, and the starting handle was fitted in clips on the heel board. The bottom of the tonneau area may have had a rubber mat on some pre-war cars, and was covered by carpet on the TC. At the rear of the tonneau was a vertical compartment for the sidescreens.

This is the correct rubber heel mat inset in the carpet in the driver's footwell, with the MG octagon logo facing sideways. Presumably the mat had been designed to fit in their larger models. (Courtesy Tim Jackson)

This was lined with black felt and had a Rexine-covered flap hinged at the bottom, fastened with a strap at the top.

Under the dashboard was found a masking panel or baffle board made from black millboard, stretching all the way forward to the toeboard and from side to side of the scuttle. The steering column had to be taken out to remove the panel; for this reason it has often been left out on restored cars, to give easier access to the wiring behind the dashboard. The accelerator pedal, mounted on the toeboard, had a roller-type hard rubber or ebonite pad.

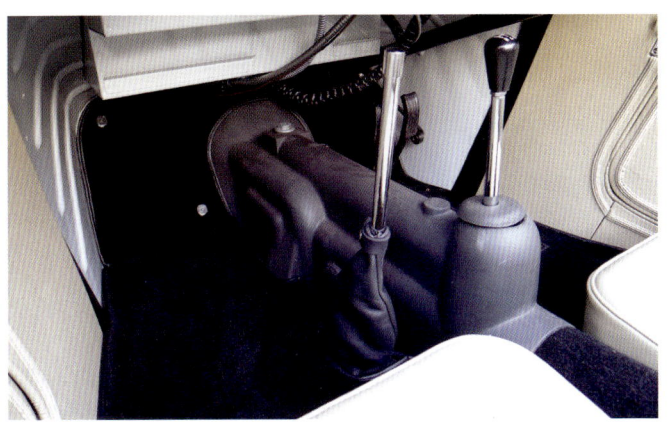

This is the rubber cover which was fitted over the remote control and gearbox tunnel, here on the TC, and this car has the correct black carpet, although it was not originally edge bound. (Courtesy Tim Jackson)

The hood frame from the inside. Most TCs had light tan frames, fawn hood covers, and fawn side screens, but early cars like this seem to have had black frames, black hood covers, and black side screens. (Courtesy Tim Jackson)

The rear side screens are fitted through small slots in the tonneau cover. (Courtesy Tim Jackson)

WEATHER EQUIPMENT

The hood and side screens were made from twill or single duck, black on pre-war cars, and usually fawn on the TC. Similarly, the hood and side screen frames were painted black on pre-war cars, and mostly light grey or tan on the TC. There were two side screens on each side: the front side screen was mounted on the door, as described above, and the rear side screen formed a quarter light behind the door. The actual windows were from mica or celluloid, with a chrome-plated beading round their edges. This beading hid the bolts used to attach the side screens to their frames.

This is how the front side screen mounted on the door. The central strap holds the signalling flap in place with a press stud. (Courtesy Tim Jackson)

A metal stiffener was sandwiched in the fabric material round the lower portion of the side screens. The lower fabric-covered half of the front side screens pivoted outwards, permitting the driver to make hand signals. A strap secured the signalling flap to the inside door panel, with a lift-the-dot on pre-war cars and a press stud on TC and later cars. The top line of the front and rear side screens formed a straight

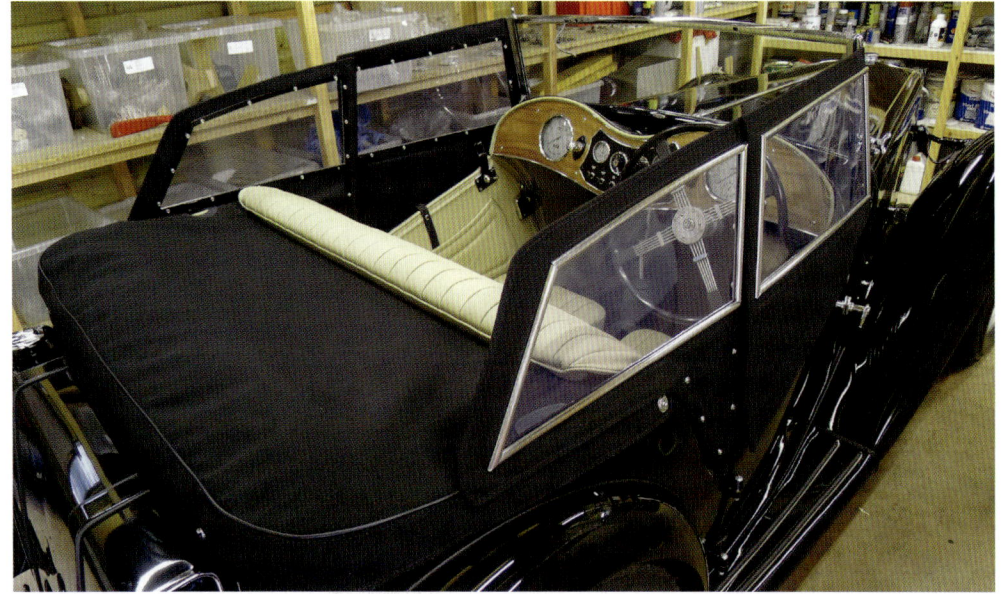

The side screens stow away in the compartment at the rear of the tonneau like this.

THE TA, TB AND TC MODELS

unbroken line, sloping downwards towards the rear. The handbooks gave precise instructions about how to store the side screens in the compartment at the rear of the tonneau, to avoid damaging the celluloid windows.

The hood frame had two bows and was attached to the inside of the body, at the top just behind the seat squab. The hood cover had a narrow celluloid rear window, originally split in two with a central vertical dividing strip, but in 1948 the TC was given a larger, one-piece rear window. At the back, the hood cover was tacked to the rear top rail of the body. A press stud on each side secured the corner flaps. When the hood was erected, dowels on the top of the windscreen frame fitted into holes on the hood front rail which was then held in place by two chrome-plated wing nut fasteners on the inside of the hood. Neither the hood nor the tonneau cover had the contrast colour piping sometimes seen on modern reproductions.

This is a comparison between TA0375 in white and TC0999 in black. Supposedly, all the pre-war cars had black hood, hood frame, and side screens, and the fawn hood frame seen on the white TA was more likely to be found on a TC. (Black TC courtesy Tim Jackson)

This late TC has the correct fawn hood, but on a black hood frame. This photo of the partially folded hood shows the later single rear window.

Like the TA, the TC seen here has the correct divided rear window in the hood. (Courtesy Tim Jackson)

With the hood raised the single rear window shows up better. This car which is in the USA has the vertical bumper guards.

61

The original half-tonneau cover was tucked over the tonneau rail on the back of the seat squab, and then retained with these straps and lift-the-dot fasteners. (Courtesy Tim Jackson)

DASHBOARD AND INSTRUMENTS

The layout of the dashboard was broadly similar on all models including the Tickford coupé. The facia panel was plywood covered in walnut veneer. Two types of veneer have been found: either in one piece with horizontal grain, or in two pieces with a symmetrical grain pattern. In 1948 the TC acquired a Rexine-covered dashboard, from approximately TC 5380. This was coloured to match the upholstery and trim. On the Rexine covered dashboard, cup washers were added to the eight screws holding the dashboard in place. Around the panel was chrome-plated beading, with Rexine piping between the dashboard and the scuttle. This piping continued downwards on either side along the door shut line, between the door pillar and the trim panel on the side of the scuttle.

The standard tonneau cover supplied with these cars was just that, only covering the area behind the seats. On pre-war cars it was made from black Rexine, also seen on early post-war cars. From approximately TC 5178 (in 1948), the tonneau cover was made from the same material as the hood. The tonneau cover was secured with four lift-the-dot fasteners below the edge of the hood. There was one on each side of the petrol tank, and one on each side of the body, in the top corner behind the door. The front of the tonneau cover was tucked over the black-painted tonneau rail on the back of the seat squab, and was held in place by elastic straps and lift-the-dots about halfway down the squab. The tonneau cover had small leather patches for reinforcement around holes for the rear sidescreen mounting points, to permit the use of sidescreens with the hood down and the tonneau cover in place. A full-length tonneau cover with a central zip was optional before the war, but does not seem to have been offered on the TC when new.

The instruments were grouped symmetrically. Starting from the left, in front of the passenger was a 5in (127mm) Jaeger chronometric speedometer, marked up to 100mph, with a five-figure total distance recorder (top) and a three-figure plus decimal trip recorder (below), with a re-setting button below the dashboard. At least on the TC, the dial is marked with the part number S.461 and the gearing of 1675 (tpm, or turns per mile). Kilometre speedometers were fitted to export cars, as required, marked to 160 km/h. Next to the speedometer was a Lucas DF41 map reading lamp, with a chrome-plated housing and a black painted base. It was switched on by turning the lamp housing.

In the centre of the dashboard was a Lucas instrument panel, made from chrome-plated sheet brass but painted black so the chrome-plating showed only on the edge. In this panel were set a Lucas ammeter (reading to +/- 20 amp), followed by a Lucas combined ignition and lighting switch. On the TA and TB this switch was a type PLC 2 which also had two positions

This is TA0375, quite an early car, but the layout of the dashboard is the same on all cars to the end of TC production.

The petrol tap marked M and R for Main and Reserve is found only on the pre-war cars.

The pre-war cars have a rev counter where the clock dial is integral with the main dial. We can also see the green Thirtilite next to it, as well as a bit of what appears to be a non-standard dual oil and water gauge.

The speedometer in front of the passenger is again similar on all cars.

We know that this instrument panel is from a pre-war car, in fact TB0415, as it has the ignition and lighting switch with two positions for low and high charge. (Courtesy Frank Langridge)

for high and low charge. These were not necessary on the TC with its automatic voltage regulator, so the switch was a type PLC 6. The ignition lock had a Wilmot Breeden barrel with a key number in the MRN range, from MRN 1 to MRN 54.

Next on the centre panel there was a Lucas combined horn push and dip switch, and finally a Jaeger oil pressure gauge. Below was a row of minor controls, with the function of each being marked in horizontal lettering on the panel directly above. Again going from left to right, they were the starter pull, the mixture (choke) control, the fog lamp switch, a two-pin plug socket for an inspection lamp, the ignition warning lamp, the panel light switch, and a screw-type slow running control or hand throttle. All switches and knobs were black.

To the right of the central panel was a Lucas "Thirtilite" device which matched the map reading lamp. This lit up green when the speed was between 20 and 30mph and went out again when one exceeded 30mph. Export cars had an additional map reading lamp in this position. In 1948, the colour of the instrument panel and of the bases of the map reading lamp and "Thirtilite" was changed from black to a metallic tan or bronze colour, probably at the time when the Rexine-covered dashboard was introduced.

In front of the driver was a 5in (127mm) Jaeger rev counter (tachometer) which was driven off a reduction box on the dynamo. It read to 6500rpm with no red line indicated. At the bottom of the rev counter dial was a clock. On the TA and TB this was a mechanical eight-day clock, and the dial was integral with the main dial of the rev counter. The TC was fitted with an electric clock, with a separate clock dial. In both cases the resetting (or winding) button protruded below the edge of the dashboard. The TC rev counter was marked with the part number, K.30. Finally, to the right of the steering column was the petrol tap with two positions, main and reserve (no off position). This was black with white lettering. On the TC it was replaced by a warning lamp which

One of the changes on the TC was that the lighting switch no longer had positions for charging, as the dynamo was now of the compensated voltage control type. (Courtesy Tim Jackson)

The TC rev counter had a dial where the clock was a separate inset dial. To the right of the rev counter is the green warning light for low fuel level.

On later TCs, the veneer facia panel was replaced by a Rexine covered panel, and the instrument panel was changed to a tan colour, with brown controls, and the lettering above each control was discontinued.

started to flash when there were around three gallons left in the tank. Very early cars had an amber light marked "PET" soon replaced by a green light marked "FUEL".

All the instruments were set in chrome-plated rims, and had silver-grey dials with dark brown figures and pointers. There was some variation in the colour of the dials, and it would seem that over the years the colour gradually became a darker silver-grey with a greener hue. The instruments had rim lighting, through apertures in the rim between the dial and the glass. Green translucent celluloid in the lighting apertures gave that ghostly green glow mentioned in contemporary accounts!

Common additions to the dashboard include a grab handle with a central octagonal badge fitted on the passenger side. There are evidently several different lengths, in that grab handles have been seen fixed by one, or two, or none, of the dashboard fixing screws. Jaeger water and oil temperature gauges were available, their design matching the standard instruments. In those days, the dealer who sold a car often fitted a plaque to the dashboard, and the plaque from the main distributor in London, University Motors, is seen quite frequently. This is rectangular, with two shields flanking a St Christopher medallion, the company name above, and the address and telephone number below.

SUMMARY OF TC INSTRUMENTS AND CONTROLS:

	Supplier	Type	Lucas service number
Speedometer with Thirtilite	Jaeger	S 461	
Rev counter with electric clock	Jaeger	K 30	
Oil pressure gauge	Jaeger	OG 54	
Ammeter	Lucas	L 29	369269
Ignition and lighting switch	Lucas	PLC 6 L 114	34018 A
Horn and dip switch	Lucas	17 A L 15	380191
Panel light switch	Lucas	PS 6 type L	314090
Fog lamp switch (as above)	Lucas	PS 6 type L	314090
Ignition warning light	Lucas	WL 3	318505
30mph dash light; green glass	Lucas	DF 41 glass DA 21	515145, 56042
Map reading light; plain glass	Lucas	DF 41 glass DA 23	545138 A, 56040
Petrol gauge tank unit	Jaeger	TA 107	
Petrol gauge warning light	Jaeger	WLP 1	

The distinctive profile of the TA Tickford drophead coupé, with the wider full-height doors on three hinges.

TICKFORD DROPHEAD COUPE BODY (TA & TB)

The Tickford coupé body was supplied by Salmons and Sons Ltd of Newport Pagnell in Buckinghamshire, a company which was later taken over by Aston Martin Lagonda, and the Newport Pagnell premises now houses Aston Martin Works, the company's heritage operation. There are various estimates of the number of Tickford coupés made. Mike Allison many years ago in *The Magic of the Marque* quoted 252 TAs and 57 TBs, total 309 cars.

In a letter written in 1961, Salmons and Sons stated that there were altogether 320 cars, but they did not split this between TA and TB models (information courtesy of Wiard Krook). I have since been given to understand that the actual Salmons records for their MG bodies do survive, although unfortunately they are in private hands and not generally accessible. I think that there were probably around 260 TAs and 60 TBs.

Oft-seen factory photos of a drophead coupé with a smooth rear end, an enclosed fuel tank, and apparently a small boot are believed to be the prototype, all production cars had a rear end with the standard external slab tank. The first Tickford bodied car was TA 2184, which started life in chassis form in March 1938 and was completed by Salmons in June, although the new model was not revealed publicly before August 1938. Production continued until August 1939. Although early post-war Tickford advertising "flew a kite" by showing drawings of what a Tickford TC might look like – with skirted front wings – no such car was ever built.

Apart from the MG chassis and engine numbers, the Tickfords were identified by a Salmons issued "job number". This was stamped on the back of the interior wooden trim pieces, on the back of the hood irons, and on an aluminium strip on the toolbox lid. As these numbers vary from at least 3673 to 5316, they must have been taken from a series shared by all Salmons-built bodies and are therefore not a guide to the production figures of the MG Midget coupés. Salmons also made Tickford drophead bodies for the SA, VA and WA MG models of the 1936-39 period, and for several Rover models.

The Midget drophead coupé was rather more civilised than the two-seater, and as one might expect carried a weight penalty of 2cwt (approximately 100kg): the TB two-seater weighed in at 15½cwt (788kg), the coupé at 17½cwt (890kg). Starting at the front end, the Tickford normally had the radiator slats painted body (as opposed to upholstery) colour, and there was a moulding along the sides of the bonnet top panels to line up with a moulding on the scuttle side and along the top of the door. The Tickford was the one TA or TB model that did have trafficators as standard, built into the sides of the scuttle. The

FACTORY-ORIGINAL MG T-SERIES

The Tickford drophead coupé had the wiper motor mounted remotely under the bonnet. Since the body is a little wider than the standard scuttle at the top, there is slightly more of a step here. Just above the wiper motor, on the toolbox lid, is the Tickford body number plate.

The door trim have wood waist rails and inset map pockets. There are wind-down windows but the door locks are the same as on the two-seater. Salmons & Sons put their coachbuilder's plate on the door trim.

The Tickford windscreen opens, as it is hinged at the top in the integral body-colour frame.

aperture may or may not have a beading round it. The Lucas trafficators had chrome-plated arms.

The windscreen pillars were fixed and painted body colour, but the chrome-plated windscreen frame (made by Perfecta of Birmingham) was hinged at the top and opened up to a horizontal position. It was adjusted on two quadrants with knurled finger nuts. The doors were full height and incorporated wind-down windows, the winders being chrome-plated with ebonite knobs in either of two different styles. The driver's door had an external key-operated lock, with the locking barrel set in the MG octagon of the door handle. While the handles were similar to those found on two-seaters, the octagonal escutcheons were mostly different, not being elongated. However, some cars had the elongated octagonal escutcheon.

The doors were wider than the two-seater doors, and had a cut-out to allow for the curve of the rear wing at the rear edge towards the bottom. They were supported on three body-colour hinges each. The door windows were guided in chrome-plated channels front and rear; the rear one was hinged and could be folded forward to horizontal above the glass when the window was wound fully down. The inside door trim panels were finished at the top with a walnut garnish rail which matched the dashboard rail at the rear edge of the scuttle. The internal door locks were similar to those found on the two-seater, but sat upon alloy backing plates 1/8in (3mm) thick which compensated for the thickness of the trim panels. In each door trim panel was a slight recess with a map pocket, which had an elasticated top.

Interior trim was generally to a higher standard than on the two-seater. There were two individually adjustable bucket-type seats with forward hinging squabs. The seats incorporated "Float-on-Air" cushions. Seat upholstery and door trims were leather with a range of colours different from the two-seater. The back of the seat squabs and the edges of the frame of the seat bases were carpeted. Wilton carpeting (with bound edges) in colours to tone with the upholstery was used. On some cars the gearbox tunnel was carpeted, and so were the

THE TA, TB AND TC MODELS

I am not sure about the "mottled" effect carpet, and I think the carpet on the back of the seats should go closer to the edge than seen here. Strapped together with the folded hood are the two wood-trimmed cant rails which fit above the door windows. This is how the starting handle is clipped to the heel board, also on the two-seaters.

Two completely separate seats are fitted. The box on the tunnel is not original.

inner sides of the scuttle. An extra map pocket may be found on the passenger's side of the scuttle. The rear wheel arches, the heelboard, and the back panel of the tonneau were fully carpeted. The bottom of the luggage area in the tonneau was covered by a rubber mat.

The top of the scuttle was flat on the coupé and finished with a walnut garnish rail. In the centre of this was an ash tray. The dashboard was recessed under the scuttle and was a different shape from that on the two-seater, although the layout was broadly similar. The dashboard was made from solid walnut (at least one car had a painted dashboard) and had chrome-plated end pieces. The speedometer and rev counter were moved downwards and outwards, and the petrol tap was re-located on a bracket behind the dashboard. One additional control on the coupé was the trafficator switch, either with a warning lamp, or of the self-cancelling type. It took the place of the map reading lamp on the two-seater.

On the coupé, the wiper motor was mounted on the left-hand side of the bulkhead under the bonnet, outboard of the toolbox, and the wipers were mounted below the windscreen. The wipers were individually controlled from two knobs on the dashboard rail. Early Tickfords had an external mirror similar to the two-seater mirror, but later cars were fitted with a small internal mirror mounted centrally below the windscreen.

The outer hood cover was mohair, available in a variety of colours. The hood was fully lined, and between outer cover and lining was a layer of rubberized waterproof material. The hood was of the three-position type, where the front part could be rolled back and secured with straps in the "de ville" position. For this purpose, the cant rails above the side windows were folded back under the hood. These cant rails

The dashboard is in wood, but with chrome-plated end pieces. The garnish rail above it is in matching wood, and features a central ash tray. The dark brown knob above the steering wheel centre is one of the wiper controls. This car has a non-original trafficator stalk on the steering column, as the original switch has been replaced by a later water temperature gauge, on the left in this photo. The gearbox tunnel should not be carpeted.

The Tickford hood had external hood irons, and a single small rear window with a chrome plated frame. Unlike the two-seater, there was a choice of hood colour.

The front part of the hood may be rolled up to leave the main hood in this de ville position. This also shows us the trafficators in the side of the scuttle, and the moulding on the bonnet which continues through the door on to the rear quarter panel.

and the vertical hood pillars behind the side windows were painted body colour. Once the front portion had been folded, the hood irons were broken and the entire hood folded back. Even in the folded position the hood sat some way above the line of the body.

At the bottom of the hood, where it was attached to the rear of the body, was chrome-plated brass pin beading. There was also chrome-plated brass beading around the letterbox-slit glass rear window, which measured approximately 3½ by 20in (89mm by 508mm). An external mirror was a good idea whether the hood was up or down! An interior lamp was fitted above the rear window on the transverse hood stick.

According to the latest register (2012) at least 177 original Tickfords survive, 141 TAs and 36 TBs. This is a considerable proportion of the total number made but is naturally insignificant compared to the number of surviving two-seaters. Patterns for the carpets, upholstery, interior trim panels and hood all exist or have been re-created, and many items of body trim had been reproduced, often by owners who have restored their cars. Complete body tubs were also made, in the 1980s, by Naylor Brothers, and also by the Cooke Group of Wigston.

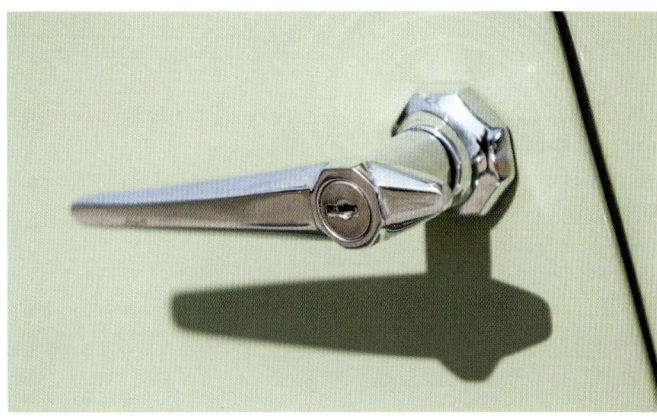

The driver's door on the Tickford has this locking handle.

The Tickford hood is fully lined, and is fitted with an interior light.

The factory-prepared TA trials cars such as this "Cream Cracker" had skimpy cycle-type wings, and 16inch rear wheels.

THE TA TRIALS CARS

After MG withdrew from racing in 1935, the company still continued to support the two well-established trials teams, the "Cream Crackers" and the "Musketeers". They had started out using PAs in 1934 and 1935, the Musketeers then used a special competition car based on the N-type Magnette, but for the 1937 season both teams adopted suitably modified versions of the TA, which they ran for two seasons, and in the case of the Musketeers, into 1939 as well. The Cream Cracker team cars were, as one would expect, finished in the classic MG colours of Cream body with Brown wings, while the Musketeer TAs were all Red.

The cars are well documented not least in Roger Thomas's book *M.G. Trials Cars* (1995) where they are listed as follows:

M.G. TRIALS CARS

Team	Season	Reg	Chassis	Engine	Name	Driver
Cream Crackers	1937	ABL 960 *	TA 0930	MPJG 1140		Toulmin
		ABL 962	TA 0932	MPJG 1177		Crawford
		ABL 964 *	TA 0934	MPJG 1192		Jones
Musketeers	1937	ABL 961	TA 0931	MPJG 1141	Athos	Macdermid
		ABL 963	TA 0933	MPJG 1181	Porthos	Bastock
		ABL 965	TA 0935	MPJG 503	Aramis	Langley
Cream Crackers	1938	BBL 78	TA 2017 chgd to EX 155/2	MPJG 2285 chgd to TPBG 1383		Toulmin
		BBL 79	TA 2018 chgd to EX 155/3	MPJG 2286 chgd to TPBG 1373		Crawford
		BBL 80	TA 2019 chgd to EX 155/4	MPJG 2291 chgd to TPBG 1397		Jones
		BBL 81	TA 2020 chgd to EX 155/5	MPJG 2595 chgd to TPBG 1384 or 792		Imhof
Musketeers	1938-39	BBL 82	TA 2044	MPJG 2267	Athos	Macdermid
		BBL 83	TA 2045	MPJG 2270	Porthos	Bastock
		BBL 84	TA 2046	MPJG 2275	Aramis	Langley
		BJB 412	TA 2518	MPJG 2771		Green

*These two cars, together with Imhof's works-prepared car TA trials car JB 9445 (a 1936 works demonstrator), were sold to the Scottish Highlanders team and repainted blue. They were trialled by various drivers in 1938.

The Cream Cracker trials TA carried two spare wheels.

On the dashboard of this trials car are the extra oil and water temperature gauges, and a grab handle. It has individual bucket seats (which look quite comfy) and basic rubber matting on the floor.

The modifications made to the TA competition cars are described below:

ENGINE ETC: Cylinder head skimmed by ³⁄₃₂in, washers of ³⁄₃₂in thickness fitted under cylinder head nuts; thin plug edge ground away; rocker brackets packed by ¹⁄₁₆in, with holes for oil feed; special valve springs and valve collars fitted to engines EX 156/1 and EX 156/3; new bottom collars; M1 needles to carburettors; tappets adjusted to 0.019in, valve cover marked accordingly; two petrol pumps with switches fitted; spare plug carriers fitted, of the six plug type; silencer moved ⅞in over to centre; exhaust tail pipe raised; accelerator stop fitted; Bowden throttle control fitted to steering column

TRANSMISSION: New gear ratios in gearbox; new type rear axle drive gear assemblies

CHASSIS: Higher front road springs, 2¼in free camber; axle straps shorter by 1in from 7⁷⁄₁₆in to 6⁷⁄₁₆in; front and rear shock absorbers of larger KN type with bottom pins reversed; those at rear also with links reversed

BRAKES: Armoured brake flexes; master cylinder with protector plates, double master cylinder pedal and push rod; brake pipe layout revised with new pipes

WHEELS AND TYRES: Double spare wheel carrier, with 4in longer packing sleeve, to take two wheels of 16in by 6in, fitted with competition tyres (i.e., "knobbly" trials tyres) and tubes; front wheels with competition tyres 4.50x19

BODYWORK AND FITTINGS: Aluminium bonnet and valances; cycle type wings and valances; rear number plate (square) on off-side rear wing; front number plate fitted 2in higher; competition number boards; door panels in aluminium; oil and water thermometers fitted (oil sump drilled and tapped for union)

Further modifications were subsequently made to the three

THE TA, TB AND TC MODELS

Musketeer cars for the 1937 Twelve-hour race at Donington, where the rear wheels were changed to N-type racing wheels; quick-release radiator caps were fitted, together with bonnet straps, special silencers and tail pipes, N-type duplex shock absorbers, and aluminium sumps. The gear ratios were changed back to standard.

The 1938 cars differed even more from standard. The new Cream Cracker cars which were given chassis numbers with the EX 155 prefixes (EX 155 being Abingdon's code for the TA) were fitted with 1548cc engines type TPBG from the VA, which were subsequently overbored to 73mm for a capacity of 1708cc. A VA-type gearbox was also fitted. By contrast, the new Musketeer cars retained their 1292cc engines, but were fitted Marshall 110 blowers, and Laystall crankshafts.

For the sake of completeness, the MG Experimental Register in the BMIHT archive at Gaydon lists two further cars with EX 155 chassis numbers:

EX 155/1, engine number 6594/1, dated to 22 February 1938
EX 155/6, was TA 2092, engine MPJG 2368 changed to TPBG 968 (i.e., a 1548cc unit)

It is not thought that these two cars were used for competition purposes.

POLICE CARS

MG cars, particularly Midgets, had been supplied for Police use since about 1930, with the Lancashire Constabulary being the biggest customer. It is not surprising therefore that the TA, TB, and TC models, also found favour with Police forces.

According to Andrea Green's book *MGs on Patrol* (1999), approximately the following numbers were Police cars:
TAs: 110 – of which 62 went to Lancashire
TBs: 18 – of which 4 went to Lancashire
TCs: 111 – of which 41 went to Lancashire

The question is how much these cars differed from standard. Typically, much of the Police equipment was fitted by the forces operating the cars. This would include signs, gongs, and radio or public address equipment. Some changes were however made to the cars at Abingdon, including larger-capacity batteries (with special cradles or battery boxes if necessary), higher-output dynamos, changes to wiring loom, and special certified accurate speedometers. The standard colour on Police cars was Black, mostly with Blue interior trim on pre-war cars. It has been speculated that one Police TA was fitted with a bored-out VA engine of 1708cc similar to the Trials TAs.

In 1939, Abingdon built a TB demonstrator with special Police equipment, BRX 266, which was photographed and included in a Police car brochure dated June 1939. On this car, the speedometer was in front of the driver, and there was an open glove pocket in front of the passenger, with an octagon-less grab handle, and a pull-out writing tray below the glove pocket. There was a Dulci public address system with a speaker mounted on the left-hand side of the bonnet,

with a microphone and control panel inside the car. The car was also fitted with a Philco radio – its aerial under the left-hand running board – a spot lamp combined with a rear view mirror on the driver's windscreen pillar, a "Police – Stop" sign at the rear, above the right-hand wing, as well as a first-aid kit and a fire extinguisher.

The ex-Police TC featured in this book, TC 0999 (yes, that chassis number is for real…) has a number of variations from standard:

• Bulkhead with oversized battery box, this and toolbox extended both left and right compared to standard car, repositioned fuel pump and ignition coil, extra holes for wiring
• Larger than usual bulge on the left-hand side of the bonnet to accommodate an oversize high-output dynamo
• Higher ratio final drive ratio of 4.875:1
• The speedometer however seems to be the standard type S 461 with 1675 tpm. I speculate this may be a replacement, since in conjunction with the higher rear axle ratio this will give inaccurate readings, contrary to the expectation of Police car speedometers.

Some Police TCs had a Police sign or loudspeaker fitted centrally on the badge bar. Some cars instead had the horn and fog lamp paired up on the left-hand end of the badge bar to make room for the loudspeaker or gong on the right-hand end.

The ex-Police TC still has the original bonnet with the extra-large bulge for the bulky Police-type high-output dynamo. The grey scuttle is typical of the early TCs, but some of the holes were unique to Police cars. The battery box was widened on the other side, as can be seen in a photo elsewhere in the book. (Courtesy Tim Jackson)

Some TCs in the USA were fitted with large direction indicator lamps on either side at the fuel tank, and had these bumper guards.

EXPORT VARIATIONS

Before the war, export variations were limited to such minor details as the provision, when required, of a kilometres speedometer, two dipping headlamps Lucas LBG 150 or LD 140 EF, and for countries driving on the right, the change-over in the positions of the horn, fog and tail lamps, all detailed in previous sections – with fog lamp on the right, and horn and tail lamp on the left. Export cars often had dry batteries type 6 LTW 11 and Dunlop Fort tyres. They typically did not have the Thirtilite, which was replaced by a second map reading lamp, or a licence disc holder.

A few TAs were sent to Australia in chassis-only form and were built up with locally made bodies, although these were probably similar to the standard two-seater bodies. Similarly a few TAs were sent to Eire in "unassembled" form – what we would now call CKD (Completely Knocked Down) exports – and after the war 84 TCs exported in CKD form were assembled by Messrs Booth Bros Ltd in Dublin (who later also assembled TDs and TFs). These CKD kits for Eire were supplied without spark plugs, tyres and tubes, and without springs, which were all sourced locally, and I expect paint and trim materials also came from local suppliers. Otherwise, it is unlikely that these Irish-assembled TAs or TCs differed greatly from the standard Abingdon assembled cars.

With the TC, a series of distinctly different export versions were recognised. The basic right hand drive export TC (type EXR) had double-dipping headlamps with twin-filament bulbs to both lamps, an extra map reading lamp in place of the "Thirtilite" and a rear view mirror positioned centrally above the dashboard. With the addition of a kilometres speedometer this model became type EXR/K. Interestingly, at least one car has been reported with a kilometres speedometer where the zero is to the top right of the dial, as opposed to the bottom left. However, these codes were not added to the chassis number on the guarantee plate, but all export cars did have an extra plate with the MG badge and the words "Made in England".

In 1948, a special model was evolved for sale to the USA and, presumably, Canada; some such cars were probably delivered in Britain for Personal Export, or may have gone to other markets, e.g. South America. Early TCs exported to North America were more or less to standard export specification. Some were fitted with bumper guards, which it is thought were added by American importers – either vertical rods front and rear, or simple horizontal full width bumpers without over riders. However, contemporary pictures of TCs in Australia or South America also occasionally show these cars fitted with bumpers. In the USA, a few TCs were re-painted in two-tone colour schemes when new, or had brake drums painted other than black.

Feedback from the important American market led to Abingdon incorporating the following alterations in export cars for the USA which were then recognised with the coding EX-U stamped after the chassis number on the guarantee plate:

- Full-width bumpers front and rear with over riders, and a central medallion to the rear bumper
- Badge bar, fog lamp, and external horn deleted
- Two Lucas windtone horns, WT6l4 and WT615, mounted under the bonnet
- Steering wheel in gold pearl finish instead of black
- Rear number-plate mounted centrally above rear bumper with Lucas number plate lamp type 467/1 (chrome-plated housing) above it
- Lucas type S.700 headlamps with twin filament bulbs, dipping to the right
- Laminated instead of toughened windscreen glass
- No "Thirtilite", but a second map reading lamp
- Rear view mirror centrally mounted on scuttle above the dashboard
- Flashing indicator lamps using the sidelamp bulb filaments
- Lucas type 482-l stop and tail lamps incorporating flashing indicators, using the stop light bulb filaments; these were bullet shaped lamps mounted on each side at the top of the petrol tank
- Flashing direction indicator switch (Lucas SD84 with built-in warning lamp) fitted in place of the inspection light sockets on the instrument panel
- Two relays fitted, Lucas model LIR L3, service number 33095 A; operation of direction indicator switch operated one of other of these relays, putting lamps on one side of car in circuit with flasher unit
- A "Tung-Sol" flashing unit was supplied and fitted in the

THE TA, TB AND TC MODELS

USA, a "slave unit" having been fitted at Abingdon
• High beam warning lamp in place of fog lamp switch
• Instrument panel re-arranged: ammeter and oil pressure gauge mounted centrally, ignition and lighting switch on the outside left, horn push and dip switch on the outside right
• Fuse box with two 50amp fuses

The fully-fledged "EX-U" model came into being only in December 1948, from chassis number TC 7380, and only 494 such cars were made before the end of TC production. Nevertheless, statistics kept by Abingdon's Production Control Department claim that 2001 "North American" TCs were made from 1947 to 1949, with 6 in 1947, 1473 in 1948, and 522 in 1949. We cannot be certain exactly how 1947 and 1948 cars to "North American" specification differed from other TCs. These statistics have led to the oft-repeated assertion that 2001 was the number of TCs actually exported to the USA, but this can be proved to be incorrect. Both production and export statistics will be found on page 82 of this book.

The fully-fledged EXU model of 1948-49 featured front and rear bumpers – with, in this case, an MG badge on the rear bumper – and these bullet-shaped rear lamps either side of the fuel tank. This car has the later type of TC fog lamp, even two of them. Other features such as the extra chrome plating are not original.

The same style of chassis plate – actually car number plate, or guarantee plate – was fitted to all cars from TA through TC. On the TA and TB, it was fitted on the front of the toolbox on the left-hand side.

This TC plate appears to be made from aluminium rather than brass. On the TC, it moved to the left-hand side of the battery box, and was accompanied by this patent plate. (Courtesy Tim Jackson)

IDENTIFICATION AND DATING (TA, TB AND TC)

The three models had chassis (or car) numbers prefixed with TA, TB and TC respectively, and the chassis number series began with 0251 for each model – as is probably well known, 251 was the telephone number of the MG factory. TA chassis numbers ran from TA 0251 to TA 3253, TB from TB 0251 to TB 0629; and TC from TC 0251 to TC 10251. The chassis number plate, or maker's guarantee plate, was found on the left-hand side of the front of the bulkhead-mounted toolbox on the TA and TB, while on the TC it was on the left-hand end of the battery box in front of the toolbox. The chassis number was also stamped on the frame itself, on the side or later the front of the left-hand dumb-iron. The only variation in the chassis number system was that TC cars to North American specification of 1948-49 had an additional code, "EX-U", stamped after the chassis number on the maker's plate.

This guarantee plate was also stamped with the engine number. The two types of engine found each had their different prefix for the engine number – MPJG on the TA, XPAG on the TB and TC. In addition the engine number was found on a plate on the engine itself. The TA had a round plate on the right-hand side of the crankcase, the TB and TC had an octagonal plate on the top of the bell housing visible from the left-hand side. TA engine numbers started from 501 and ran up to at least 3503. TB engine numbers also started from 501 and ran up to 883, with TC engine numbers following in the same sequence, from 884 to at least 10923.

Finally each car had a body number. The body number plate was attached to the left-hand (passenger side) body pillar inside the scuttle. This plate carried a body type number, which was B.269 (1936-37 TAs with narrow rear wings), B.270 (1937-39 TAs with wide rear wings, and TBs), B.278 (TA and TB Tickford coupés), or B.280 (TCs). No records exist of the body numbers for individual cars, but it is thought that the B.269 body numbers for the early TAs ran from 100 to 1090, with the B.270 body numbers also starting with 100. The body number stamped on the plate was followed by the body maker's batch number. Please refer to the Tickford section for a description of the Salmons Tickford body job numbers.

As previously mentioned, TC export cars carried a special "Made in England" plate adjacent to the chassis number plate. All TCs also had a patent number plate, listing the numbers of

On this TB, the car (or chassis) number was stamped in the outside of the left-hand front dumb-iron, but on the TC, it is on the front face of the same dumb-iron. (TC, Courtesy Tim Jackson)

THE TA, TB AND TC MODELS

The engine number plate was always octagonal. It is plain brass, but this example was badly discoloured, prior to restoration. On the TA it was fitted on the right-hand side of the crankcase, on the TB and TC on the left-hand side of the bellhousing. (Courtesy Tim Jackson)

This is how the body plate was mounted on the wooden frame member inside the scuttle in front of the passenger door on the TC. (Courtesy Tim Jackson)

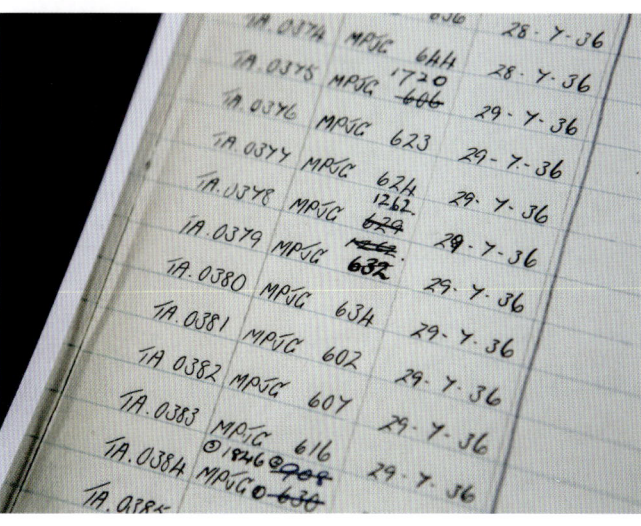

The MG Company recorded the issue of each guarantee plate in the ledgers still preserved by the MG Car Club – car number, engine number, and date, plus a column for comments, for instance if an engine was changed.

patents embodied in the construction of the car.

The following list of first chassis numbers issued in each year is taken from the ledgers giving the dates of issue of guarantee plates to each car (found in the archives of the MG Car Club). Although these dates are mostly slightly earlier than the actual production dates, they are nevertheless a good guide to dating individual cars. As far as the TC is concerned, the annual production figures implied by this series of chassis numbers do not quite match the figures compiled by Abingdon's Production Control Department found in the next section of this book. The reason is that the guarantee plates were usually issued at the start of the production process and this is reflected in the dates in the guarantee plate ledgers, but Production Control only counted a car towards their statistics when it came off the line, which could be several days later.

It is worth pointing out (and this applies to all T-types) that the engine and body numbers were not issued in strict numerical order by the sequence of chassis numbers, therefore the difference between the chassis number and the engine number will vary between cars of the same model. As far as the pre-war cars were concerned, if a car was fitted with a replacement engine by the factory when new or nearly new, quite often a new guarantee plate with the new engine number would be issued. Several examples of TA cars with such engine changes can be documented in the guarantee plate ledger. These replacement engines appear also to have had the MPJG prefix. Reconditioned factory replacement engines fitted in post-war years tend to have five-figure numbers, prefixed with A if of standard bore size, B if first overbore size, etc.

PRODUCTION DATES

TA	Jun 1936	TA 0253	first production TA; 0251 and 0252 were prototypes
	Jan 1937	TA 1016	
	Jan 1938	TA 2044	
	Mar 1938	TA 2187	first chassis for Tickford coupé
	Jan 1939	TA 3061	
	Apr 1939	TA 3253	the last TA
TB	May 1939	TB 0253	first production TB; 0251 and 0252 were prototypes
	Oct 1939	TB 0629	the last TB
TC	Sep 1945	TC 0252	first production TC; 0251 was a prototype
	Jan 1946	TC 0352	
	Jan 1947	TC 2052	
	Jan 1948	TC 4412	
	Dec 1948	TC 7380	first car identified as EX-U specification
	Jan 1949	TC 7503	
	Nov 1949	TC 10251	the last TC

75

PRODUCTION CHANGES (TA, TB & TC)

The number in the first column is either a chassis number (prefix TA, TB or TC) or an engine number (prefix MPJG for the TA, XPAG for the TB and TC). The engine number series started with 501, and it is likely that axle number series did as well, but I think the body number series started with 101. Much of the information on TA production changes has become available thanks to the research of Paddy Willmer for his book *MG T-Series in Detail* (2005), using the rare contemporary MG Service Newsletters issued by the factory.

MPJG 684   August 1936
Synchromesh in place of "crash" gearbox, with slightly changed ratios.

MPJG 697   August 1936
Three ring pistons in place of four-ring pistons.

TA 0500   September 1936
Moulded rubber tool trays added to tool boxes; canvas roll for smaller tools discontinued.

TA 0616   September 1936
New rear exhaust pipe, without the auxiliary expansion chamber.

TA 0652   September 1936
Modified engine fume pipe.

TA 0682   September 1936
Wooden support block for jack fitted in tool box.

TA 0717   October 1936
Rubber pads added to brake and clutch pedals.

MPJG 1048   October 1936
Oil cup on water pump in place of Stauffer greaser.

TA 0824   November 1936
Modified petrol tap and pipe from tap to pump.

MPJG 1139   November 1936
Modified oil filter cover.

MPJG 1245   December 1936
Improved valve springs, interchangeable with original.

MPJG 1294   January 1937
Modified clutch cover plate.

TA 1074   February 1937
New type of front shock absorbers, housing marked AR, instead of AC; interchangeable with original, in pairs.

TA 1250 (approx) April 1937
Body type B.269 was replaced by body type B.270, with narrower petrol tank and wider rear wings (for details, see bodywork section).

TA 1253   April 1937
Improved type of swivel pin oil seal, with felt washer. In the later parts list, this appears as a new type of king pin with felt washer, from front axle no. 1501.

TA 1254   April 1937
Single-row thrust bearing for rear axle bevel pinion replaced by double-row front thrust bearing. In the later parts list, this appears as a modified bevel pinion housing and front ball bearing, from rear axle no. 1501.

TA 1255   April 1937
Stronger steering arms fitted.

MPJG 1514   April 1937
New type of oil filter; separate oil delivery pipe from filter to block deleted.

TA 1306   May 1937
Return spring fitted to hand-brake cross shaft.

MPJG 1605   May 1937
Triple instead of double valve springs.

MPJG 1637   May 1937
Pushrods of improved material specification.

TA 1657 (and earlier cars TA 1632-1647) August 1937
New double bracket for offside engine tie strap, to accommodate different positions of nut securing strap to engine front bearer plate.

TA 1770   October 1937
Centre-laced wire wheels replace side-laced wire wheels, with increased offset to wheel, which caused the track to be widened by about 5/16 in.

TA 1877   November 1937
Modified carburettor controls.

TA 1926   November 1937
Modified carburettor suction chambers.

TA 1990   December 1937
Return spring fitted to carburettor slow running control.

MPJG 2430   March 1938
New crankshaft with a second oilway in the main bearing journals.

TA 2187   March 1938
First chassis to be fitted with Tickford body.

TA 2232   March 1938
Flexible section added to oil pressure gauge feed line.

TA 2249   March 1938
New prop shaft part number A 1070, interchangeable with original, part number A 843. This probably coincides with prop shaft flange nuts increased from ½in BSF to ⅝in BSF, from rear axle no. 2501, as quoted in the Parts List.

TA 2253   March 1938
Grouped chassis lubrication nipples introduced. Individual greasers on spring trunnions and brake cables ceased with TA 2252.

TA 2254   March 1938
New type of front spring with seven leaves.

MPJG 2514   March 1938
Rubber spacer for plug leads deleted.

MPJG 2532   March 1938
New crankshaft main bearings with offset oil grooves

MPJG 2592   April 1938
Water pump spindle located with peg.

MPJG 2622   April 1938
Oil deflecting plate added to front of camshaft.

TA 2486   June 1938
Clutch pedal bracket fitted with clevis pin.

TA 2518   July 1938
All chassis grease nipples changed from Enots to Tecalemit. New type of grease gun in tool kit.

MPJG 2847   August 1938
Modified valve spring cap with packing ring.

MPJG 3053   October 1938
Modified rocker shaft bracket supports.

TA 2882   November 1938
Telescopic steering column fitted to two-seater (always found on drophead coupé). Steering box ratio altered from 8:1 to 11:1.

TA 3208   March 1939
Coupé only: internal rear view mirror in place of external one.

PRODUCTION CHANGES (TA, TB & TC)
There were a number of modifications on the TA which appear in the Service Parts List but which cannot be directly related to a chassis or engine number, as the change point given relates to the number of the component or sub-assembly:

From front axle no. 2154: possibly around TA 1900, November 1937
Introduction of bolt anchor bracket for steering knuckle and steering arm.

From rear axle no. 2570: possibly around TA 2320, April 1938
New bevel pinion housing.

From body no 507 (B.269): possibly around TA 0657, September 1936
Carpet over gearbox replaced by moulded rubber cover.

From body no. 629 (B.269): possibly around TA 0779, October 1936
Rubber draught excluder with retainer fitted around base of brake and clutch pedals.

From body no 1790/10554 (B.270):
D-shaped tail lamp and new rear number plate; possibly around TA 3200, March 1939, or from the start of the TB.

The modifications made to the TB over the TA have been described in detail in the appropriate sections of the text. There were not very many modifications made to the TB during its short production run, but the Service Parts List indicates the following:

TB 0307   May 1939
Modified crankshaft pulley.

XPAG 645   June 1939
Revised design of tappet cover and studs for same.

Again, the modifications made to the TC from the outset of production in 1945 are listed in the text. During the TC's production run the following modifications were made to the TC, in so far as they can be related to a chassis or engine number:

XPAG 2020   September 1946
Cast aluminium rocker cover, incorporating oil filler with clamp, replaced pressed steel rocker cover with snap-on oil filler.

TC 1850   November 1946
Diamond pattern headlamp glass introduced as replacement for, or alternative to, horseshoe pattern glass. From this point onwards, headlamp glasses became more domed, and the section of the rim was changed.

XPAG 2720   January 1947
Changes to oil filter and pipes.

TC 2196   January 1947
Speedometer cable re-routed, cable housing improved.

XPAG 2966   February 1947
Cast aluminium rocker cover discontinued, original pressed steel rocker cover re-introduced.

TC 3414   August 1947
Control box changed from Lucas RF91, with fuses inside cover, to RF95/2, with exposed fuses.

TC 3856   October 1947
Hydraulic piston dampers added to carburettors.

TC 4251   December 1947
Tapered packing pieces added between front axle and springs, reducing castor angle from 8° to 5½°.

TC 4739   February 1948
Fog lamp changed from Lucas FT27 to SFT462. Revised design of tail lamp.

TC 5039   March 1948
Redesigned steering box drop arm, less felt washer.

TC 5086 (approx) March 1948
Plain sill tread plates were introduced after 4836 bodies had been made. The TC Service Parts List is quite clear that the first 4836 bodies had sill tread plates, part numbers B.269/120 (right-hand side) and B.269/121 (left-hand side). These must have been of the pre-war type plates lettered "The M.G. Car Company". The new sill tread plates were part numbers B.280/134 (right-hand side) and B.280/135 (left-hand side).

TC 5178 (approx) April 1948
Fawn instead of black tonneau cover.

TC 5380 (approx) April 1948
Rexine-covered dashboard replaced walnut veneer dashboard. Instrument panel in metallic tan with black lettering replaced black panel with white lettering.

TC 5732 (approx) June 1948
Body-coloured bulkhead and red engine introduced, replacing grey bulkhead and engine. The bulkhead now has shallower flutes.

TC 7380   December 1948
Introduction of 'EX-U' model with modifications as detailed in the section on export variations.

There were a number of modifications to the TC which cannot be referred to a specific change point by chassis or engine number; they have been described by Mike Sherrill in *TCs Forever* (1990). As previously described in the section on the interior trim, there were two different types of seat. The door trim panels changed from leather to Rexine, either in 1946 or in 1948, depending on who you believe! There was also a change to the front wings. Early TC wings had a deeper cut-back to the swan-neck at the leading edge of the wing where it swept down to meet the dumb-iron; this wing was shaped like that of the pre-war cars. On later models, the cut-back was reduced, pulling the edge of the wing further forward. There were some changes to the hood frame side members, which had an off-set at the front on early cars, missing on later cars, and later on, a change to the pivot point on the hood frame by the mount on each body side of the tonneau behind the seat squab. These and other changes, in particular those which affected the body, were not well documented, and cannot be referred to a precise chassis number, even if a change point by body number is known, since bodies were not fitted to chassis in body number order.

This TB has been fitted with a number of optional extras, including the wheels painted red rather than silver. The rear-mounted luggage carrier is a useful addition.

OPTIONAL EXTRAS (TA & TB)

The following "approved extras" were offered on the TA and TB:
Aero screen, one or two (two-seater only)
Bonnet strap
Built-in jacks, front and rear
Bulb carrier
Battery acid level indicators
Cigar lighter
Double-dipping headlamps (for Continental use)
Fire extinguisher (Pyrene Junior)
Full-length tonneau cover with zip (two-seater only)
Inspection lamp
Horn and dipper switch fitted on arm on steering column
Luggage carrier (two-seater only)
Master battery switch
Number plates in aluminium (pair)
Oil temperature gauge by British Jaeger
Radiator shield, in black or colour
Radio, Philco, six or seven valve types
Radio aerial, telescopic type
Reversing lamp
Second spare wheel (less tyre and tube), and attachment
Speedometer in kilometres (for Continental use)
Spot lamp, with bracket
Steering wheel, by Ashby, or by Bluemels
Stone guards for headlamps
Stop and tail lamp on left-hand side (for Continental use)
Trafficators (two-seater only; standard on coupé)
Water temperature gauge by British Jaeger

The oil and water temperature gauges matched the size and design of the oil pressure gauge and ammeter. If fitted, they were typically set at the two extremities of the dashboard.

For details of special colour and trim finishes, please see the section on colour schemes.

Aero screens were really intended for competition (or for show-offs...).

THE TA, TB AND TC MODELS

The "Midge" mascot was a popular after-market accessory.

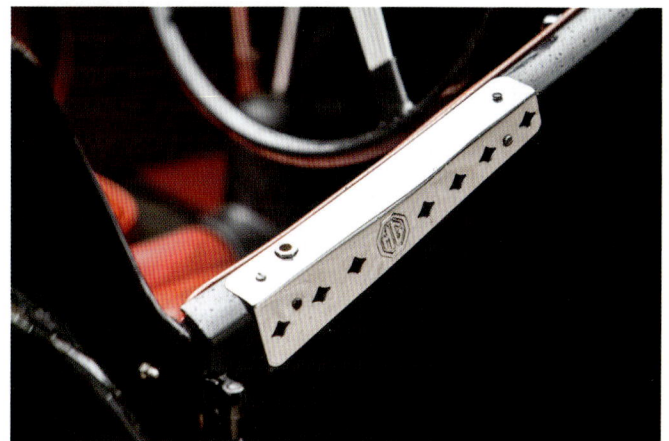

Similarly, I expect the door top protector was an after-market item.

Passenger grab handles of various types can be seen fitted on many cars. This TB has one of the popular dealer badges, from the Colmore Depot in Birmingham; the car was actually registered in Leicester, where Colmore also had a branch.

OPTIONAL EXTRAS (TC)

It seems that the list of options was drastically pruned after the war, if you wanted a TC, you had to take it or leave it as it came! I have only been able to verify the following extras being quoted:

Luggage carrier

Smiths Radiomobile radio CMK 56 (installed under the dashboard)

The absence of a full-length tonneau cover was remarked upon in a road test of the TC in The Motor in 1947, and was ascribed to the then-current shortage of material. I do believe that a full-length tonneau cover did become available a little later.

The Boyce Moto-Meter (the UK equivalent was the Wilmot-Breeden Calormeter) was commonly fitted by many American owners. This is a reproduction, marked MG, by Moss Motors Ltd.

The ultimate in competition parts would be a supercharger; several makes were suitable for the T-types. This is an Arnott, fitted to a TC in the USA. By the way, this car seems to have a non-original steering box.

COMPETITION PARTS (TA)

The following competition parts were listed for this model:

High compression ratio cylinder head (7.3:1)
Stiffer valve springs
Bracket to raise oil filter 2½in, with pipes
Steel sump
Two alternative sets of lower gearbox ratios
Special front springs
Lower rear axle ratio of 5.375:1 (8/43)
Brake tandem master cylinder
Special hand throttle (slow running) control
Twin independent petrol pumps, with control switch
Larger shock absorbers, or Luvax P.6 piston type shock absorbers
Square rear number plate and competition number board
Spare sparking plug carrier
4.00-16 wheels with 6.00-16 tyres, or 4.50-16 wheels with 6.50-16 tyres
Cycle type wings and special side fairings, in steel or aluminium
Aluminium bonnet with louvres to bonnet tops
Supercharger assembly and special carburettor

Most of these parts were undoubtedly aimed at the trials fraternity wishing to emulate the successes achieved by the factory-sponsored TA trials teams, notably the "Cream Crackers" and the "Three Musketeers". Please refer to the separate section (pages 169-171) dealing with the detailed specification of the works-prepared trials cars.

COMPETITION PARTS (TB & TC)

For a detailed description of tuning of the XPAG engine, please see the section which appears on page 116. Many of the non-engine parts listed above for the TA were undoubtedly also available for the TB, but were probably not available after the war. It is, however, worth mentioning that the TB and TC could be equipped with a higher final drive ration of 4.875:1 (8/39) as found on the TA, and the wider 16in wheel continued to be available for the TB and TC models. In the 1950s, an aluminium cylinder head for the XPAG engine was made by Derringtons, and this can be fitted to TB and TCs. Much later reproductions have been made, with valve set inserts, which apart from being suitable for unleaded fuel, can also offer a considerable increase in performance.

PRODUCTION AND EXPORT FIGURES, TA & TB

No particularly detailed production figures exist for the pre-war MG cars, so the following table for TA and TB models has been based solely on the guarantee plate issue ledgers held by the MG Car Club Archive at Abingdon. These ledgers basically only give the engine number and the date of issue of the guarantee plate, which is approximately the build date. The ledgers do not show the type of body fitted to individual cars, so the split between two-seaters and coupes use below has been based on the assumed figure of 320 Tickford-bodied cars. All cars are assigned to the year according to the dates of issue of the guarantee plates. The Tickford bodied cars will have been completed rather later by Salmons, but precise dates are not known. I have assumed there was only one TA Airline coupé, TA 0355 in 1936, but see section on special-bodied cars. Officially there were no chassis-only deliveries, other than for export, mainly to Australia. The Australian chassis have been counted as two-seaters, as have the unassembled cars exported to Eire. The resulting figures are as follows:

PRODUCTION FIGURES, TA & TB						
	1936	1937	1938	1939	Total, all years	
TA two-seater	764	1028	794	156	2742	
TA Airline coupé	1	-	-	-	1	
TA drophead coupé	-	-	223	37	260	Total TA 3003
TB two-seater	-	-	-	319	319	
TB drophead coupé	-	-	-	60	60	Total TB 379
All models	765	1028	1017	572	3382	

At this time MG's export sales were handled by Nuffield Exports Ltd, and calendar year statistics exist from 1937 onwards. According to this, the major export markets were as follows (no split possible between TA and TB)

EXPORT FIGURES, TA & TB						
	1937	1938	1939	1940	Total, all years	
Australia	49	24	34	6	113	incl. 10 chassis
Germany	25	30	24	0	79	incl 13 d/h coupés
Malaya	20	11	9	7	47	
S. Africa & Rhodesia	10	9	8	3	30	
Belgium	12	3	1	0	16	
Switzerland	8	5	3	0	16	
Eire	8	4	0	0	12	
Netherlands	4	3	4	1	12	
Canada	11	0	0	0	11	
Hong Kong (China)	3	2	0	6	11	
USA	6	3	1	1	11	
Denmark	2	5	3	0	10	
New Zealand	6	2	1	0	9	
Sweden	8	1	0	0	9	
Argentina	2	3	1	2	8	
Total of above	174	105	89	26	394	83.4% of total
Total of all exports	212	126	107	27	472	
(of which d/h coupés)		(3)	(28)		(31)	

It seems likely that around 100 further cars were exported during 1936.

PRODUCTION AND EXPORT FIGURES, TC

The single TC prototype (which was probably a re-worked TB, the 1939-40 works demonstrator registered CJB 59) had chassis number 0251. Production cars commenced with 0252 and ran to 10251, which equals 10,000 cars made. The following statistics were kept by the Production Control Department in the Abingdon factory:

PRODUCTION FIGURES, TC	1945	1946	1947	1948	1949	Total, all years
Home market	34	1001	1146	297	930	3408
Export, RHD	47	638	1194**	1278	1340	4497
Export, North America	0	0	6	1473	522	2001
Chassis only, RHD	0	0	0	1	9	10
CKD cars, RHD (for Eire) *	0	36	0	36	12	84
All specifications	**81**	**1675**	**2346**	**3085**	**2813**	**10,000**

*CKD cars – Completely Knocked Down kit cars which were assembled abroad

**In 1947, Abingdon quoted 1026 RHD export cars and 168 LHD export cars. As the TC was never made with left-hand drive this must be a mistake! In the table above, these 168 cars have been counted together with the RHD export cars however; they may have been to a special specification, for example, for the USA; but the EX-U model was only introduced in December 1948.

The following were the major export markets, according to Nuffield Exports' statistics:

EXPORT FIGURES, TC	1945	1946	1947	1948	1949	Total, all years
USA	0	20	234	1143	423	1820
Australia	2	108	165	599	900	1774
S. Africa & Rhodesia	0	83	139	241	154	617
Switzerland	2	59	142	130	75	408
Canada	0	6	20	247	97	370
Belgium	0	27	122	104	33	286
Malaya	0	27	31	66	55	179
India & Pakistan	0	49	54	31	6	140
Argentina	10	70	24	1	0	105
Eire	6	0	36*	36*	12*	90
Brazil	0	0	3	55	6	64
West Germany	0	0	0	5	59	64
Sweden	0	10	50	0	0	60
Ceylon	0	19	11	8	8	46
Hong Kong (China)	0	3	17	10	16	46
Egypt	0	19	10	10	5	44
Total of above	**20**	**500**	**1058**	**2686**	**1849**	**6113 (92.7%)**
Total of all exports	**23**	**610**	**1162**	**2815**	**1983**	**6593**

* CKD cars

COLOUR SCHEMES, TA & TB

From 1936 to 1938, the following were the standard colours on the two-seater:

>   **Saxe Blue**, with Blue trim
>   **Racing Green**, with Green trim
>   **Emgee Red** (or possibly Carmine Red), with Red trim
>   **Cream**, with Red trim
>   **Black**, with Blue, Green, Biscuit or Red trim

The hood, sidescreens and tonneau cover were black. The carpets were black. The wheels were finished in silver.

In August 1938 the drophead coupé was launched and things became a great deal more complicated. The standard colour schemes in 1938-39 are listed on the right:

STANDARD COLOUR SCHEMES 1938-39

Paint	Trim, 2-str.	Hood, 2-str	Trim, coupé	Hood, coupé
Apple Green	Green	Black	Biscuit	Green
Black	(any)	Black	(any)	Black
Coral Red	Red	Black	Maroon	Red
Duo-green	Biscuit	Black	Biscuit	Green
Light Grey	Grey	Black	Grey	Grey
Maroon	Maroon	Black	Brown	Maroon
Metallic Grey	Grey	Black	Grey	Grey
Saxe Blue	Blue	Black	Grey	Blue

Notes: Duo-green: Light green body, dark green wings and fairings.
Metallic Grey: Metallic on body, non-metallic on wings and fairings.

Carpets remained black on the two-seater but were to tone with the trim on the drophead coupé. Wheels were silver as standard but could be finished in special colours to order (cost £1.1.0 for the set). The drophead coupés could be fitted with hoods in special colours to choice from the standard range. It was possible to have a car finished in a two-tone scheme, in any combination of two standard colours, on the body and on the wings and fairings respectively. Cars could also be finished in any Nobel stock colour, including metallic finishes and white on the two-seaters, at extra cost. Trim could be chosen from any standard colour if desired, or in any colour from Connolly's Vaumol range at extra cost.

The TB colour schemes were basically as for the late TAs. However, green trim was discontinued, replaced by biscuit trim on green two-seaters, and so was brown trim, replaced by maroon trim on maroon drophead coupés. Red and green hoods were replaced on TB drophead coupés in these colours by fawn hoods, and fawn was offered as an alternative hood colour on drophead coupés in all other body colours as well.

COLOUR SCHEMES, TC

The colour range was much simplified after the war, to the extent that at first the TC was available only in black, with a choice of beige, green or red trim. By approximately May or June 1946, two paint colours were added, and a sales brochure published at this time lists:

>   **Black**, with Vellum Beige, Shires Green,
>   or Regency Red trim
>   **Regency Red**, with Regency Red trim
>   **Shires Green**, with Shires Green trim

In 1947 or 1948, two more colours were added. The complete range was now:

>   **Black**, with Regency Red, Vellum Beige
>   or Shires Green trim
>   **MG Red**, with Regency Red or Vellum Beige trim
>   **Shires Green**, with Shires Green or Vellum Beige trim
>   **Sequoia Cream**, with Regency Red
>   or Shires Green trim
>   **Clipper Blue**, with Vellum Beige trim

The carpets were black, and the hood and side screens usually fawn but black on some cars. The tonneau cover was black, changed to fawn in 1948. The wheels were silver.

During 1949 the colour range was revised, and the following colours were used on the last TCs as well as on the TDs through to 1951 (see colour list later in this book):

>   **Black**, with Red, Beige or Green trim
>   **MG Red**, with Red or Beige trim
>   **Almond Green**, with Beige trim
>   **Ivory**, with Red or Green trim
>   **Clipper Blue**, with Beige trim

As has been pointed out previously (in the section on the TA/TB/TC cooling system), the radiator slats were painted to match the upholstery colour, but with some variation depending on whether the upholstery and trim were to tone with the body, or in a contrast colour.

The pre-war paints were supplied by the Nobel company (the dynamite people!) and it is likely that they would now be rather difficult to re-mix. I have never come across any mixing formulae, and the colours are not recognised by present-day paint manufacturers. Attempts have been made at correlating these old colours to BMC colours of the 1950s and 1960s, but I believe this can only result in approximations. The best solution might be to try to match a sample – but after more than 70 or 80 years, any paint will have faded. The post-war colours are simpler to deal with, and a table of latter-day paint code numbers appears in the colour section for the TD and TF models.

THE TD AND TF MODELS

The drawing of the exploded TD chassis shows us many of the features, including the actual frame design, the independent front suspension, etc. The scuttle hoop was added early in the production run. The H-shape spare wheel carrier was replaced by a simpler bracket on the TF, and the TF also had a different radiator with the filler cap under the bonnet.

In this second major section of the book, the various aspects of the TD and TF models are dealt with mostly together under joint headings, since the cars were virtually identical under the skin. This include the XPAG engine of the TF 1500, as the only difference was the bore. However, the dashboards and instruments differed between the two models, so they have been dealt with separately for the TD and TF.

CHASSIS

The TD chassis was a completely new design compared to the TC, but was in many respects derived from that of the Y-type. In fact the prototype TD used a shortened Y-type chassis, with the wheelbase reduced from 8ft 3in to 7ft 10in (2183mm, as on previous T-types). The two main side members were now fully boxed in, and tapered towards the front in plan view. Between the front wheels there was a substantial box section crossmember which carried the independent front suspension, the steering gear, the front engine mounting, and the radiator. In addition there were three tubular cross-members – at the rear of the gearbox, at the front mounting points of the rear springs, and at the rear end of the chassis.

Unlike both the TC and the Y-type, on production TDs the chassis side members were swept above the rear axle, with a reduced cross-section. After the first 100 TDs had been made, a tubular section hoop was added above the front tubular crossmember to improve scuttle stiffness. There were originally three body mounting points on each side, two on chassis outriggers below the door, the third behind the rear axle. In 1952, a fourth body mounting point was added on each side, at the foot of the scuttle hoop. The body was also attached directly to the scuttle hoop. There was a substantial pillar carrying the steering column, mounted on the left- or right-hand chassis side member, depending on whether LHD or RHD was specified. The entire chassis with its attendant brackets was finished in petrol-resistant matt black paint.

The TF chassis was in all fundamental respects the same as the TD chassis, except for revised engine mounts. There were no changes to the chassis during the TF production run. As on the earlier T-types, the bolts and nuts used throughout the chassis and associated parts had BSF threads and hexagons with Imperial measurements, with the exception, as noted in the following, that the wheel studs and nuts, together with threads in the prop shaft and rear axle, changed to Unified threads in December 1951 (see list of TD production changes on page 122). The engine continued to have metric threads.

FRONT SUSPENSION

The independent front suspension on the TD had been designed by a young engineer called Alec Issigonis, together with the draughtsman Jack Daniels, working for Morris Motors at Cowley before the war, and had first gone into production on the Y-type in 1947. Their inspiration had come from the original Cadillac independent front suspension introduced on 1934

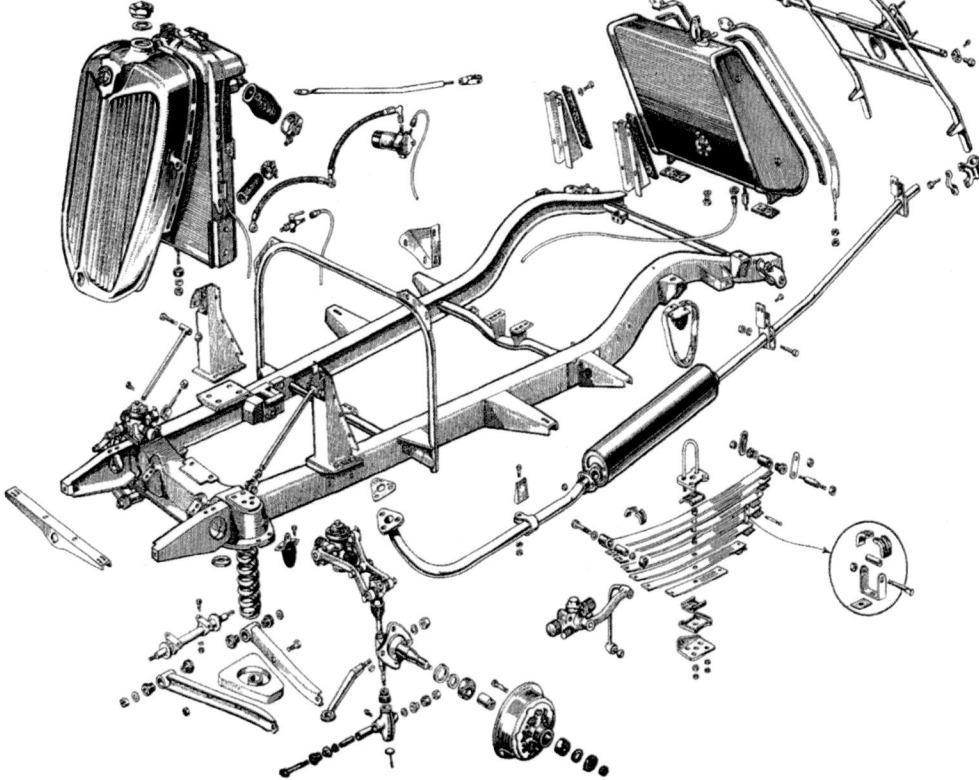

THE TD AND TF MODELS

models. It was a straight-forward coil and double wishbone lay-out, and a key feature borrowed from the Cadillac design was that the wishbones were of unequal length. Significantly, this particular suspension set-up was to endure with very little change until the last MGB was made in 1980.

The lower wishbone was mounted in rubber-bushed bearings on the chassis. A plate between the wishbone arms carried the coil spring which at the top fitted into the inverted "cup" formed by the end of the front chassis cross member where it overhung the side member. The upper wishbone was formed by the lever arms of the hydraulic shock absorber, mounted on top of the coil spring housing. Originally, Luvax Girling type PVA 6X shock absorbers were used, but in 1953 a change was made to Armstrong type IS 9 dampers, which were also fitted on the TF. It is not known exactly when the Armstrong dampers were introduced. The vertical wheel bearer which connected the outer ends of the wishbones doubled as the king pin. The camber angle was +/-1°, the castor angle was 2 ° and the front wheel toe-in was nil. The king pin angle was 9-10½°.

Suspension parts were generally painted black but the Armstrong shock absorbers fitted to later TDs and to TFs were left in unpainted alloy, although still with black lever arms. There were no changes to the front suspension on the TF model.

REAR SUSPENSION

Conventional semi-elliptic leaf springs continued to be used for the rear suspension, with seven leaves interleaved with rubber. The springs were mounted in rubber-bushed bearings on the outside of the chassis, the front bearings being mounted on chassis outriggers at the point of the middle tubular crossmember. These outriggers also doubled as body mounting points. At the rear end, the springs were attached to the rear chassis legs by shackles. Luvax Girling type PVA 6 (and later Armstrong type DAS 10) lever arm type hydraulic shock absorbers were fitted to the outside of the chassis side members in front of the rear axle. The springs passed underneath the rear axle casing. A rebound strap was attached to each chassis side member, passing underneath the axle. There were no changes to the rear suspension during the TD/TF production run.

STEERING

As with the front suspension, the rack-and-pinion steering gear was borrowed from the Y-type. The steering rack was mounted on the front chassis cross-member, ahead of the front hubs. At either end of the rack was a short track rod. These protruded through circular holes in the chassis side members and were shrouded in rubber dust excluders.

The steering column incorporated a rubber-bushed universal joint. The column was telescopically adjustable for reach, with a clamp just below the steering wheel and a chrome-plated concertina spring covering the actual telescoping part. There was also a certain amount of adjustment for rake, on the bracket where the column was attached to the scuttle hoop.

The standard TD steering wheel with three wire spokes, each with four wires paired two and two.

The Bluemels Brooklands steering wheel remained and remains a popular alternative to the standard wheel, as seen here on an early TD. The brown rim is typical of the post-war version of the Brooklands wheel.

The TF steering wheel centre or "manette" in close-up, with the silver and cream MG medallion. Note that this steering wheel hub has probably been repainted but the gold colour is correct.

The steering column was always painted black.

The 16½in (419mm) diameter steering wheel had three equally spaced spring spokes; each spoke with four separate spring wires, paired two and two. The steering wheel rim was in mottled plastic, usually light brown or bronze. The hub was painted metallic bronze and incorporated a plastic MG medallion, with silver letters and edge on a cream background, set in a dark brown surround with a chrome ring. The steering ratio was 13.75 to l, and there were 2¾ turns lock to lock.

In October 1951, from chassis number TD 11111, the inner track rod end housing on the steering rack was changed, and in March 1953, from chassis number TD 25973, the tie rod end design was changed for a new type with improved seals. The steering gear was carried over on the TF with no further changes.

BRAKES

Another important innovation on the TD compared to the TC was that the Lockheed hydraulic brakes were now of the twin leading shoe type at the front. The drum size was 9in (229mm) with linings 1½in (38mm) wide. The total friction area was 99.45sq in (642 sq.cm). The linings were Ferodo MR19 on the TD, Ferodo DM7 on the TF. The combined supply tank and master cylinder was under the floor as before, directly activated by the vertically mounted brake pedal.

The brake and clutch pedals shared a joint moulded rubber dust excluder, and had flat pads with oval, grooved pedal rubbers. Two different types of pedal arms were used on the TD. The later type had a spacer between the pedal arm and the pedal itself, and on cars fitted with this type of pedal arm, the clutch and brake pedals were also off-set rather more to the left in relation to the accelerator pedal. This allowed more space around the pedals for ease of operation.

The rear brake drums had a single cylinder, floating on the back plate, incorporating a bell-crank for handbrake operation. Two separate cables linked up with the handbrake lever, which was still of the fly-off type, but which was now mounted horizontally on the prop-shaft tunnel between the seat cushions. The lever was chrome-plated, with a black plastic grip and a chrome-plated button. The handbrake bracket was painted black and had two exposed adjusting nuts at the back.

The original brake drums were bolted and riveted to the hubs, but from chassis number TD 4251 in November 1950, the hub and brake drum assembly became a one-piece casting. The brake drums were normally painted black. There were no further changes to the braking system during the TD/TF production run. On the wire-wheeled TF, however, different brake drums with non-integral hubs were used.

REAR AXLE

The TD was the first MG to be fitted with a hypoid bevel rear axle with semi-floating half shafts, of a standardized Nuffield design, also used on Morris and Wolseley cars. The axle casing was in two pieces, split vertically just to the left of the centre line of the differential. The standard rear axle ratio was 5.125:1 (8/41). However, alternative rear axle ratios of 4.875: 1 (8/39) and 4.55:1 (9/41) were available as optional extras. The 4.875:1 ratio was standard on the TD Mark II model (see the section on the Mark II), and was carried over on the TF models. The other two ratios remained available as options on the TFs. The rear axle casing was painted black.

WHEELS AND TYRES

When the TD was introduced, it was stated that with the adoption of independent front suspension and rack and pinion steering, the steering arms and links would project so far into the plane of the wheel that it would complicate the arrangement of spokes if wire wheels were used – which one may question – so the TD was offered only with a deeply dished disc wheel, size 4Jx15. The wheels were attached to five studs which were integral with the brake drums. Originally, the wheels were plain, but in 1950 pierced or drilled wheels with 15 round ventilation holes were introduced. This supposedly happened from chassis number TD 0501 in January 1950, yet it does seem that some later cars still had the solid type of wheel. The wheels were always finished in silver paint.

The TD had chrome-plated hub caps, with an MG medallion where the background to the letters was painted red. Tyres were by Dunlop, size 5.50-15, fitted with inner tubes. A single spare wheel was fitted as standard equipment. The tubular spare wheel bracket in the form of a letter H was mounted on the chassis at the rear of the petrol tank, and attached to the rear of the body at the top. A special spare wheel carrier for

The handbrake was completely different from the earlier cars. It had a chrome-plated handle with a black plastic grip, and was mounted horizontally between the seats. Here it is in the on position. However it is still of the "fly-off" type.

The early TDs had this solid disc wheel, fitted on five studs, and with a hub cap which had the MG medallion. This car runs on radial tyres, as is now common practice.

The pierced wheel was soon introduced on the TD. This car probably should have hub cap medallions with the red infill. As it is a Mark II, it has the black-and-white enamel badge on the spare wheel hub cap, and we can just see the H-shape of the spare wheel mounting bracket.

two spare wheels could be obtained as an optional extra.

One modification worth listing is that from chassis number TD 12285, in December 1951, the threads on the wheel studs and nuts were changed from BSF to Unified (SAE) threads. It took until chassis number TD 12419 to change similarly the thread on the spare wheel studs and nuts!

When the TF was introduced in 1953, suddenly MG had overcome the complications of fitting wire wheels, and the TF was available with either disc or wire wheels, despite the steering arms and links being apparently identical to those on the TD. The explanation may be found in the fact that the hubs were different so the front track on a wire wheeled car was increased by 7/16in (11mm) and the rear track by 13/16in (21mm), and each wheel effectively moved a little further out. The disc wheels were the same as those found on the TD, but the hub caps were now made of stainless steel and the MG medallions were left with a plain background. The hub cap on the spare wheel had a larger black and white MG enamel

We are now looking at a TF, which should not have MG medallions with red infill on the hub caps, but it illustrates that the TF had a different spare wheel mounting bracket from the TD.

medallion, of the same type as that fitted to the radiator (this was also found on the last TD Mark II cars – see the Mark II section on pages 113-115). On the TF, the spare wheel carrier was a simple triangular bracket, like that fitted to the TC. A double spare wheel carrier was not quoted.

The wire wheels were also size 4Jx15, fitted with 5.50-15 tyres. They had 48 spokes (16 outer and 32 inner) and were painted silver. I doubt that chrome-plated wire wheels were available but unsurprisingly, they have become popular in later years. They were attached by chrome-plated two-eared knock-ons with the MG logo. Wire wheels were very popular on the TF, especially in the American market, and of the 9600 TFs, 6463 cars (or 67.3%, just over two-thirds) had wire wheels. Supposedly a wire-wheeled TF should have a letter "W" after its chassis number but I question whether this is correct for all cars. The design of the wire wheel was changed from chassis number TF 6887 in August 1954, to incorporate a deeper-dished inner flange.

TF tyre equipment was as for the TD, with some known variations on certain export models (see separate section). One car is shown in contemporary factory photographs shod with Dunlop racing tyres, but these were never quoted as official optional equipment. Whitewall tyres became available, and were in particular fitted to quite a few TF 1500s for America. Apparently, the 5.50-15 tyre size is now not available, so the nearest cross-ply equivalent is 5.60-15. Nowadays many cars run perfectly happily on radial tyres. The suggested equivalent sizes are 155R15, or 165R15, or low-profile 165/80R15. Radial tyres are likely to offer increased tyre life, but with the usual penalties of harsher ride and increased tyre noise.

Once the TF had appeared, MG rather surreptitiously offered a "service kit" (part number ACG 5163) to convert TDs to TF wire wheels, incorporating the hubs, wire wheels and so on from the TF, so the most legitimate wire wheeled TDs would be those that use the appropriate TF parts. Quite a number of TDs were and now are fitted with other proprietary wire wheels; thus the Arnolt seen at the Turin Motor Show in 1953 had wire wheels, possibly by Borrani, as did many other Arnolts. It is still debated whether some of the last TDs were fitted with wire wheels from the factory, but I feel that it is more likely that late TDs held over in dealer stocks could have been converted before delivery to customers, which seems to have happened in the USA.

These wire wheels are not the correct original type: firstly they have been chrome-plated, and secondly they have got 60 rather than 48 spokes. Some cars now even run on 72-spoke wire wheels. But the knock-ons are correct, including the special one for the spare wheel with the enamel badge.

THE TD AND TF MODELS

The TD engine inherited features both from the TC and the Y-type engines. The colour scheme of red block and head, with silver-green rocker cover, continued; the silver colour here is possibly too silver, it should have a green tinge, and the engine red is rather bright. The snap-on oil filler cap was now at the front, and the engine number plate towards the front on the right-hand side of the crankcase. The oil bath air cleaner was new. The right-hand radiator stay running in front of the inlet manifold had a kink to give clearance to the front carburettor.

The scuttle or bulkhead was now always body colour. The battery sat on an open shelf in front of a smaller toolbox. Two windtone horns were mounted on the bulkhead. The plug caps here look like the original type. This car has been fitted with a flasher unit and flasher relay of the type normally seen on the TF (to the right of the horn).

ENGINE

The XPAG engine as first employed in the TD could best be described as a cross-breed between the TC engine and the single-carburettor XPAG/SC engine used in the Y-type. MG no doubt wished to standardize components, so the TD had the rocker cover with the snap-on type oil filler at the front from the Y-type. The Y-type sump was also fitted, with the full depth of the sump carried further forward, instead of the stepped front end of the TC sump. The flywheel housing was similar to the Y-type, and so were the engine mounts and such ancillaries as the starter and dynamo. On the other hand, the twin carburettors and the high-lift camshaft were inherited from the TC, and the power output of 54.4bhp was exactly the same as on the previous model.

On all TDs, the engine and gearbox were painted red, including the cylinder head, the sump, the gearbox lid and so on. The rocker cover was painted a silver grey-green colour. Ancillaries such as the starter motor, the dynamo, the air cleaner and the exhaust pipe were black. The air manifold was left in natural aluminium. The carburettor balance pipe may be either

89

The fixed bonnet sides on the TF do nothing for accessibility, or photography! This early car still has the under-bonnet fuel pump. The horns have been moved but there is now a remote wiper motor. The rocker cover should be silver-green, not red. There are individual pancake-type air filters for the carburettors, which have shorter bodies than on the TD.

Another change on the TF was that there was an under-bonnet filler cap for the pressurized cooling system. The plastic sheath for the oil filler cap chain is believed to be correct, but the jubilee clamps on the radiator hoses are not.

black or engine red, and the exhaust manifold was aluminized.

A small change from the start of TD production was a new combination of starter ring gear and pinion, now with 93 and 10 teeth instead of 120 and 9 teeth, which slightly affected the gearing. The new starter motor was smaller and is not directly interchangeable with that on the TC. However, the internal diameter of the starter ring of 10 3/8 in (264mm) was not changed, so the new starter motor in combination with the new starter ring gear can be fitted to the earlier engines.

A major change which occurred to engine specification during the TD production run was the introduction of a bigger flywheel and an 8in (203mm) diameter clutch, replacing the original 7¼in (184mm) clutch, necessitating also an enlarged flywheel housing. This took place from engine number XPAG/TD2 9408 in July 1951. Note that the revised engine was given the distinguishing prefix XPAG/TD2; the original engine prefix had simply been XPAG/TD.

It may also be noted that whereas early TD engines had the engine number plate on the flywheel housing, visible from the left as on the TC engine, later TD engines had this plate on a square plinth on the right-hand side of the crankcase, where it is also found on all TF engines. It is possible that the changed

THE TD AND TF MODELS

On this TF 1500, the fuel pump has been moved to the chassis at the rear, but this car has a filter in the fuel line. There are some non-original MG badges on the rocker cover – note in silver – and above the exhaust manifold there is what I guess is a heat shield, which is not original.

This car has the correct wire clamps for the radiator hose, but has modern plug caps. The darker red engine colour is more correct. Note the position of the body number plate on top of the toolbox lid; it should be on the underside of the lid. The bonnet strut on the right is not original.

position of this plate took effect from engine number XPAG/TD2 9408. Further detail changes which took place during the TD production run will be found in the summary of changes at the end of the TD/TF section on pages 122-123.

In January 1953, from engine XPAG/TD2 24116, a new camshaft was introduced, with valve timing revised as follows:

VALVE TIMING
Early camshaft to engine 24115 also found on TC
Inlet opens   11 degrees BTDC
Inlet closes   57 degrees ABDC
Exhaust opens   52 degrees BBDC
Exhaust closes   24 degrees ATDC

Late camshaft from engine 24116 also found on TF
Inlet opens   5 degrees BTDC
Inlet closes   45 degrees ABDC
Exhaust opens   45 degrees BBDC
Exhaust closes   5 degrees ATDC

The valve timing was now the same which had been introduced in about July 1951 on the Y-type, and was intended to give quieter running and more torque. The tappet clearance was changed to 0.012in (0.30mm), with a new tappet clearance plate fitted to the rocker cover. Valve lift was increased to 0.327in (8.3mm).

Details of the specially tuned engine found in the TD Mark II model are described elsewhere, but it should be borne in mind that it was basically the Mark II engine specification which was adopted for the TF model in 1953, with engine type XPAG/TF. The TF therefore had the cylinder head depth reduced from 76.75mm to 75.16mm for the higher compression ratio of 8.1:1, and was fitted with the larger valves and bigger carburettors of the Mark II. Accordingly, the TF's power output matched the Mark II at 57bhp.

This was still not enough for some customers, and a year after the introduction of the TF, MG launched the TF 1500 with a 1466cc version of the XP-engine, now known as the XPEG. The increase in capacity was achieved by opening out the bore to 72mm which necessitated siamesing the front and rear pairs of cylinders respectively, losing the water space between the cylinders. The depth of the cylinder head returned to 76.75mm but the compression ratio was increased to 8.3:1, and the power output was improved to 63bhp at 5000rpm.

IGNITION SYSTEM

The distributor was a Lucas model DKY 4A or DKYH 4A with automatic centrifugal advance and retard, in three slightly different forms; on the early TD it was service number 40162, on later TDs with high-lift cams in the distributor it was service number 40162E (or a letter subsequent to E), and on the TF it was service number 40367A, according to the workshop manual. Actually, in October 1952 from engine number XPAG/TD2 20942 a new distributor D2A4 was introduced, with a shorter stem and cotter bolt fixing, rather than clamp fixing. This required a small modification to the block to incorporate the cotter fixing for this distributor. The contact breaker gap was 0.010 to 0.012in, increased to 0.014 to 0.016in on models with high-lift cams.

The ignition coil was type Q12L on the TD and early TFs, service number 45020; it was changed to type LA12 on later TFs. Originally the TD used Champion L10S plugs with ½in (12.7mm) reach, but from engine number XPAG/TD2 22735, in November 1952, ¾in (19mm) reach Champion NA8 were specified, and these were also used on the TF. The Mark II was fitted with Champion NA10 plugs. All plugs were 14mm size and the plug gap was quoted as 0.020 to 0.022in. Ignition timing was TDC.

CARBURETTORS AND FUEL SYSTEM

The carburettors were very little changed from the TC to the TD, except that the control linkage was slightly different. Otherwise they were the same SU type H2 (1¼in) slightly inclined semi-downdraught carburettors, with standard needle ES and 0.090in jets. A single SU electric fuel pump, type L, was mounted on the right-hand side of the front of the toolbox on the bulkhead. The air cleaner was an AC oil-bath type mounted on top of the rocker cover, this being an immediate recognition point of the under bonnet layout of the TD compared to the TC.

On the TF, the larger 1½in carburettors, type H4, from the Mark II model were used, although with shorter body castings. The TF carburettors had hexagonal brass tops without slots. Individual Vokes pancake air filters, painted black, were mounted directly on the carburettor air inlets. In February 1954, from chassis number TF 3495, piston dampers were added to the carburettor dashpots. There was apparently no change to the carburettor specification on the TF 1500 model. The standard needle for all TFs was GJ, with 0.090in jets.

SU CARBURETTOR NEEDLES:		
	TD	TF
Rich needle	EM	HI
Standard needle	ES	GJ
Weak needle	AP	GL

At first the TF had a low pressure type fuel pump mounted on the scuttle similar to the TD, but from chassis number TF 1501, in December 1953, a high pressure or HP-type pump was fitted. This was mounted on the right-hand chassis side member in front of the rear wheel. Earlier cars could be modified, and many probably were.

The filler cap, here on a TF, is similar to earlier models. On the TD and TF it has an MG logo on the release lever. The tank is similar in principle, with painted-over chrome end plates, and body-colour straps with chrome brackets.

THE TD AND TF MODELS

The contrasting radiator badges on the TD, brown and cream, and the TF, black and white. The TD also has painted radiator slats, but the TF's are chromed. And the filler cap on the TF is a sham, as the real filler cap is under the bonnet.

On both the TD and TF, the fuel tank was strapped to the back of the chassis in the manner of the earlier cars, but it was immediately obvious that the TD tank, compared to that of the TC, was more triangular in section, as the spare wheel was leaning forward at a more acute angle. Tank capacity was 12.5 imperial gallons (approximately 57 litres) of which 2.5 gallons (just over 11 litres) were "reserve" – when the low fuel warning lamp on the dashboard would light up.

The fuel tank and its retaining straps were painted body colour. The end plates were also painted body colour but were chrome-plated underneath; this showed up on the end plate edges which were left unpainted. The end plate retaining nuts were chrome-plated. The fuel filler cap on the left-hand side was in natural stainless steel, and was of the quick-release type, with an MG logo on the chrome-plated release lever. The TF fuel tank was very similar to that on the TD, but the spare wheel was angled slightly further forward so the tank was again a slightly different shape.

EXHAUST SYSTEM

On the TD, the exhaust system was rubber-mounted, so the flexible section of the front down pipe found on the TC was discontinued. The flange where the front pipe was attached to the silencer had three bolts on the TD as opposed to two bolts on the TC. On the TF the front pipe simply pushed on to the silencer inlet and was fastened with a clamp. The diameter of the tailpipe was increased on the TF model.

COOLING SYSTEM

This was one area of major difference between the two models. The TD used the same cooling system in principle as the previous T-types (although the parts are not interchangeable), but the TF had a pressurized cooling system, with an eared 4 lbs radiator cap under the bonnet. The octagonal cap still fitted on the outside was a sham! Another change was the introduction of a convoluted top radiator hose on the TF. Also, because the TF had a lower bonnet line, it was necessary to lower the height of the radiator core on this model, but the thickness of the core was increased to compensate. A different type of thermostat was fitted on the TF, being inset in the water outlet of the engine.

The radiator and header tank were painted black (in an eggshell or semi-matt finish) on both models. While the TD had a black four-bladed fan, some experts believe the TF had a red fan. The radiator shell was chrome-plated on both models. On the TD the radiator slats were painted. They often matched the upholstery colour, but on red or green cars with beige trim the radiator slats could be body colour. The paint finish on the slats has been described as "semi-gloss". Late Mark II models (see the Mark II section) had chrome-plated slats. The MG badge on the TD radiator shell was brown and cream, changed on late Mark II cars to black and white. All TFs had chrome-plated slats and the black and white badge.

A Morris Motors Radiators Branch plate on the header tank of the TF 1500.

TRANSMISSION

As on the TC, this comprised a single dry-plate Borg & Beck clutch, a four-speed gearbox (with synchromesh on the top three ratios) and a short, open Hardy-Spicer prop-shaft with universal joints. The flywheel and clutch housing, and the gearbox, were painted the same red as the engine, but the extension for the remote control gearlever was left in natural aluminium. The prop shaft was painted black.

The closest relative to the TD/TF gearbox was that found on the Y-type, which had the same gearbox casing and the same internal ratios. However, the Y-type gear lever was a cranked lever coming straight out of the back of the gearbox.

The following table gives the internal and overall gear ratios for the TD and TF, the internal ratios being the same but the overall ratios being altered with the higher rear axle ratio on the TF. In addition, the overall ratios are given for the 4.55:1 rear axle which was an option on both TD and TF.

GEARBOX RATIOS:

	Internal Ratios TD and TF	Overall Ratios TD (not Mark II)	Overall Ratios TD Mark II TF and TF 1500	Overall Ratios with optional 4.55:1 rear axle
First & reverse	3.50:1	17.938:1	17.063:1	15.925:1
Second	2.07:1	10.609:1	10.091:1	9.419:1
Third	1.385:1	7.098:1	6.752:1	6.302:1
Top	1.00:1	5.125:1	4.875:1	4.55:1

I am not sure that either of these gear lever gaiters is completely correct, and the carpet should be black on both cars. The clutch and brake pedals were completely different from earlier cars. They now had oval ribbed pedal rubbers of a common Nuffield design

Later TDs had the foot-operated dip switch seen here. All TDs and TFs had oval pedals but the pedal rubbers here are not original and seem to have been fitted upside down?

As previously mentioned, from engine number XPAG/TD2 9408 in July 1951, the clutch diameter was increased from 7¼in to 8in (184mm to 203mm). In May 1952, some slight changes were made to the gearbox. From engine number XPAG/TD2 16482, a snap ring was added to the front of the top and third shift rail, and this rail was lengthened with extra support at the back of the remote control housing. From engine number XPAG/TD2 16978, a key was added to the speedometer drive worm gear. The only other transmission modification worthy of note occurred in November 1952 when the clutch operation was changed from cable to rod, at engine number XPAG/TD2 22717 and chassis number TD 22251. Also, from then on a stop bolt was added to the pedal bracket to limit clutch pedal travel.

ELECTRICAL EQUIPMENT AND LAMPS

This was all manufactured by Lucas. The single 12 volt battery, type GTW 9A (GTW 9A/2 on the TF), was mounted in an open battery box on the bulkhead. The box was lined with a wooden tray. The battery retaining bar was fastened with ordinary (as opposed to wing) nuts and had a rubber strip stuck on the back. The bar was not quite a right angle in section. Battery capacity was 51 AH. Some export cars had different batteries, or were supplied with dry batteries, or none at all. Apparently there was a Police version of the TD which had not only a large capacity battery but also a bigger battery box to accommodate it. This version was also fitted with a high output dynamo and a somewhat modified wiring loom. The electrical system was wired positive to earth. The wiring loom was insulated with rubber, covered in braided cotton with colour coding.

The normal dynamo was type C 39 PV DA41 on the original TD; later TDs and TFs had a dynamo type C 39 PV/2. The starter motor was type M 35 G/1 L3/1; both this and the

THE TD AND TF MODELS

The TD still had separate headlamps with block-pattern lenses, mounted on body-colour brackets. A Lucas medallion was inset in the headlamp shell.

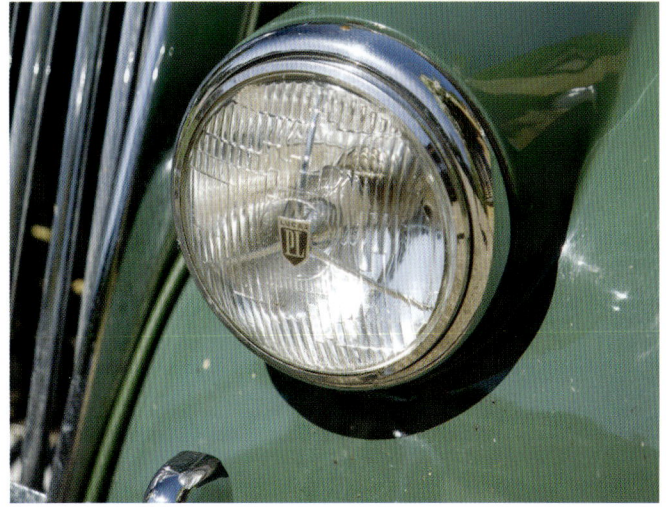

Both of the TFs photographed have variants of Lucas tripod headlamps. These were and obviously still are popular, but are not original; the TF should have F.700 headlamps with block-pattern lenses similar to the lenses on the TD.

Grouped together on the left-hand side of the TF bulkhead are the regulator with separate fuse box, the flasher relay and flasher unit, and the black-painted coil. This also shows the bonnet lock, and the non-original bonnet strut.

dynamo were painted black. The voltage regulator fitted to the early TDs was type RF 95/2 with exposed fuses, similar to that fitted to the later TCs, but from chassis number TD 8142, in June 1951, it was changed to a type RB 106/1 with a separate fuse box, type SF 6, still with only two fuses. This was carried over on the TF.

Regardless of minor differences to suit various export markets, all TD headlamps were type S 700 with block lenses. Early home market cars to TD 7623 in May 1951 had a "dip and switch" system like the TC, later home market cars and all export cars were fitted with twin filament dipping bulbs to both lamps. Today, all cars in the UK must have double-dipping headlamps. Early cars had a headlamp dipping switch on the instrument panel, it was later replaced by a foot dipper from TD 18883 in August 1952.

The headlamp mounting brackets were similar to those used on the TC and were painted body colour. The TD was found with both chrome-plated and painted headlamps; the latter may still have chrome-plated rims. It is not possible to state specific change-over points by chassis numbers, but it can be

TD REPLACEMENT BULB CHART (from workshop manual)

Application	Lucas no.	Watts
Headlamp, home, left-hand lamp, early model	300 dip left	36/36
Headlamp, home, right-hand lamp, early model	162	36
Headlamp, home, both lamps, later models; and RHD export	354 dip left	42/36
Headlamp, LHD export	301 dip right	36/36
Headlamp, export Europe and North Africa (not France)	360	45/35
Side lamps, not including direction indicator lamps	207	6
Stop/tail lamps (symmetrical bayonet or reversible fitting)	189	6/24
Stop/tail lamps (offset bayonet or non-reversible fitting)	361	6/18
Number plate lamp (early cars: two; later cars: one bulb)	989	6
Ignition, fuel, and headlamp beam warning light	970 (2.5 volts)	0.5
Fog lamp if fitted	323	48

TF REPLACEMENT BULB CHART (from workshop manual)

Application	Lucas no.	Type	Watts
Headlamp, home and RHD export (dip left)	354	Pre-focus	42/36
Headlamp, LHD export, and USA (dip right)	301	Pre-focus	36/36
Headlamp, European export (except France)	360	Pre-focus	45/35
Headlamp, vertical dip	370	Pre-focus	45/40
Side lamps, including direction indicator lamps	369	S.C.C.	6/18
Stop/tail lamps (offset bayonet or non-reversible fitting)	361	S.B.C.	6/18
Number plate lamp	222 or 989	M.C.C.	4
Fog lamp if fitted	323	Pre-focus	48
Panel light, fuel warning light, and flasher warning light	987	M.E.S.	2.2
Ignition warning light	985 or 987	M.E.S.	2.2

The early TDs had the triangular or wedge-shaped Lucas rear lamp, the same type as found on other Nuffield cars of the period, for instance the Morris Minor.

The side lamps were the same Lucas type 1130 on both the TD and the TF, carried over from earlier cars.

The same chrome-plated standard Lucas number plate lamp was fitted on both the TD, seen here, and the TF.

suggested that the painted lamps were probably used owing to the chromium shortage during the Korean War – although strangely, no other chrome plating was deleted from the TD's specification! Most TD headlamps had a countersunk Lucas medallion but this was discontinued on the final chrome-plated lamps. The TF's built-in headlamps were type F 700. The side lamps on both models were type 1130, similar to those found on the earlier models.

Originally, the TD had stop/tail lamps which were triangular or wedge-shaped when seen from the side, of the type 471 which was also found on the Morris Minor and other Nuffield cars. They were fitted with glass lenses which often broke, so many cars are now fitted with replacement plastic lenses of a lighter red colour, although the plastic lens was introduced only after this type of lamp had ceased to be fitted on the TD. From chassis number TD 21303 in October 1952, round stop/tail lamps type 488 were fitted. These were mounted on a chrome-plated plinth and were also found on the TF.

The number plate lamp was type 467/2 on all cars, originally with two bulbs but with only one bulb on later TD and all TF cars; the change point is not known. It was always chrome-plated. Flashing direction indicators which were built into the side lamps, and the stop/tail lamps, were found on North

THE TD AND TF MODELS

Rear reflectors were introduced on the TF 1500. This is the correct position, on the black rubber mount which is shaped to suit the angle and curvature of the body so that the reflector is vertical.

On later TDs, this rear lamp with a round lens in a chrome-plated housing was introduced, and then carried over on the TF.

American specification TDs from chassis number TD 22371 in 1952, and on all TFs; in the tail lamps, they worked by flashing the higher-wattage stop lamp filament. It is possible that the flashers were introduced from TD 22315, as several other sources say, but that some changes were then made from TD 22371. Just to completely confuse the issue, TD 22315 was apparently made out of sequence on 4 December 1952, while TD 22371 was made on 25 November.

Two windtone horns were fitted, type WT 614 on the TD and type WT 618 (or possibly still WT 614?) on the TF. On the TD, they were mounted on the bulkhead under the bonnet, the high-note horn on the right and the low-note horn on the left. On the TF they were relocated below the radiator in front of the chassis cross-member. The fog lamp was now an extra; if fitted,

	TD: Lucas model	TD: Lucas service number	TF: Lucas model	TF: Lucas service number
SUMMARY OF LUCAS ELECTRICAL EQUIPMENT (from *Motor Trader*):				
Battery	GTW 9 A	-	GTW 9 A-2	-
Dynamo, early TD	C 39 PV	22257 A		
Dynamo, late TD and TF	C 39 PV/2	22265 A	C 39 PV/2	22265 B
Control box, early	RF 95/2	37065 E		
Control box, late	RB 106/1	37138 A	RB 106/1	37138
Fuse box (with the later control box)	SF 6	37132 A	SF 6	033240
Starter motor	M 35 G/1	25022 D	M 35 G	25022
Coil	Q 12 L	45020 A	Q 12	45020
Distributor, early TD	DKY 4 A	40162 A		
Distributor, late TD and TF	D2 A4		D2 A4	40367
Headlamps, dip left RHD	S 700	50995 E	F 700	51344
Headlamps, dip right LHD	S 700	50755 E	F 700	51345
Headlamps, non-dipping	S 700	50798 A		
Headlamps, Europe			F 700	51346
Headlamps, France			F 700 EF	51411
Headlamps, USA			F 700	51467
Side lamps	1130	52030 A	1130	52134
Fog lamp(s) optional	SFT 462		SFT 576	55128
Stop/tail lamps, early TD	471	53200 A		
Stop/tail/flasher lamps, late TD and TF	488		488	53178
Number plate lamp	467/2	53093 E	467	53093
Starter switch	ST 19	76423 A	PS 19 *	31248
Lighting and ignition switch	PLC 6	34018 A		
Lighting switch			PPG 1	31251
Ignition switch			SS 5	31187
Stop lamp switch			HL 2	31082
Fog lamp switch			PS 19 *	31248
Panel light switch			PPG 1	31126
Flasher switch			TPS 1	031296
Dipper switch			FS 22	31284
Horn push			HP 19	76205
Flasher unit			FL 3	35003
Flasher relay			DB 10	33117
Screenwiper	CW 1	732480	CRT 12	75144
Horn, low note	WT 614	69011 E	WT 614	69011
Horn, high note	WT 614	69012 E	WT 614	69012
Ammeter			CZU 34	36181

*I think one of these must be an error in the *Motor Trader* service guide.

it was type SFT 462 on the TD, and type SFT 576 on the TF. It is possible that the TF could be fitted with a matching long-range driving or spot lamp of type SLR 576 as an alternative (or in addition to the fog lamp).

The TD had a windscreen wiper motor type CW 1 DA34 mounted on the passenger side at the top of the windscreen

The TD has its wiper motor mounted on the top of the windscreen frame. On the early car seen here it was in front of the passenger, but it was moved to a central position on later cars.

On the TF the wiper motor was sensibly mounted remotely under the bonnet, and the wipers were mounted in the scuttle below the windscreen.

As a consequence of the relocated wipers and wiper motor, on the TF the wiper control knobs were in the glove boxes.

frame at first, but centrally from chassis number TD 22315 in 1952, thus obviating the need for changing the position of the wiper motor for LHD cars. The motor housing was finished in crackle black with a chrome-plated control. The two wiper arms and their connections were chrome-plated. By contrast, the TF had a remote wiper motor type CRT 12 mounted under the bonnet, with cable drive to the wipers mounted on the scuttle below the windscreen.

A 1953 Service Parts List amendment actually quotes "reflex reflectors" fitted to the rear bumper of late North American specifications TDs but this seems doubtful. Rear reflectors, type RER2 were found on all TF 1500s, as they became a legal requirement in the home market around the time the model was introduced in 1954. I do not think this type was fitted to any TDs, or any earlier home market TFs, but may have been found on some export model TF 1250s. They were fitted to the top corners of the body at rear, outboard of the fuel tank, on rubber plinths which were wedge-shaped to compensate for the curvature of the body.

BODY AND BODY TRIM

The overall impression of the TD compared to its predecessor was of a much lower, wider and squatter motor car. Obviously the smaller disc wheels with the fatter tyres contributed to this image. In fact, with the new chassis, the front and rear wheel tracks were wider, and the TD was also wider than the TC in terms of overall and interior width. Some 4½in (114mm) were added to the width of the body in the area of the seat, so the TD was rather more comfortable than the TC.

In principle there was very little difference between the TD body and those found on the earlier models. One had to open the bonnet to appreciate one major difference – this being that the bulkhead was now always painted body colour, having been added to the body by Morris Bodies Branch at Coventry. The lidded battery box of the TC was replaced by an open battery box or shelf, cut into the sloping bulkhead, with the toolbox still behind it. The bonnet itself followed the style of the TC, but the centre bonnet hinge was now made from stainless steel.

The front valance between the chassis horns was plain without louvres. The front valance hexagonal bolts were painted body colour, but the cross-head screws were chrome-plated. The front wings came much further down in front than the TC wings. The TD running boards had three strips but the innermost strip was very short and was found only at the front, owing to the tapering shape of the running board in plan. At the rear was a body-coloured valance which formed a shelf with a central depression for the spare wheel.

All TD and TF models were fitted with full-width chrome-plated bumpers front and rear. The bumper blade section was a simple curve, and the blades had pointed (not squared-off) ends. Ribbed overriders were fitted, of a type also seen on other Nuffield cars of the period. There was originally no piping between the bumpers and the overriders. The rear edge of the overriders should be flush with the rear edge of the bumper blade; some reproduction overriders are not deep enough, so that their rear edge is forward of the edge of the bumper blade.

Behind the bumper blades were full-width strengthening bars painted black, as were the brackets which were attached with ½in (12.7mm) thick spacers to the front chassis horns on the TD. Spacers were interposed where the front bumper brackets were attached on the TF, through the front wings. At the rear, spacers were found on the bumper brackets on both models. A starting handle bracket was incorporated in the front bumper. The badge bar of the TC was relegated to the options list.

The front bumper and overriders on this TD are correct, but there should not be any piping between them. The badge bar (and fog lamps) seen here were optional; they rather obscure the front valance. The radiator slats should be coloured to match the interior trim, and the piping between wing and body should be body colour.

On this TF, the wing piping is correct in body colour, and there is no piping behind the overriders. The radiator slats were chrome-plated on all TFs.

All TDs and TFs had this type of curved external door handle with the triangular escutcheon. They did not originally have locks but locking handles have long been available, as seen on the black car.

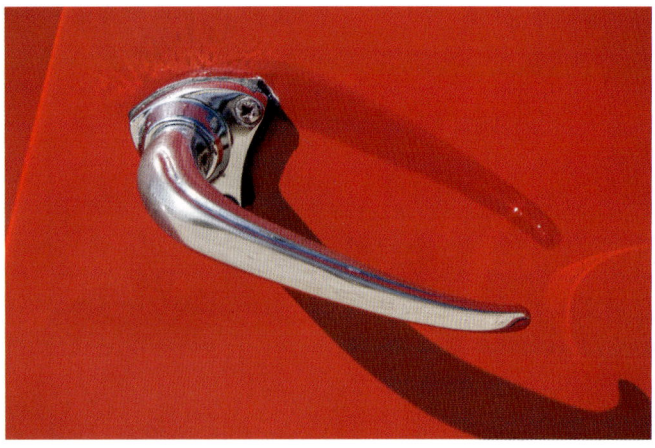

The TD running boards had these three tread strips with rubber insets.

On the TF, the tread strips were of a different type and continued well up on to the front wings. The rear wings now had this distinctive flare, stretching forward to meet the running board.

The door handles of the TD and TF were completely different from those found on earlier T-types, being of a style common to the Y-type, and fitted with a triangular escutcheon. At the rear, the TD had a square backing plate for the number plate, mounted on the driver's side of the car, with the number plate lamp above it. It was, however, often omitted on export cars, or replaced by a simpler bracket which could be adjusted to cope with different sizes of number plates.

The Auster windscreens fitted to the TD and TF were similar in design but not identical. The TF screen was raked a little further back. On both cars, the bottom of the windscreen stanchion should be flush with the panel break line on the side of the scuttle. Cross-headed Phillips screws were used for the first time on the TD windscreen frame. The windscreen glass was toughened on home market TDs, laminated on export cars. All TFs had laminated windscreen glass. A final point to note on both the TD and the TF is that the tread plates at the bottom of the door openings were plain, without the company name.

The TF looked radically different from the TD, although the main section of the body tub was very little changed. The front end was all new, dominated by the forward-mounted, raked radiator shell, and the bonnet line was lowered towards the front. The front wings were new, the most obvious change

This windscreen-mounted mirror is very much like that found on the TC, here fitted on a TD, where it would be an optional extra. This car also has non-original wind deflectors.

THE TD AND TF MODELS

The windscreen is basically similar on both the TD and TF. This grey TD has been fitted with another type of mirror, and again with non-standard wind deflectors. The wing nut and quadrant for folding the screen are similar to earlier cars.

Wing mirrors are a popular and useful addition; this is the contemporary Lucas type.

being that the separately mounted headlamps of the TD had been replaced by headlamps faired into the wings. The wings were also pulled down more at the front, and their section was more domed.

The running board was still separate. Between the wing and the running board was black rubber piping, also found at the rear of the bonnet and the bonnet side panels. Each running board had three plain chrome-plated tread strips without rubber inserts. The two outer strips were 31in (787mm) long, the inner one 20½in (521mm) long. The three tread strips ran well forward up the front wing, the inside one running furthest, with the front ends of the strips being set on a diagonal line across the wing.

The shape of the rear wings was also altered. At the front of each rear wing a flare was added to join the rear of the running board, with black rubber piping. The rear end of the rear wing was pulled further back and was raised slightly in relation to the level of the rear bumper. The void below the spare wheel was filled by a very deep shelf-like rear valance which completely filled the area between the petrol tank, the wings and the bumper.

At the front, with the radiator shell coming so much further forward, there was only the narrowest of valances behind the bumper. The TF bonnet was still of the centre-hinged two-piece type, but the bonnet sides were fixed and only the tops opened, which compromised engine access. Each bonnet side had twelve short louvres, split in two groups with three at the back and nine a little further forward. Between the louvres, and towards the front end of the bonnet side, were two chrome-plated push-button bonnet locks on each side. There was a chrome-plated trim strip to the edge of the bonnet top on each side. It may be noted that the beading found between the radiator and the wings was somewhat fatter than the ordinary wing beading.

The TD bonnet is very similar to that on the TC, with 21 louvres and two bonnet lock handles featuring the MG logo.

101

The TF bonnet sides are fixed, and have twelve short louvres each. There are two press-button bonnet locks each side, the rearmost between the louvres, and a chrome trim strip on the edge of the bonnet panel above.

On the TF 1500 there is a badge on either side of the bonnet, just behind the front bonnet lock.

No doubt to compensate for those fixed bonnet sides, the TF was given removable louvred aluminium panels fitted inside each front wing. They were supposed to ease access to the starter motor and the oil filter (with, as one commentator put it, appropriate malediction aimed at the body designer!). The TF rear number plate was of the oblong type, mounted centrally above the rear bumper, with the number plate lamp above it. As far as the TF 1500 was concerned, the only external recognition points were the rear reflectors previously mentioned, and small enamel badges on each side of the bonnet. They read "TF"-1500 in black letters on a white background.

A detail of the much-improved door hinges, here on a TF.

TOOL KIT

The toolbox on the bulkhead was lined in cream felt and had two lids hinged in the centre. Two different types of hinges have been reported, with a change in 1951 from a "finger" type of hinge that will only fold one way, to a simple "piano" hinge, but there was no change in the part number. A comprehensive set of tools was provided, as detailed below (the TF and TD tool kits were essentially the same, but I have included both early and late part numbers).

The reader of the handbook was warned that the tools supplied may vary or be omitted from time to time, as a result of the steel supply situation or design modifications. The starting handle was stowed in the interior of the car, on the back of the seat squab on the TD, and to the rear panel of the tonneau on the TF.

SUMMARY OF TOOL KIT

	TD, early and late part no.	TF	Notes
Tool roll complete with tools	S 78/35; AJJ 584	AJJ 584	
Wheel brace (pressed wheels) for BSF thread wheel studs and nuts	SK 2741		13/16in to TD 12284 in Dec 1951.
Wheel brace (pressed wheels) for UNF thread wheel studs and nuts	ACA 5217	ACA 5217	¾in from TD 12285 in Dec 1951
Copper hammer		ACG 5037	For wire wheels; TF only
Ring-type tappet spanner	S 78/2; SK 1118	SK 1118	
Jack and jack handle	A 1337	A 1337	The jack was a screw-type usually by King Dick
Ring spanner for cylinder head nuts	2368; 81782	81782	TD and TF 1250 only
Lockheed bleeder drain tube	S 78/25	7H 7064	Some sources state this was optional
Tappet feeler gauge, .019in (0.48mm)	S 78/31; AJJ 582		
Ditto, 0.012in (0.30mm)	500929	500929	From engine no. XPAG/TD2 24116 in Jan 1953
¾ lbs hammer.	P 330/130; AJJ 282	AJJ 282	
Pair of combination pliers.	P 330/104; AJJ 279	AJJ 279	
Grease gun, Enots or Tecalemit.	180954	180954	
Tool roll, canvas, without tools	S 78/29; AJJ 580	AJJ 580	
Adjustable spanner	S 78/30; ACG 5283	ACG 5283	
Two tyre levers	P 330/126; AJJ 281	AJJ 281	
Tyre valve spanner	S 78/11; AMK 9958	AMK 9958	
Distributor screwdriver and feeler	S 78/12; 2H 1697	2H 1697	
Tyre pump	S 78/22; AJJ 578	AJJ 578	
Set of three box spanners			Not marked with sizes
1/4in x 5/16in	794 A; ET 140	ET 140	
3/8in x 7/16in	794 B; ET 141	ET 141	
1/2in x 9/16in	794 C; ET 142	ET 142	
Tommy bar for box spanners	P 330/110; AJJ 280	AJJ 280	
Set of three open spanners *			
1/4in x 5/16in	792 A; 41273	41273	
3/8in x 7/16in	792 B; 41274	41274	
1/2in x 9/16in	792 C; not listed	41275	
Screwdriver	S 78/9; AJJ 575	AJJ 575	
Starting handle	MG 862/439;	X 22401	

*Some open spanners were marked with both BSF and Whitworth sizes; some sources quote different combinations of sizes for the two ends of the same spanner, thus: 3/16in x 1/4in; 5/16in x 3/8in; 7/16in x 1/2in.

On this car, the early TD with beige trim, I wonder if the outermost flute on the seat cushion is slightly too wide. The door threshold plate with the company name is not correct for any TD or TF model; but as one expert puts it resignedly, "everybody has them"... the threshold plates should be plain aluminium.

On the later TD with red trim, the seat flutes look more even. On both cars we can see the bound edge of carpet behind the hand brake.

INTERIOR TRIM

The TD interior (with the exception of the dashboard, and the position of the handbrake) would be immediately familiar to an owner of an earlier T-type. There was the same type of seat, with two separate cushions and a one-piece squab, and the same style of door trim panels. The carpeting, black Karvel with mostly unbound edges, was similar. However, the gearbox tunnel was now carpeted (over a steel pressing) and the exposed carpet edges behind the gearlever, and over the handbrake bracket, were bound in Rexine. There was a small plug with carpet cover, giving access to the gearbox dipstick.

Behind the seat, the heel board was uncarpeted and painted black. The bottom of the tonneau was made from three pieces of plywood of different sizes, of which only the centre portion lifted out for access to the rear axle. On some cars it was covered in carpet fixed with press studs, on others not. As before, the floor carpet had underfelt, but this was lacking on the toe board, which was pressed steel and was usually painted black. The gearlever had a sewn leather gaiter.

Most of the interior trim panels were in Rexine covered plywood, but an exception was in the region of the scuttle hoop, where the panelling was in moulded fibreboard to fit around the hoop. Sometimes the front half of the sides of the

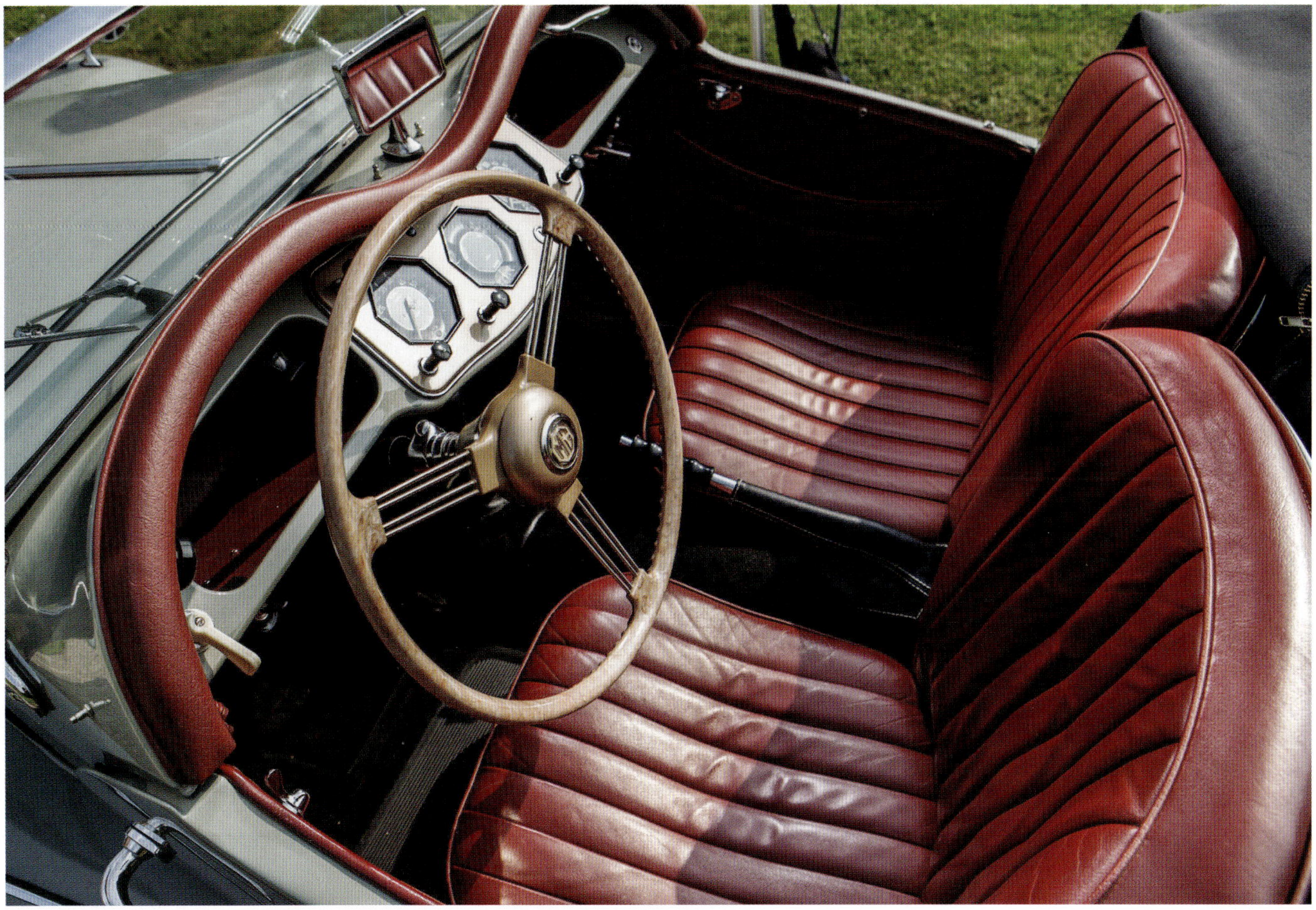

The TF had two individual bucket seats, with squabs folding forward.

The TD door trim is very much like the earlier cars, and the TF was again similar, but both of these cars had a new triangular bracket for the front side screen mounting point. We can see how the seat cushions go under the squab.

foot wells was covered in carpet. Under the dashboard was still the Rexine-covered scuttle masking panel or baffle board. The starting handle was now attached to the back of the seat squab with three clips, below the tonneau cover rail.

Inside the TF, the most important change from the TD was that two individual bucket type seats were now fitted. They were individually adjustable with a lever at the bottom outside front corner of each seat cushion. The seat frames were hinged to the floor at the front so that the seats could be tilted forward. The TF tonneau rails (which were now painted tan rather than black) on the backs of the seats doubled as convenient grab handles for this purpose. The wearing surfaces and the edges of the cushions were upholstered in leather, with the edges and the backs of the squabs in Rexine. The stitching pattern had seven flutes to each squab but only six to the cushion, in each case with border panels which were rather wider than the individual flutes.

Other small changes on the TF concerned the position of the starting handle, which was now clipped to the rear body panel at the back of the tonneau, and the heel board which was now covered in carpet. Finally, the under-dash masking panel did not now extend to the full width of the scuttle.

Fairly early in the TD production run, sometime in 1950,

FACTORY-ORIGINAL MG T-SERIES

The tonneau rail on the back of the TF seat is also convenient to grab hold of when you want to tilt the seat forward. The rail should be tan or beige, not chrome as seen here, and not necessarily trim colour either.

In the floor of the tonneau on the TF is a compartment for storing the side screens with a cover hinged at the rear, held by a strap fastening on to a press stud. The compartment itself is lined with black felt. This is the correct storage for the TF starting handle; on the TD it was mounted on the back of the seat squab.

it appears that a change was made from a flat to a grained Rexine. Furthermore, it is likely that at some time during the TF's production run a change was made from the old Rexine trim material to the then new Vynide (PVC) material. Unfortunately, there are no part number changes in the Service Parts List to document either of these changes, and the body material specification is singularly unhelpful. It may in fact be that Vynide was used right from the start of TF production.

WEATHER EQUIPMENT

The hood was always made from biscuit coloured single duck on the TD and TF, with the hood frame painted light tan. Originally, a two-bow hood frame similar to the TC hood frame was fitted, but from chassis number TD 20374, in 1952, a three-bow frame was fitted, and this was carried forward to the TF models. At the same time the shape of the side screens was changed. The early type of front side screen had the top

The TD originally had this two-bow hood similar to the TC, with a tan hood frame. Although the side screens are not fitted here, we can see how the top line of the side screens would be in a more or less straight line downwards from front to rear.

On the later three-bow hood, there is a clear break in the line of the side screens. A black hood was not fitted originally, but many later replacement hoods are black.

line of the screen sloping down towards the rear, and this was continued in the line of the rear side screen. With the three-bow frame, the top and bottom lines of the celluloid in the front side screen were both horizontal and thus parallel, and the top line of the rear side screen was at a steeper angle. Because of the steeper rake of the windscreen, the TF side screens were different from those on the TD. There was a small patent number plate at the top inside the front side screens. The hood cover had a single rear window measuring approximately 8in by 24in (203mm by 610mm).

The usual half tonneau cover, tucking over the black-painted tonneau rail at the back of the seat, was standard on the TD. It is likely that the full length tonneau cover was offered as an optional extra but I have not actually been able to document

The rear window in the hood was quite a useful size, although I suspect that this is a little too large.

If the hood is black, the tonneau cover should be as well. This is the full-length tonneau cover, which was probably an optional extra.

On the TF, the three-bow hood was continued, and this is the correct colour for hood cover and side screens

this to my satisfaction; however, the 1958 parts list quotes two alternative tonneau covers, one of which is described as "full size", part number 300597. The other tonneau cover was originally part number MB 50208, later AFH 3739. The tonneau compartment was lined in black felt. The side screens were still stored in a vertical compartment at the back of the tonneau, as on the TC and earlier models. On the TF, the side screens were stored in a horizontal compartment in the floor of the tonneau. This was lined with black felt and had a Rexine-covered lid hinged at the back.

Another full-length tonneau cover, black this time, showing the position if the passenger seat is not occupied.

While the black hood fabric is not original, this shows the tan coloured hood frame, and we can just see how the front hood bow is hinged to the centre bow.

These TF side screens are very correct, again excepting the black fabric. However, the patent plate is missing, although you can just spot the two tiny holes where it should be fitted, in the top frame of the front side screen.

The later TD (in fact a Mark II model) has the correct finishes for the TD, with a painted instrument panel, and a Rexine-covered dashboard. This car is fitted with flashing direction indicators, hence the white control under the edge of the dashboard, and the extra warning lamp in the centre of the instrument panel. There is now a foot-operated dip switch. The mirror is of the type found on all TDs and TFs.

DASHBOARD AND INSTRUMENTS: TD

As this is one area where the TD and TF models were completely different, I will consider the two cars separately. The TD dashboard was similar in shape to the TC, and, like the later TC dashboards, it was made from plywood, covered in Rexine to match the upholstery colour. The layout was completely changed, with both of the main instruments now in front of the driver, and a glovebox in front of the passenger. The dashboards on RHD and LHD cars were complete mirror images. Thus the speedometer was always towards the outside of the car and the rev counter towards the centre, and similarly the positions of minor gauges and switches on the central panel were reversed on LHD cars.

Looking at a RHD car, starting from the right (which would be starting from the left on a LHD car), the speedometer read to 105mph and incorporated a five-figure total distance recorder as well as a three-figure and decimal trip recorder, with a trip reset button under the dashboard. The rev counter read to 6500rpm and incorporated an electric clock. The instruments had silver-grey dials and brown figures and pointers. Some variation did occur to the colour of the dials. They were set in chrome bezels.

The early TD instruments were of the chronometric type with flat dials and were similar to those found on the TC, but the correct mph speedometer will be marked with part number S.516 and the gearing of 1600 TPM (cable turns per mile). The kilometre version is believed to have been marked S.516/K. The TD rev counter was marked K.45. From chassis number TD 10751, in October 1951, they were replaced by magnetic instruments with a flat centre and a dished outer circle to the dial; the speedometer was now marked S.S.598, and the rev counter X.65021/4 and 2-1 K.45. It is possible that not all instruments carried the reference number on the dial, or that instruments without numbers may be reproductions. The instruments were made by British Jaeger, which had been a subsidiary of Smiths since 1929. The traditional green rim or edge lighting was still used.

This early TD has had the paint stripped off the instrument panel, and the Rexine from the dashboard. The instruments are of the early chronometric type, as found on the TC, with flat dials, and the small gauge on the right is just for oil pressure. The headlamp dip switch is built together with the horn push.

The dual oil and water gauge was fitted to the later TDs, with the odd combination of centigrade for the water temperature but pounds per square inch for oil pressure.

The rev counter of the later magnetic type, and the speedometer, have this characteristic design of dial, with a dished outer circle, and a flat centre.

The central instrument panel was very similar to that of the TC. It was chrome-plated but this showed only on the raised lip around the edge, with the centre of the panel painted in the same metallic bronze colour which was used on the steering wheel hub. Again, looking from right to left (or the other way on a LHD car), the first instrument was a Jaeger oil pressure gauge with its pointer sweeping from 0 at top right-hand quarter clockwise to 160lb/sq in. On cars from chassis number TD 13914, this gauge was replaced by a combined oil pressure gauge and water temperature gauge (previously quoted as an optional extra). Next to this was a Lucas ammeter, originally reading to +/- 20 amp, but from chassis number TD 10751 it was replaced by a +/- 30 amp gauge. The design and colour of the two smaller gauges followed the larger ones.

Next to the ammeter was a combined horn push and dip switch, on a black bezel with white lettering. In August 1952, from chassis number TD 18883, this was replaced by just a horn push, as the dip switch was changed to a foot-operated type, mounted to the left and above the clutch pedal. Last in the top row on the instrument panel was the combined ignition lock and light switch, its black bezel lettered OFF-S-H. The ignition key number (in the MRN range, numbers from MRN 1 to MRN 54) was stamped on the front of the lock barrel.

In the bottom row on the panel, from right to left on a RHD car, was a red ignition warning lamp, followed by a green warning lamp for low fuel level (2.5 imperial gallons, or 11.4 litres). Then there was the pull-operated starter, an inspection lamp socket, the choke pull, a switch for fog lamp(s) if fitted, and lastly the panel light switch. This was originally a simple on/off switch, but from chassis number TD 10751 it was changed to a rheostat type switch. There was no indication of the functions of the knobs and switches.

On North American export TDs from chassis number TD 22371, in November 1952, there was an additional control in the shape of a switch for the flashing direction indicators, this was a self-cancelling switch of the dashpot or air valve type, mounted under the dashboard on the driver's side. These cars also had a warning lamp mounted centrally on the instrument panel, the hole for which was covered by a blanking plug on cars not fitted with direction indicators.

In front of the passenger, the glovebox was made from flock-sprayed cardboard. The inside and outside of the lid were covered in Rexine matching the dashboard, the lid having chrome-plated beading and an octagonal bakelite knob. The lid hinges were also chrome-plated. The factory fitted radio, an HMV Smiths Radiomobile valve unit, had its control unit installed in the glovebox.

All the instruments had chrome-plated bezels. There was chrome-plated beading around the whole dashboard panel and Rexine-covered rubber piping around the top of the panel where it butted up to the scuttle. This piping continued down to the door lock and further down following the front edge of the door on either side. The rear view mirror was mounted centrally on the top of the scuttle, and had a chrome-plated back and stem.

A mostly original dashboard on a left-hand drive TF, though the panel should be red to match the interior, rather than body colour. The open glove boxes are lined with leathercloth, and there is a wiper control in each of them. The grab handle is correct. The mirror is the same type as on the TD. The telescopic adjustment on the steering column shows up well. Please excuse the modern gear lever which operates a five-speed box.

DASHBOARD AND INSTRUMENTS: TF

Where the earlier models had the dashboard set flush with the edge of the scuttle, on the TF the dashboard was set well back under the scuttle, at an angle to facilitate the reading of the instruments. The rear top edge of the scuttle was finished with a strip of foam padding covered in leathercloth to match the upholstery colour. The dashboard itself was in painted metal, red on cars with red or biscuit trim, green on cars with green trim. The two open gloveboxes in front of the driver and passenger were made from millboard, lined with leathercloth to match the upholstery.

In the centre was the instrument panel, painted metallic bronze with a chrome-plated beading surround. There were three instrument dials, set in octagonal chrome-plated bezels. The black dials were actually round but with a white octagonal line round the centre, and white figures and pointers. The main

Here we can compare the detail differences between a right-hand drive and a left-hand drive TF, which are basically that the rev counter and speedometer have changed places, and so have the starter and choke controls. All the controls have octagonal knobs. The central combination dial on the LHD cars has an identification number, missing on the RHD car.

On the TF, the black horn button is mounted under the scuttle, above the white control for the direction indicators. This car has an extra non-standard switch under the dashboard.

At the other end of the dashboard is a hole matching that for the indicator switch; it is simply filled by an MG medallion.

instruments were similar to those found on the Y-type saloons, but were not quite the same. The positions of the speedometer and rev counter were changed over on a LHD car.

Looking at a RHD car from left to right first came a 105mph speedometer (with numbers in increments of ten from 10 to 100), with the trip meter now above and the total odometer below, and an electric clock inset at the bottom. In the centre was a combination dial, with a water temperature gauge on top left reading to 110° C, an oil pressure gauge on top right reading to 100 lb/sq in, and an ammeter at the bottom, reading to +/- 30 amp. The combination dial was marked at the top with part number X.58958/2 and RA.144; it is similar to the Y-type dial but this is marked X.58958 PA.108, and the Y-type combination instrument of course included a fuel gauge, not a water temperature gauge. The individual gauges were also marked but these numbers can only be seen if these gauges are removed from the main dial. Nearest to the driver was a rev counter marked to 6500rpm (still no red line), with a red main beam warning lamp at the bottom of the dial. The instruments were all by British Jaeger, except for the Lucas ammeter.

Above the instruments was, in the left corner, a panel light switch marked P which in its second position switched on two map reading lamps, mounted under the scuttle in front of the driver and passenger. In the centre were three warning lamps – blue for low fuel level, red for the ignition, and green for direction indicators. In the top right corner was a switch marked A for auxiliary, which could be used for fog lamp(s) if fitted. Below the instruments were the choke pull marked C, a two-stage light switch marked L, the ignition lock (with an FA key number, ranging from FA 501 to FA 625), and the starter pull marked S. The five knobs and switches were octagonal, black with white letters, and set in chrome-plated bezels. On LHD cars, the choke and starter controls changed places.

There was a knurled knob for the wipers in each glovebox, that on the driver's side being the master switch for the electric motor, and that on the passenger side merely connecting the wiper on that side to the drive mechanism. The horn push was on the driver's right (left on a LHD car) under the scuttle, and the self-cancelling direction indicator switch at the end of the dashboard just below this. The matching hole at the opposite end of the dashboard was covered with an MG medallion. The dip switch was foot-operated. There was a chrome-plated grab handle under the scuttle on the passenger side. The rear view mirror, also chrome-plated, was mounted centrally on the top of the scuttle.

If a radio was fitted, the control unit occupied the glovebox in front of the passenger, as on the TD. A heater was never fitted as standard on the TF, but certain heaters were approved for installation, and at least two cars were fitted with heaters by the factory (see list of optional extras at the end of this section).

EXPORT VARIATIONS

In the TD/TF range there was no such distinctive model as the TC/EX-U. Rather, the different export models were permutations of a number of specification differences. Most obvious was whether a car had right- or left-hand drive, and a miles-per-hour or kilometres-per-hour speedometer. As previously mentioned, the LHD TDs had a mirror-image dashboard, while on a LHD TF just the two main instruments were changed over.

Another permutation depended on the type of headlamps fitted. Basically all of these cars had S.700 or F.700 headlamps (TD and TF respectively) but they were supplied in different versions to suit different markets, as follows:

RHD cars, home and export: dip to the left
RHD cars for countries driving on the right: dip vertically
LHD cars, except North America and France: dip vertically
LHD cars for North America: dip to the right
LHD for France: dip vertically or to the right, with special yellow glass

Furthermore, there is evidence that some cars for the USA were supplied without the actual headlamp units but with empty shells for local fitting of sealed beam units. Sealed beam headlamps and turn signals were required by law on new cars in many American states from 1952, if not earlier, and to comply MG cars might have had to be modified by local dealers prior to sale. Later North American TDs and all TFs had flashing indicators fitted from the factory.

Some export cars were supplied with a different battery, Lucas type GTZ9A/1 or GTZ9A/2, which was dry-charged from the factory. On cars to certain destinations (Australia, New Zealand) and on CKD cars, a battery was usually not fitted.

Reinforced six-ply tyres were found on cars supplied to African markets, and Dunlop "Green Label" tyres were

THE TD AND TF MODELS

The TD Mark II had a larger air filter and different inlet manifold, larger carburettors with shorter bodies, and most notably, twin fuel pumps.

On the ignition side there is less to point out, as we just cannot see whether the ignition coil is of the sports type!

fitted to cars for certain European markets. Again on cars to Australia, New Zealand and on CKD cars, tyres and tubes were usually not supplied.

The rear number plate and lamp were mounted on the left on a LHD TD, but the number plate was often omitted or replaced by a bracket on export cars. Also as mentioned previously, export TDs had laminated windscreens whereas home market cars had toughened windscreens. Cars for France had a special type of laminated glass. Finally, rear reflectors may have been fitted to some export cars before they became standard on all cars, from the start of the TF 1500 model.

TD MARK II OR TD/C MODEL

The first tuned competition TD (registered FMO 885) was built in early 1950 and was given to Dick Jacobs to race, in the Tourist Trophy and elsewhere. This car incorporated all of the features that we now associate with the Mark II model, but also had lightweight bucket seats which were not part of the normal Mark II specification, although some cars did have the bucket seats. A genuine Mark II model can be identified by its chassis number prefix, TD/C, and on later cars from engine number 17029, in June 1952, by the engine number prefix, which at that time became XPAG/TD3.

The later Mark II cars had small badges on either side of the bonnet, and chrome-plated radiator slats. The radiator badge should be black and white, not brown and cream. Just behind the headlamp, we can see the small bulge added to give clearance to the larger inlet manifold.

These Andrex friction shock absorbers were fitted to most of the Mark II cars, here seen fitted to the front suspension spring pan.

The production Mark II had its engine tuned to give 57-61bhp, more or less as to Special Tuning Stage 1/1A. The cylinder head was machined from the standard depth of 76.75mm to 74.37mm, which increased the compression ratio from 7.25 to 8.6:1. The valve diameter was increased by 3mm – inlet from 33 to 36mm, exhaust from 31 to 34mm. Stronger valve springs were fitted. The 1¼in carburettors were replaced by H4 1½in carburettors, the intake manifold was bigger, and a larger air cleaner was fitted. Later Mark II cars had a different distributor with a revised advance curve, also quoted as an optional extra for non-Mark II cars. Some cars were fitted with a sports ignition coil, and all Mark IIs had two fuel pumps, the second one mounted on the outer side of the toolbox, slightly behind the standard fuel pump. A manual ignition advance/retard control was fitted.

As far as the chassis was concerned, the final drive ratio was raised from 5.125:1 to 4.875:1, and in addition to the normal hydraulic shock absorbers, adjustable Andrex friction shock absorbers were fitted front and rear, although possibly not on all cars.

There were originally no body modifications, but from chassis number TD/C 22613, in December 1952, the Mark

THE TD AND TF MODELS

The Mark II models usually had this grab handle fitted under the dashboard on the passenger side. By the way, it should be pointed out that the car photographed was originally left-hand drive as were most Mark IIs, but has been converted, to the correct specification.

II was given enamel badges reading "Mark II" on either side of the bonnet and on the rear bumper. To distinguish the car from the standard model, Mark II models were now given chrome-plated radiator slats (they stayed painted on the ordinary TD), and the MG badge on the radiator nosepiece was changed (again only on Mark IIs) from brown and cream to black and white. A radiator type badge was now fitted also to the hub cap of the spare wheel of the Mark IIs. Some of the later Mark II models for export may have had reflectors fitted on the rear bumper.

Further changes in December 1952 included a reduced compression ratio of 8.1:1, with the cylinder head depth now being 75.16rnm. This was the cylinder head carried forward on the TF model. The air intake manifold was enlarged, and a small bulge was added to the right-hand bonnet side panel for clearance. A tubular section grab handle was mounted under the dashboard on the passenger side.

The same optional extras were available on the Mark II as on the standard TD, including the even higher final drive ratio of 4.55:1, and the engine could obviously be tuned even further by the various Stages described by the factory.

The first production Mark II was a right-hand drive export car built in May 1950 with chassis number TD/C 1123. Only a few more cars were built in this year, although they included the three works racing cars (registered FRX 941, FRX 942 and FRX 943) which were raced at Silverstone and in the TT by Dick Jacobs, George Phillips and Ted Lund. Mark II production was only increased to substantial levels when MG began making them for the American export market in January 1951.

Various figures have previously been quoted for Mark II production, in particular a total figure of 1022 cars, but research carried out by the author using the TD guarantee plate issue ledgers kept in the MG Car Club archive has revealed that 1710 cars can be identified as Mark II models through being listed with the TD/C chassis prefix in these records. The breakdown of Mark II production should be compared this with the total TD production and export figures found elsewhere in this book. While there is no indication of the destination of the left-hand drive chassis in the record ledger, I think they both went to Germany.

Of the revised Mark II model made from December 1952 onwards, there were 315 cars. The last Mark II was chassis number TD/C 29909, a North American LHD export car, which is thought to be still in existence. This was built on the last day of TD production, 17 August 1953.

PRODUCTION FIGURES MARK II					
	1950	1951	1952	1953	Total, all years
Home market	4	0	2	45	51
Export, RHD	24	11	4	12	51
Export, LHD	2	0	0	11	13
Export, North America	0	459	977	157	1593
Chassis only, LHD	1	0	0	1	2
All specifications	**31**	**470**	**983**	**226**	**1710**

It should be pointed out that the original Jacobs car, FMO 885, is unlikely to be included in the statistics above, which are based only on production cars. Another car which may not be included, is George Phillips' streamlined 1951 Le Mans car, EX.172 registered UMG 400, although this seems to have been a Mark II, with chassis number TD or TD/C 5336 (see section on specials on page 147).

A Mark II badge was also fitted to the rear bumper on these later cars, and it is possible that these reflectors were fitted originally.

ENGINE TUNING (XPAG/XPEG)

In 1949, the MG company first issued the Special Tuning booklet for the XPAG engine. Later issues were updated so that precise instructions were available for all models, including the XPEG engine in the TF 1500. While it is unlikely that many owners of road-going cars will now wish to tune their engines, it is worth giving a brief account of the various stages of tuning which could be said to be part of the original specification of the T-series cars.

Although MG would happily sell you the necessary parts, the company was at pains to stress that they could not supply new cars in tuned form, nor would they undertake to tune owners' cars. Customers were warned that super-tuning as described in the booklet would invalidate the guarantee on a new car, and that here, as elsewhere, "Power Costs Money". It must also be remembered that the original tuning booklets were written at a time when the only fuel available was "pool" petrol of 70 or (with luck!) 80 octane rating, so all sorts of weird and wonderful fuel mixtures were recommended which we can forget about these days. Or does someone fancy having a go at running a supercharged TD on lead-free 80 octane aviation fuel? They claimed it was possible.

Stage 1 was fairly simple. It called for an increased compression ratio of 8.6:1 which meant machining the cylinder head, by various amounts depending on model. The depth of TB, TC and TD heads was reduced from 76.75 to 74.37mm; TF 1250 heads from 75.16 to 74.37mm; and TF 1500 heads from 76.75 to 76.25mm. The head, the ports and the manifold were polished; otherwise the engine was left more or less as standard. A Stage 1 XPAG engine should give 60-61bhp, and the XPEG engine 65bhp.

An additional Stage 1A applied to the TB, TC and TD models. The compression ratio was again raised to 8.6:1 but Mark II size valves were fitted. By using special sodium-cooled exhaust valves, the engine could still be run on 70 octane fuel. With 1½in carburettors (needle LS1) and a Lucas BR12 sports ignition coil, around 61bhp could be expected.

Stage 2 involved machining the cylinder head down to 73.575mm, the minimum depth recommended for all XPAG 1250cc engines. On the TF 1500 XPEG engine, the finished depth should be 75.50mm. In all cases, this would raise the compression ratio to 9.3:1. On TD and earlier engines, the larger valves were fitted. With Champion LA11 plugs, power output should be 63-64bhp, and if 1½in carburettors were fitted this should improve to 66-68bhp. For TF models already fitted with the larger valves and 1½in carburettors, 64bhp could be expected, and 67bhp from a TF 1500.

With Stage 3, we enter the world of racing. This involved fitting TD and earlier engines with special pistons, in conjunction with a standard cylinder head, for a compression ratio of 12:1. With standard 1¼in carburettors (0.100in jets and GK needles), LA14 racing plugs and ignition retarded to 4° ATDC, the result should be 73bhp. The use of a competition cylinder head gasket and the dual fuel pump set-up was recommended. If in addition larger valves were fitted, power should be 76bhp. With 1½in carburettors (0.125in jets and VE needles), 80bhp should be available; and with VJ needles, running on pure alcohol, 83bhp was within reach.

For the TF (1250cc), Stage 3 involved the 9.3:1 compression ratio and a semi-racing camshaft (part no AEG 122); with few other modifications, this should yield 66bhp. For the TF 1500, this camshaft should be used together with a 9.45:1 compression ratio (machining the cylinder head down to 75.16mm) The result should be 70bhp. On Stage 3 tuned TF engines, the oil pressure should be increased to 80 lbs/sq in, and a special distributor fitted.

Stages 4 and 5 of TB/TC/TD engine tuning both called for the installation of a Shorrock (or Nordec) supercharger, belt-driven from the crankshaft pulley. With a single 1½in carburettor, 69 to 75bhp could be expected depending on the fuel used. In Stage 5, the supercharger installation was combined with the 9.3:1 compression ratio and the larger valves, resulting in 88bhp – or, if using a 1¾in H6 carburettor, up to 97bhp. While definitive evidence one way or the other is impossible to find, I doubt that many cars were actually supplied from the factory with a supercharger installed; however, two TD Mark IIs were fitted with a supercharger from the factory, according to the guarantee plate issue ledgers.

The supercharger installation was not quoted for the TF, but TF Stage 4 tuning involved the additional fitting of a four-pipe exhaust system, and, for 1500 engines, a high overlap racing camshaft (part no. 168551). The compression .ratio was increased to 10.7:1 by machining the cylinder head to a finished depth of 73.575mm (the minimum recommended depth also for the XPEG engine).with either 1½in or 1¾in carburettors, 79 or 82bhp were within reach.

The parts required to carry out the various stages of tuning were available from MG's service department, as were a range of Champion and Lodge plugs suitable for racing, the Lucas high performance BR12 ignition coil, and even a Lucas 4 V.R.A. vertical magneto suitable for XPAG and XPEG engines. Other useful gadgets are quoted in the list of optional extras for the TD model, but they could obviously equally easily be fitted to other T Series cars. It may be noted that wider wheels of 16in diameter were available for TB and TC models. An interesting non-factory option was the aluminium cylinder head offered by Derringtons, which has been re-manufactured in later years.

The enthusiast who wishes to know more should consult MG's Special Tuning booklets: L/8 (with supplement L/8/l) for early XPAG engines; L/10 for the XPAG/TD engines; and L/17 for the XPAG/TF and XPEG engines. Articles in *The Autocar* for 18 and 25 July 1952 and by Eric Blower in the Nuffield magazine *Motoring* for July and August 1957 are useful. The same Eric Blower put this information in his famed *MG Workshop Manual* as well.

THE TD AND TF MODELS

The car number plate on the TD is similar to the plate on the TC, and also has the engine number stamped in. However, there is an additional space below the car number for stamping the code for specification found on export cars; it is left blank on home market cars.

IDENTIFICATION AND DATING: TD

A TD chassis number is prefixed with the letters TD, or TD/C on the Mark II model. Two TD prototypes had chassis numbers TD 0250 and TD 0251. The first production car was TD 0252 and the chassis number series ran to TD 29915, which equals 29,664 cars made (compare the production figure table on page 126). The maker's guarantee plate was fixed on the left-hand side on the front of the toolbox. There was space below the chassis number for a code used only on export cars. The different codes found here may be interpreted as follows:

EX-R   Export car with right-hand drive and mph speedometer
EX-RK   Export car with right-hand drive and kph speedometer
EX-L   Export car with left-hand drive and kph speedometer
EX-LM   Export car with left-hand drive and mph speedometer
EX-U   Export car to North American specification (to March 1950)

From March 1950 to approximately August 1951, the following codes were used on North American cars:
EX-L-U   North American export car with left-hand drive
EX-R-U   North American export car with right-hand drive

From approximately May 1951 on some cars, and from August 1951 on all cars, the North American codes were changed to the following:
EX-L-NA   North American export car with left-hand drive
EX-R-NA   North American export car with right-hand drive

North American cars were usually fitted with a miles-per-hour speedometer, but if a kilometres speedometer was fitted (for export to Mexico) the code may have been amended to **EX-L-NA-K**.

Apart from on the guarantee plate, the chassis number should also be stamped in the chassis frame itself, on the vertical outside surface of the left-hand front chassis horn which carries the front bumper, but usually hidden by the front wing and valance. Here it is prefixed by TD, but the detailed specification code was not stamped.

On this later TD Mark II, the car number prefix has had a C added, here the additional code EXL/NA is stamped in below the car number, and the engine number prefix is XPAG/TD3. This is not the correct location for the car number plate, but the body number plate is correctly located. There should be a small plate saying "Made in England", with an MG logo, on the end of the toolbox.

The engine number was also stamped on the guarantee plate. In addition, it was found on an octagonal plate on the engine itself, originally fixed to the left-hand side of the flywheel bell housing, later moved to the right-hand side of the crankcase. The engine number series began with 501 and ran to at least 30287. The following engine number prefixes may be found:

XPAG/TD Engine numbers from 501 to 9407, with 7¼in clutch
XPAG/TD2 Engine numbers from 9408 upwards, with 8in clutch
XPAG/TD3 Mark II engines only, from engine number 17029 upwards (earlier Mark II engines had standard prefixes)

In addition, engines on left-hand drive cars to approximately February 1952 had the letters LHX following the engine prefixes quoted above. The LHX code seems to have been dropped on later engines, and no equivalent code is found in the engine number of any right-hand drive car. In theory, the engine number should on average be 250 higher than the chassis number, but much wider variations did occur.

Each car also had a body number plate, on the left-hand side of the bulkhead by the toolbox. This quoted the body type number; the body number itself and the body batch number. No records of the TD body numbers exist and the numbers found on individual cars would be difficult to make sense of, without much further research. A typical body number plate reads as follows:

Body type   22381
Body number 1373/49378

This particular plate is from an early 1950 car, and it is thought that the first set of figures in the lower line (1373) is the actual body number. However, it is the second number, in this case 49378, which has been found stamped in the main body frame side timber, just inside the left-hand door threshold. The body type number 22381 appears to be common to all TDs.

On the left-hand end of the toolbox on export cars was another plate with the MG badge and the legend "Made in England" (similar to TC export cars). This plate was deemed superfluous as far as home market cars were concerned! Finally there was a plate quoting patent numbers above the maker's guarantee plate.

An approximate guide to dating a TD is given by the following list of the first chassis numbers issued in each year, taken from the guarantee plate issue ledgers. For this reason, these numbers do not quite match the annual production figures (compare the table on page 126).

Nov 1949	TD 0252 (first production TD)
Jan 1950	TD 0349
Jan 1951	TD 5170
Jan 1952	TD 12578
Jan 1953	TD 23635
Aug 1953	TD 29915 (the last TD)

THE TD AND TF MODELS

The TF had this new type of car number plate. The engine number prefix was now XPAG/TF, on the 1250cc-engined model. The patent number plate here is the same as on the TD.

IDENTIFICATION AND DATING: TF

In April 1952, on Morris and Wolseley cars built at Cowley, the new unified Nuffield car number prefix system was brought into use. Abingdon did not catch up with this system before the autumn of 1953, when it was introduced on the TF, the MG Magnette ZA and the Riley Pathfinder, which were all then going into production. The Nuffield car or chassis number system prescribed a five character alpha-numeric prefix of three letters and two numbers. The series of numbers for each model began with 501 which was the traditional starting number for Wolseley and later Morris cars, in the same way that MG's traditional starting number had previously been 251. It may be noted that the Wolseley factory's telephone number in Birmingham was East 1501!

The maker's guarantee plate on the TF was found on the left-hand side of the bulkhead at the end of the toolbox and quotes both the chassis (or car) number, and the engine number. A TF chassis number prefix would normally start with the letters HD, H for MG Midget and D for open two-seater bodywork. These were followed by a third letter which indicated the paint colour and may be decoded as follows:

A – Black
B – Grey or later Light Grey (Birch Grey)
C – Red (MG Red)
E – Green (MG Green, or Almond Green)
H – CKD finish (primer), found on CKD cars
P – Ivory

Next was a number which indicated the specification class, as follows:

1 – right-hand drive home market cars
2 – right-hand drive export cars
3 – left-hand drive export cars
4 – North American export cars, usually with left-hand drive
5 – CKD cars with right-hand drive
6 – CKD cars with left-hand drive

The final number in the prefix indicated the paint finish, and the following may be found on a TF:

3 – all-cellulose paint finish (normal on green TFs)
5 – primer finish, found on CKD cars
6 – cellulose finish on body, and synthetic finish on wings (normal on TFs in all colours other than green)

A number 4 would indicate metallic paint finish, but although some TFs were finished in Metallic Green, these still had the figure 3 in the prefix.

Typical code examples would be HDE 13 (a green home market car) or HDC 46 (a red North American car). One car that did not have the normal prefix was a home market TF delivered in chassis-only form which simply had a prefix HK 1, the K indicating chassis form, and of course the letter

Another example of the TF car number plate, with the engine prefix XPEG for the 1500 model. This plate is so nice that I wonder whether it may be a reproduction. This car has a new type of patent plate, but despite being left-hand drive, lacks the "Made in England" plate.

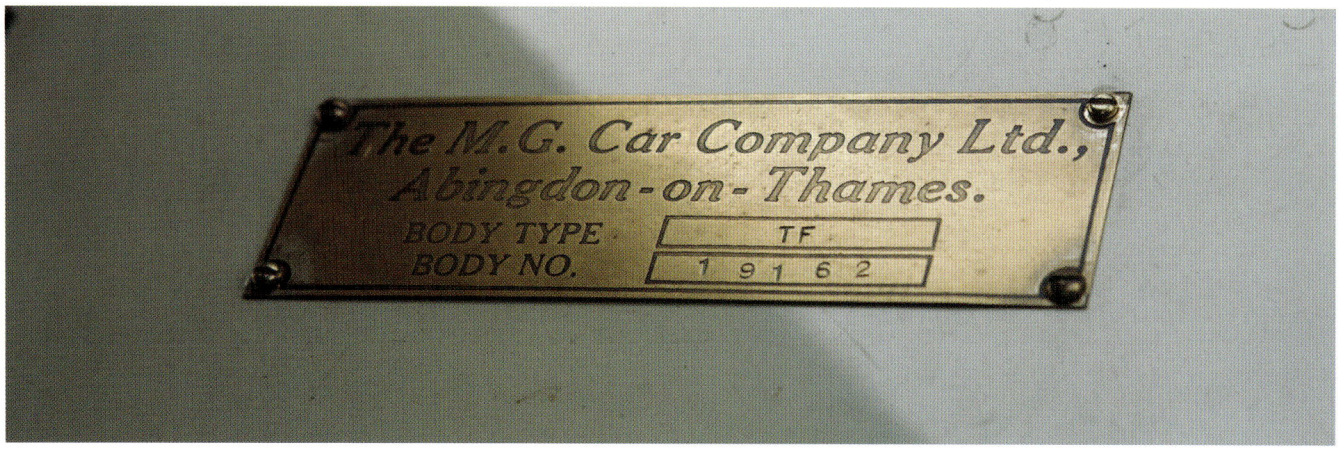

The body number plate on a TF; in fact it should be fitted to the underside of the toolbox lid.

and number for the paint were omitted. This was incidentally HK 1 5271 built in May 1954. The TF chassis number prefix system has sometimes erroneously been referred to as the BMC system. In fact, the very different BMC system was introduced later, and first appeared on MG cars in 1959.

The prototype TF was given chassis number TF 0250; this car was registered KBL 296 and was later rebuilt by MG as the TF 1500 prototype. A preproduction car with chassis number TF 0251 is also still in existence. Production cars, however, started from chassis number 501 and continued to 10100, so 9600 cars were made.

The engine number stamped on the guarantee plate was repeated on the octagonal plate on the right-hand side of the crankcase. The TF 1250 engine prefix was XPAG/TF; the engine number series continued from the TD engine numbers, starting with 30301 and running to at least 36516. On the TF 1500, the engine number prefix was XPEG, and these numbers ran from 501 to at least 3936.

On the body number plate, the body type was described simply as TF. Again no records exist of the body numbers, but they seem to be typically around 10,000 higher than the chassis numbers. The body plate was found on the inside of the left-hand toolbox lid. A patent number plate was found near the guarantee plate. On the TF, the chassis number was stamped in the frame in the same place as on the TD. Here it will be prefixed simply TF, if at all.

The following list of first chassis numbers by year is, like the previous similar lists in this book, taken from the guarantee plate issue ledgers in the MG Car Club archive at Abingdon. These ledgers document the date that the guarantee plate was issued to each car, and are therefore no more than an approximate guide to exact dates of production. Indeed the TF production ledger in the BMIHT archive at Gaydon gives slightly different first numbers for each calendar year. For exact production figures, please see the table on page 127.

September 1953	501 (first production TF)
January 1954	2178
July 1954	6501 (the first TF 1500)
September 1954	6950 (the last TF 1250)
January 1955	8644 (8644 is the lowest number in 1955, but it may be noted that chassis numbers 8671 to 8682 were allocated out of sequence on 3 January 1955 so they are the first cars built in 1955; 8644 to 8670 followed on 4 January)
April 1955	10100 (the last TF)

From July to September 1954, the two models were produced side by side. The following batches of chassis numbers were allocated to TF 1500 models:

6501-6650	150 cars
6751-6850	100 cars
6951-10100	3150 cars

The total number of TF 1500 cars was thus 3400, leaving 6200 TF 1250 cars.

The following were the CKD cars, which all had numbers allocated in batches of five cars at a time:

TF 1250 with RHD for Eire:
two batches in January and February 1954:
2910 to 2914, and 3390 to 3394

TF 1500 with LHD for Mexico: fifteen batches from November 1954 to March 1955:

1954:			1955:		
7876 to 7880	Nov 1954	5	9063 to 9067	Jan 1955	5
8032 to 8036	Nov 1954	5	9303 to 9307	Feb 1955	5
8178 to 8182	Nov 1954	5	9658 to 9662	Mar 1955	5
8385 to 8389	Dec 1954	5	9663 to 9667	Mar 1955	5
8433 to 8437	Dec 1954	5	9783 to 9787	Mar 1955	5
8457 to 8461	Dec 1954	5	9930 to 9934	Mar 1955	5
8599 to 8603	Dec 1954	5	9960 to 9964	Mar 1955	5
			9990 to 9994	Mar 1955	5
		35			40

Note that two of the Mexican batches had consecutive chassis numbers. The Mexican cars were to North American specification but had kilometres speedometers.

THE TD AND TF MODELS

OPTIONAL EXTRAS: TD

- External mirror, Desmo no. 44P1, with convex glass and double-jointed arm.
- Luggage carrier (the external mirror was always supplied when a luggage carrier was fitted).
- Double spare wheel carrier. Two types, depending on whether a luggage carrier was fitted or not. With distance piece if competition tyres were fitted.
- Competition tyres, 6.00-15 Dunlop Fort, on 4.50Jx15 wheels (ventilated type).
- Badge bar and fog lamp mounting (including two mounting brackets for lamps).
- Lucas type SFT462 fog lamp.
- Combined oil pressure gauge and water temperature gauge (standard from TD 13914).
- Shock absorbers with special low setting or double hydraulic shock absorbers.
- Additional Andrex friction shock absorbers (standard on Mark II model).
- Alternative rear axle ratios, 4.875:1 (8/39) (standard on Mark II) or 4.55:1 (9/41).
- Drawbar attachment (quoted in 1958 parts list); the maximum towing capacity was 15cwt or 763kg.
- Oil temperature gauge (quoted in 1958 parts list).
- Competition clutch (for either 7¼in or 8in clutches).
- Manual ignition control (usually fitted on Mark II).
- Radio, usually a Smiths Radiomobile or HMV of various types. Control unit fitted in glovebox, power unit/amplifier and loudspeaker mounted under scuttle.
- Radio aerial, fitted to the side of the scuttle.
- Extra fuel pump and duplicated fuel lines (standard on Mark II, and recommended fitting if engine was to be tuned).
- Wire wheel replacement service kit (ACG 5163), incorporating TF wire wheels, hubs, etc. Believed offered only after TF had been introduced, and production of the TD therefore ceased.

A range of competition and engine tuning parts were also available, for details see the section on engine tuning on page 116. A very wide range of locally-sourced extras and accessories were available in the USA, also later for the TF, and may often have been fitted to cars when sold new, but are strictly speaking not "factory original".

OPTIONAL EXTRAS: TF

- Wire wheels 4Jx15, including hubs, special rear axle with standard 8/39 ratio, and special spare wheel carrier.
- Alternative rear axle ratios, 5.125:1 (8/41) or 4.55:1 (9/41), for either disc wheel or wire wheel cars.
- Speedometer gear and pinion 6/14 for 9/41 rear axle.
- Speedometer gear and pinion 5/13 for 8/41 rear axle.
- Andrex friction shock absorbers, front and rear.
- External mirror, or luggage carrier and mirror (as for TD).
- Badge bar and fog lamp mounting.
- Fog lamp (Lucas SFT576) or spot lamp (Lucas SLR576).
- Full-length tonneau cover with zip, in biscuit "imitation mohair".
- Radio and aerial (remarks as for TD).
- Whitewall tyres; possibly Dunlop racing tyres.

The following heater kits were approved by MG for fitting to the TF: Smith's no CHS 4532; Delaney Galley no. S.1; Key Leather Co no KLA 360. At least two North American export cars were fitted with heaters by the factory, HDA46 2802 had the Delaney heater, HDA46 2803 had the Smiths heater.

When the luggage carrier was fitted, as here on a TF, there was also an external rear view mirror.

PRODUCTION CHANGES: TD

The number in the first column is either a chassis number, prefix TD, or an engine number, prefix XPAG/TD or XPAG/TD2.

Mark II chassis and engine numbers ran in the same series as the ordinary TD model.

This information is based on the following Service Parts Lists:
Parts List L.11 second issue 1951
print date May 1951
Amendment number 1 dated July 1951, and amendment number 2 March 1953
Parts List AKD 834 also marked second issue June 1958; this has many new BMC part numbers superseding the original numbers

TD 0351   December 1949
Scuttle hoop (also called "dash stiffener") added to chassis, with attendant changes to masking board and dash casings.

TD 0501   January 1950
Pierced (or drilled) wheels replaced solid (so-called ventilated) wheels.

TD/C 1123   May 1950
First Mark II model.

XPAG/TD 2985   July 1950
Purolator canister type oil filter replaced Wilmot Breeden oil filter, new cylinder block part number.

TD 4237   November 1950
Rubber pad added to footwell on driver's side on LHD cars, with attendant change to floor board and carpet.

TD 4251   November 1950
One-piece combined casting for hub and brake drum introduced, replacing separate riveted parts.

XPAG/TD 6180   February 1951
Change to carburettors on Mark II model

TD 6035   February 1951
Outer front wheel bearing grease retainer: press-on steel cap replaced felt washer type.

XPAG/TD 6483   February 1951
Modified water pump with integral seal.

XPAG/TD 6533   February 1951
Sliding hub assembly for top and third gear in gearbox changed (according to the 1958 parts list).

XPAG/TD 7576   April 1951
Oil suction filter in sump moved to central position for better pick-up.

TD 7624   May 1951
Dip left headlamps on home market cars.

TD 8142   June 1951
Lucas control box RB106/1 with separate fuse box SF6 replaced control box RF95/2. Dynamo with pulley and brackets, and locking bolt for dynamo (the number may be an error for engine number XPAG/TD 8142, as the 1958 parts list says the dynamo change occurred at "chassis number E 8142").

XPAG/TD 9008   June 1951
Exhaust rockers improved with longer bosses and bushes, to match the inlet rockers which were not changed.

XPAG/TD2 9408   July 1951
8in diameter clutch replaced 7¼in diameter clutch. New flywheel, new starter ring gear with larger internal diameter of 10¾ in (273mm) but still 120 teeth, larger bell housing and stronger clutch fork shaft. Engine number prefix changed. Oil pipe from block to head changed to be common with Y-type.

XPAG/TD2 10900   September 1951
Shorter dipstick tube, new dipstick.

TD 10751 (LHD)   October 1951
TD 10779 (RHD)
New magnetic instruments (speedometer, rev counter and ammeter), speedometer and rev counted with dished outer rings to dials, ammeter reading to +/- 30 amp; rheostat switch for panel lights. Attendant change to facia board, at least on RHD cars.

TD 11111   October 1951
Redesigned housing for inner tie rod on steering rack.

TD 12285   December 1951
Threads on wheel studs and nuts, and throughout prop shaft and rear axle, changed from BSF to Unified.

TD 12419   December 1951
Spare wheel studs and nuts, threads changed from BSF to Unified.

TD 13914   February 1952
Combined oil pressure and water temperature gauge replaced the original oil pressure gauge.

XPAG/TD2 14224   February 1952
Modified oil pump, oil filter with replaceable element introduced.

XPAG/TD2 14948   March 1952
New sump in finned aluminium. Capacity increased from 9 pints (5 litres) to 10½ pints (6 litres).

XPAG/TD2 15372   April 1952
Modified oil sump suction filter with a strap bolted to the baffle plate.

XPAG/TD2 15861   May 1952
New clutch lining with improved friction.

XPAG/TD2/16482   May 1952
New top and third shift rail to gearbox, with snap ring, and extra support at the back.

XPAG/TD2 16978   May 1952
Key added to speedometer drive worm gear

XPAG/TD3 17029   June 1952
Mark II engine prefix changed to XPAG/TD3. Mark II engines from now on fitted new cylinder head casting with round water holes. Standard engines still had the earlier type cylinder head.

XPAG/TD2 17298   June 1952
Shorter pushrods with longer adjusting screws.

TD 17548   June 1952
High beam warning lamp added to speedometer.

XPAG/TD2 17969   June 1952
New cylinder block with round water passage holes, new cylinder head gasket, but this still had oval holes.

XPAG/TD2 18291   July 1952
Improved material specification for exhaust valves.

TD 18883   August 1952
Foot-operated dip switch and new horn push replaced the combined horn push and dip switch. New battery tray.

TD 18959   August 1952
Change to speedometer on Mark II model (according to the 1958 parts list).

TD 19300 (RHD)   August 1952
TD 19900 (LHD)   September 1952
New harness with change to dip switch cable. On LHD NA export cars, reflex reflectors part number 500817 added to rear bumper (the reflectors seem to be quoted only in Service Parts List amendment no. 2).

TD 20374 (LHD)   September 1952
TD 20696 (RHD)   October 1952
Three-bow hood frame replaced two-bow hood frame; side screens revised to suit.

XPAG/TD2 20942   October 1952
A new distributor D2A4 was introduced, with a shorter stem and cotter bolt fixing rather than clamp fixing. This required a small modification to the block to incorporate the cotter fixing.

XPAG/TD2 20972   October 1952
New oil pump end plate incorporating priming plug.

TD 20749   October 1952
Additional body mounting point each side of chassis.

TD 21303   October 1952
Round rear lamps replaced triangular type, and rear wings modified to suit.

TD 22251   November 1952
XPAG/TD2/22717
Rod operated clutch linkage replaced cable operation, and clutch stop bolt added.

TD 22315   November 1952
Wiper motor moved to centre of the windscreen frame.

TD 22371   November 1952
Flashing direction indicators fitted on cars to North American specification (see Service Parts List amendment no. 2 and later parts list). Instrument panel changed on both RHD and LHD with a hole to fit warning lamp on LHD cars, RHD cars have a "plug button" filling this hole. Change to grommet for harness through dash on LHD cars.

TD 22407   November 1952
Floorboards and dash casings changed.

XPAG/TD2 22735 November 1952
Cylinder head with round water passage holes, as already used on Mark II (see XPAG/TD3/17029 above), now also introduced on standard engines, and new cylinder head gasket with round water holes. L10S plugs (¾in reach) replaced NA8 plugs (½in reach).

XPAG/TD3 22978 December 1952
On Mark II engines, compression ratio reduced from 8.6:1 to 8.1:1.

TD/C 22613   December 1952
Special trim package for Mark II model; compression ratio on Mark II engines lowered.

XPAG/TD2 24116 January 1953
New camshaft, as used subsequently on TF. Revised valve timing, improved torque at lower revs. Tappet clearance altered from 0.019in to 0.012in, and new tappet clearance plate to rocker cover.

XPAG/TD2 24489 January 1953
XPAG/TD3 26744 March 1953
Points gap clearance changed from 0.010/0.012in to 0.014/0.016in. This change may actually have occurred when the new distributor was introduced at XPAG/TD2 20942, compare above.

TD 25973   March 1953 (or 25976?)
New type of tie rod outer ends with improved seals.

XPAG/TD2 26364 March 1953
New type of oil suction filter.

TD 26180   March 1953
Headlamps for France now quoted as a special type (according to the 1958 parts list).

XPAG/TD2 26635 March 1953
New type of oil pump body.

XPAG/TD2 27551 April 1953
New crankshaft, made from EN.100 steel.

XPAG/TD2 27867 May 1953
XPAG/TD3 27996
Height of valve spring faces reduced, valve guides slightly more protruding.

XPAG/TD2 28167 May 1953
Holes drilled for locking wire in heads of bolts for rocker shaft supports.

TD 28950   June 1953
Change to the flexible brake hoses, two at front, one at rear, on North American cars only; part number 68680 replaced by TF type, part number ACG 5087 (according to the 1958 parts list).

I have been advised that in 1952, there was effectively a change to the TD rear axle. I speculate this happened because the new MG YB saloon then adopted the same standard Nuffield hypoid bevel axle as the TD, but as the YB still featured the built-in Smiths Jackall jacks, this had to have an additional small bracket on the axle casing to locate a hydraulic pipe for the jacks. It seems that this bracket was also found on TD axles from then on, albeit obviously not used, but was probably discontinued when the TF appeared, as the YB had then gone out of production.

PRODUCTION CHANGES: TF

The fairly extensive changes made from the TD to the TF at the start of TF production are detailed the body of the text. Therefore only modifications made during the TF production run are listed here, with as usual a chassis number (prefixed in the following list simply with TF) or an engine number (prefix XPAG/TF or XPEG) in the first column. TF 1500 chassis numbers continued in the TF series, but there was a new series of engine numbers for the XPEG engine.

The reference for this section is the TF parts list second issue AKD 804 dated to March 1958.

XPAG/TF 31263 December 1953
Oil pump modified with hole drilled in priming plug, to make pump self-priming.

TF 1501   December 1953
XPAG/TF 31537
Low-pressure fuel pump (SU L-type AUA 25) mounted under bonnet replaced by high-pressure pump (SU HP-type AUA 57) mounted on chassis side member in front of right-hand rear wheel arch. Wiring loom altered to suit. Change to instrument panel.

XPAG/TF 31857 December 1953
Modified ignition high-tension cables.

XPAG/TF 31943 December 1953
Reduced internal diameter to lower banjo oil coupling on oil pipe from oil gallery to cylinder head.

XPAG/TF 33024 February 1954
Modified oil suction pipe and sump.

TF 3495   February 1954
Piston dampers added to carburettor dashpots.

TF 3811   April 1954
Improved front wheel grease retainers on cars fitted with wire wheels.

TF 4760   April 1954
The track rod end, on the taper end, was changed from a BSF thread to Unified thread. The tie rods were unchanged and remained with a BSF thread to the end of production. The ball socket greaser was changed on LHD cars from TF 4910.

TF 6501   July 1954
XPEG 501
First TF 1500 car with 1466cc engine. TF 1500 badges added to bonnet sides, and reflectors to rear of car (new legal requirement in the UK).

TF 6887   August 1954
Wire wheels with deeper dished inner flange.

TF 6950   September 1954
Last TF with 1250cc XPAG/TF engine.

TF 8146   November 1954
New casting for body of horns; the horns were still known to Lucas as type WT618.

The large MG logo was cast into the early XPAG engines, until replaced by a W in a diamond shape in 1952. The block casting number 24142 tells us this is a block from an early TC. (Courtesy Tim Jackson)

The point of this engine number plate is that it is marked TD3, as it is an engine from a TD Mark II. Otherwise the plate is the type found on all XPAG and XPEG engines. The location on the right-hand side of the crankcase towards the front is common to TDs and TFs.

EVOLUTION OF THE XP ENGINE FAMILY

As indicated in the introductory chapter, the XP engine was introduced in 1140cc form in the Morris Ten Series M (XPJM engine) in October 1938 and the Wolseley Ten (XPJW engine) in February 1939, with the 1250cc size XPAG engine adopted for the MG TB in April 1939.

On the XPAG engines, the water holes between block and head were originally oval, and the block had a cast-in MG logo. TB engine numbers ran from XPAG 501 to XPAG 882. The TC engines started from XPAG 883, and the only major modification was that a timing chain tensioner was added. TB block and head casting numbers are not certain, but on the TC, the XPAG engine was originally block casting number 24142, which subsequently was changed to 24146 without any apparent modification, and the head was casting number 22952.

In 1947, with the introduction of the Y-type saloon, things got a little more complicated. The Y-type engines had a prefix of XPAG/SC (SC for single carburettor) and their engine number series commenced with 10001. The block and head castings were the same as on the TC but there were some detail differences, and a different camshaft with 0.256in (6.5mm) valve lift.

In 1948, MG introduced the YT tourer model which had its engine fitted with twin carburettors and the higher-lift camshaft from the TC. YT engines had prefixes of XPAG/TL (on LHD cars) and XPAG/TR (on RHD cars), but their engine numbers were taken from the series of numbers for the "SC" engines, so the commencing numbers were XPAG/TL 11604 and XPAG/TR 12026.

In late 1949, the TD commenced production with engine number XPAG/TD 501, incorporating some minor modifications already found on the Y-type engine. On both TD and Y-type, the starter ring gear was now changed, and a new smaller starter motor fitted. The corresponding Y-type

The octagonal engine number plate on original-fitment engines is well enough known. These interesting plates are from a BMC factory reconditioned service replacement XPAG engine, fitted in a 1939 TB but obviously supplied much later.

engine was XPAG/SC 14023. The block and head castings stayed the same.

In July 1950, when a new oil filter was introduced from XPAG/TD 2985 and XPAG/SC 15405, there was an attendant modification to the block casting which became 24445, still with oval water holes and MG logo.

In July 1951, a major modification was the introduction of the 8in (203mm) clutch, on both the TD and the Y-type, with a change to the engine prefixes where a number 2 was added, from XPAG/TD2 9408 and XPAG/SC2 16916. The block and head castings stayed the same.

In November 1951, the first engine fitted to a YB saloon was XPAG/SC2 17131.

In June 1952, the TD Mark II engine was given its own prefix, XPAG/TD3 from engine number 17029, which appears to coincide with the introduction of a head casting number 168422 with round water holes, at first only on the Mark II.

In July 1952, from engine number XPAG/TD2 17969 and XPAG/SC2 17463, a new cylinder block casting number 168421 was introduced with round water holes, to match the cylinder head introduced previously on the Mark II engine. At this time, the blocks lost their MG logo which was replaced by a W in a diamond shape, in anticipation of the forthcoming Wolseley 4/44 using the same basic engine.

In November 1952 on the TD, the Mark II cylinder head with round water holes casting number 168422 was introduced also on the non-Mark II cars, from engine numbers XPAG/TD2 22735, but only in February 1953 on the YB, from engine number XPAG/SC2 17994.

Around the same time, the Wolseley 4/44 was introduced with engine numbers commencing from XPAW 501, however series production only began in February 1953. Because of the front suspension cross member on the 4/44, the XPAW engines had a different sump mounted towards the front of the engine and in consequence a different oil pump pick-up, and a different location for the dip stick. Despite the change to the dipstick location, the XPAW engine used block casting 168421, or 22500, and head casting 168422.

In July 1953, the YB saloon ceased production and it is believed that the highest engine number was XPAG/SC2 18456.

In September 1953, the TF was introduced with engine numbers from XPAG/TF 30301, block casting 168421, and head casting supposedly 168425, although it seems that 168422 continued to be used, with the "2" ground off and a "5" stamped in.

In July 1954, the TF 1500 engine of 1466cc was introduced, with block casting AEF 117 with the W logo, and head casting AEF 118, both with round water holes. Part numbers with three-letter prefixes starting in this case with A were allocated under the new BMC part number system.

The information given here is a much abbreviated version of Roger Wilson's compendium *History of the MPJG XPAG and XPEG Engines and Transmissions* published by the MG Car Club T Register in 2012 and 2014, to which the reader in search of more details is directed.

PRODUCTION AND EXPORT FIGURES: TD

There were 29,664 production TDs (compare previous section), of which at least 1710 cars were Mark II models (see Mark II section on page 113). The following statistics were kept by the Production Control Department in the Abingdon factory:

PRODUCTION FIGURES: TD

	1949	1950	1951	1952	1953	Total, all years
Home market	2	149	385	246	874	1656
Export, RHD	96	1268	940	371	280	2955
Export, LHD	0	142	292	285	237	956
Export, North America	0	2810	5756	9901	5021	23,488
Chassis only, RHD	0	4	0	2	3	9
Chassis only, LHD	0	6	48	13	90	157
CKD cars, RHD	0	388	30	20	5	443
All specifications	98	4767	7451	10838	6510	29,664

Of the 103 LHD chassis in 1952-53, 101 were for Bertone-bodied Arnolt-MGs. CKD cars were exported to South Africa (345 cars) and Eire (98 cars).

MAJOR EXPORT MARKETS: TD (Nuffield Exports statistics in the BMIHT archive)

	1949	1950	1951	1952	1953	Total, all years
USA	6	2495	4988	9009	3509	20,007
(of which Mark II)			(467)	(959)	(129)	(1555)
West Germany	0	124	126	345	653	1248
Canada	2	233	358	170	383	1146
Australia	8	292	405	87	112	904
Belgium	0	218	164	46	73	501
Switzerland	0	219	134	44	27	424
France	0	16	17	94	223	350
South Africa	0	331	15	1	0	347
(of which CKD)		(330)	(15)			(345)
Japan	0	14	191	51	30	286
Malaya	3	28	38	54	58	181
Brazil	0	6	0	143	0	149
Rhodesia	3	25	86	15	17	146
Sweden	0	44	27	42	18	131
The Netherlands	0	33	70	9	15	127
Venezuela	0	11	22	36	45	114
Eire	0	45	30	20	5	100
(of which CKD)		(43)	(30)	(20)	(5)	(98)
Total of above	22	4134	6671	10166	5168	26,161
Total of all exports	30	4431	7084	10936	5823	28,007
(of which Mark II)			(480)	(976)	(212)	(1668)

PRODUCTION AND EXPORT FIGURES: TF

Of the 9600 production TFs, there were 6200 TF 1250s and 3400 TF 1500s. The following statistics have been compiled by the author by going through the actual production ledger. It reveals that there were rather fewer home market TFs than had previously been thought and it also gives the precise split between TF 1250 and TF 1500 models to each specification:

PRODUCTION FIGURES: TF

	1953 TF 1250	1954 TF 1250	1954 TF 1500	1955 TF 1500	Total, all years TF 1250 and TF 1500	
Home market	77	736	47	197	1057	
Export, RHD	123	1084	19	503	1729	
Export, LHD	61	359	24	48	492	
Export, North America	1374	2374*	1826	661	6235	*incl 2 RHD cars
Chassis only, RHD	0	2	0	0	2	home market
CKD cars, RHD	0	10	0	0	10	for Eire
CKD cars, LHD	0	0	35	40	75	for Mexico
All specifications	**1635**	**4565**	**1951**	**1449**	**9600**	

MAJOR EXPORT MARKETS: TF (Nuffield Exports statistics in the BMIHT archive)

	1953 TF 1250	1954 TF 1250	1954 TF 1500	Total, 1953-54 TF 1250 and TF 1500
USA	611	1614	1506	3731
Australia	20	793	0	813
West Germany	226	393	85	704
Canada	12	262	0	274
France	46	125	7	178
Switzerland	16	62	5	83
Belgium	5	70	0	75
Mexico (CKD)	0	60	15	75
Sweden	13	60	0	73
Italy	1	62	0	63
Venezuela	20	40	0	60
Rhodesia	5	54	0	59
New Zealand	0	53	0	53
(French) Morocco	3	44	0	47
Malaya	0	46	0	46
Japan	17	26	0	43
Total of above	995	3764	1618	6377
Total of all exports	**1114**	**4275**	**1643**	**7032**

unfortunately the export figures for 1955 are not available.

COLOUR SCHEMES: TD & TF

When the TD was launched, it was offered in the same range of colour schemes which had been available on the final TCs, as follows:

Black, with Red, Beige or Green trim
MG Red, with Red or Beige trim
Almond Green, with Beige trim
(Green trim optional on 1951 models)
Ivory, with Red or Green trim
Clipper Blue, with Beige trim

Some TDs finished in Almond Green had metallic paint on the body and matching solid green paint on the wings and valances (as had been the case with the pre-war Metallic Grey colour on the TA and TB models).

In late 1950, the following two additional colours became available on the TD:

Autumn Red, with Red or Beige trim
Sun Bronze (metallic), with Red or Green trim
Autumn Red was a much darker colour than the bright MG Red.

The range of seven paint colours lasted only through the 1951 model year, and for 1952 and 1953 the TD was offered in the following colours:

Black, with Red or Green trim
MG Red, with Red trim
Woodland Green, with Green trim
Ivory, with Red or Green trim
Silver Streak Grey (metallic), with Red trim

Woodland Green was a darker green colour than Almond or MG Green, and is sometimes also known as MG Racing Green. In 1953, Beige trim was re-introduced as an option on cars in Black, MG Red and Woodland Green, but only on home market specification cars. Since Silver Streak Grey has been reported even on a 1950 car, it is possible that it had been introduced earlier, replacing Clipper Blue.

The TF was available in the following colour schemes throughout the production run from 1953 to 1955, with no changes:

Black, with Red, Green or Biscuit trim
MG Red, with Red or Biscuit trim
Almond Green (or MG Green), with Green or Biscuit trim
Ivory, with Red or Green trim
Birch Grey, with Red trim

Some TFs were finished in metallic Almond (or MG) Green. An American correspondent has stated that he believes some TFs were finished in the darker Autumn Red rather than MG Red; well, it is not impossible...

On both the TD and TF, the colours for other components followed the pattern set with the TC: hoods and side screens in biscuit; carpets in black; tonneau cover normally in biscuit but possibly in black; and wheels, whether disc or wire, in silver. On the TD, the radiator slats were painted to match the upholstery (but see remarks in the TC colour list and in the section on the TD cooling system), the exception being late Mark II cars with chromed-plated slats, also found on all TFs.

Cellulose (lacquer) paint continued to be used on the TD. TFs were finished in a combination of cellulose paint on the body and synthetic (enamel) paint on the wings and valances. The reason for this was probably that synthetic paint had greater resistance to chipping. However, green TFs were finished entirely in cellulose; there may have been problems getting an exact colour match with the two different types of paint in green, particularly when metallic green was used. The underside of the wings was finished in body colour.

The only T Series model for which records are preserved showing the colours of individual cars is the TF. I have gone through the TF records to establish how many cars were painted in the five different colours and have come up with the following figures: Red, 3190 cars (33%); Black, 1882 cars (20%); Ivory, 1712 cars (18%); Green, 1521 cars (16%); Grey, 1207 cars (12%). The eagle-eyed reader will immediately have spotted that there are 88 cars (1%) unaccounted for. Of these, 85 were the CKD cars; one was delivered in the chassis-only form; and two were special colour orders, of which one was delivered in primer (with Red trim), and one car was actually finished from the factory in White with Black trim. There may equally well have been a few special colour orders among the TDs – although I am inclined to think that contemporary pictures of two-tone TDs in the USA were the results of quick on-the-spot re-sprays by local dealers before delivery to customers.

Most post-war colours are still recognised by paint manufacturers, and the following table lists the colour code numbers from ICI in the UK (which should still be recognised by Nexa), or from Ditzler, Dupont, Rinshed-Mason, and Martin Senour in the USA (some of the paint codes which I have quoted here are to be found on websites The Original

PAINT CODES TD & TF

MG colour name	MG part number	BMC code	ICI (Belco)	Ditzler PPG	Rinshed-Mason	Dupont (Lucite, or Dulux)	Martin Senour
Almond Green (MG Green)	S4/148		3483 (solid) 2007 (metallic)	44159 47705	BM 076	8195 LH 93-96223 H	20214
Autumn Red	S4/146	RD.6	2145 or 2752	50930	BM 108 R	43077 92-83450 H	20216
Birch Grey		GR.3	2507	31918	BM 002		
Black	S4/145	BK.1	0122 (cellulose) 2340 (synthetic)	9000	A 946	99	
Clipper Blue	S4/151		3300	12297	BM 042	93-25888	25286
Ivory	S4/147	YL.5	2700	81271	BM 127	83449	25235
MG Red	S4/150	RD.14	9448	71993	BM 121 R		25011
Sequoia Cream			4138 (?)	80203			
Silver Streak Grey	S4/163	GR.25	2209	72030 or 33676	BM 027		25280
Sun Bronze	S4/149		2653 or 2027M	23662		34759	
Woodland Green	S4/164	GN.29	0191 or 9767	2246	BM 078	8194 LH 93-98249	20561 (?)

MG TD and The Original MG TF).

According to paint codes listed in the TF production ledger, Birch Grey, Black, and MG Red were originally supplied by ICI. The TF ledger quotes a code for Green of 228855 ME (ME = metallic?), and for Ivory of 225765 for cellulose, and 15285 for synthetic. I am not certain from which paint manufacturer these codes are.

I am not sure whether Sequoia Cream and Ivory may be the same colour, nor MG Green and Almond Green – and I am not convinced that the TC colour Shires Green is the same as either MG or Almond Green. This table does not always distinguish between metallic and non-metallic MG and Almond Green. I believe that the "Almond Green" used on the TC/TD/TF is not the later BMC "Almond Green" (GN.37), and the "Clipper Blue" used on the TC/TD is not the later BMC "Clipper Blue" (BU.14); these later colours were used for instance on the Morris Minor and the Mini in the 1960s.

Ever since an article in *Safety Fast!* in the 1960s, there have been attempts at equalizing early MG paint colours with later BMC colours. This is perpetuated by current parts specialists, but forgive me for remaining a little sceptical. However, it may well be that it is now difficult or impossible to get a modern paint which exactly matches the shade of the original cellulose paint.

SPECIALS AND SPECIAL-BODIED CARS

The cars described in this chapter strictly speaking don't really meet the criteria for "Factory Original", since with few exceptions they were not produced completely in the MG factory. However, it is worthwhile including descriptions of many cars which were built, or bodied, mostly in period, on MG chassis and using MG engines. In other words, these are typically cars one would normally describe as special-bodied, most famously the Arnolt-MG.

There were inevitably many other special MGs or cars based on MG chassis, particularly for racing, which remain obscure since their full histories have yet to be researched. Some had lightweight bodies, some had different engines, and many probably had both. Other specials, such as Ken Miles's cars in the USA, and the Canelas-MG in Portugal, simply used MG engines and sometimes other components in unique chassis.

Then there were many small-scale manufacturers of sports cars which used MG components, typically the XPAG or XPEG engines, but which had completely different chassis and bodies, such as the Cooper-MG, the Kieft, the later Lester-MGs, the Lister-MG, some early Lotuses, the Tojeiro, and the TVR-MG. As they were promoted under their own manufacturers' names they really fall outside even the rather flexible parameters adopted for the cars discussed in the following.

SPECIAL TAs

First of all, mention must be made of the very first TA, chassis TA 0251, which was one of the two prototypes, registered CJO 618. TA 0251 was built as early as March 1936. It has a unique body where the petrol tank is hidden by a well-rounded tail; it was not, in my opinion, a particularly attractive design, and presumably Cecil Kimber did not think so either, as it remained a one-off, and the following cars reverted to MG's traditional slab tank. However, TA 0251 is important historically and is fortunately preserved, since 1976 in the ownership of Colin Fitzgerald in Vancouver, Canada. The next car and second prototype, TA 0252, registered CJO 617, did not differ from production cars to the same extent. It survives, in unrestored form, having been taken off the road in the 1960s, and is featured in this book.

The TA Airline should strictly speaking not be listed in

The first TA prototype had this unusual rear end treatment, and it is also worth noting the dashboard, which is just like that of the superseded PB model. (from growninengland.co.uk/mg-van)

In 1936, MG issued a small leaflet for the TA Airline, which was illustrated with this photo of TA 0355 in the original two-tone colour scheme.

SPECIALS AND SPECIAL-BODIED CARS

Later on, the Airline was repainted in red. (From growninengland.co.uk/mg-van/)

Eventually, TA 0355 was restored in yellow and black, a colour scheme which it still retains. Note the bonnet with extra louvres and a different handle, which is unique to this car.

the section on special cars either, since it was made by MG with a catalogued body, but it was a one-off. For the P- and N-types MG had offered the Airline coupé with a very pretty streamlined two-seater body designed by HW Allingham and made by Carbodies in Coventry.

The story goes that the original order had been for 50 bodies, of which (according to many sources including the Airline Registry) 28 had been fitted to PA chassis, 14 to PB chassis, and 7 to NA/NB chassis, total 49, leaving 1. This left-over is presumed to have been the body fitted to chassis TA 0355. However, an HRG was fitted with a near identical body in 1938, and it has also been suggested that MG built a second TA Airline.

The Airline with chassis TA 0355 was built in July 1936 and has led a varied but well documented life. It was registered in December 1936 under MG 4952, one of the Middlesex marks issued through University Motors in London. It was originally two-tone green but was repainted red in the 1960s and in 1972 migrated to North America, where it acquired its present striking black and yellow gold combination.

The car came back to Europe in 1986. For many years it was in the collection of Wolfgang Fischer in Switzerland and was registered in Zürich under ZH 50354 or ZH 21247. It was offered at the Bonhams sale in the Grand Palais in Paris in February 2011, and since 2012 has been owned by Colin Schiller and Tony Slattery of Brisbane, Australia.

I am probably at fault for having perpetuated the idea that MG made two Airlines which I assumed both dated to 1936. I am now inclined to agree that there was only one Airline in 1936. It does however seem that there was at one time a second TA Airline, which carried the Berkshire registration mark AMO 802 dating to mid-1937 and which was apparently chassis TA 2210, built in March 1938.

A photograph stated to have been taken in 1953 surfaced in *Enjoying MG* magazine in 2012. It has not been established whether this car had the Airline body fitted originally, or later, and its ownership history is not fully documented. While the Airline body is said to have been scrapped in the 1970s, the chassis of TA 2210 still exists, and was later built up as a "Q-type special" by the late Freddie Yhap which he raced in the early 2000s.

The best-known of the special-bodied pre-war cars is TA 0730 of October 1936, the Park Ward bodied TA drophead coupé registered KPB 999 (issued in Surrey in February 1946). It is believed that the car was built with a standard body. Probably soon after the end of World War Two the car was rebodied by Charles Ward, the son of the founder of Park Ward, for his own personal use.

Originally it had short front wings and a modified standard MG radiator, as seen in an article in *The Autocar* of 9 August

The Park Ward TA was originally built with short wings and a standard radiator.

Here is the Park Ward TA with the longer wings and a streamlined cowl over the radiator.

When the car was rediscovered it had reverted to the standard radiator and was therefore at first restored in this form, but it has later been fitted with the cowl again.

1946, and was finished in black, with sky-blue wheels and upholstery. Unusual features included electric window lifts and an Arnott supercharger. Charles Ward subsequently had it modernised, with longer front wings and a streamlined cowl over the radiator.

When in 1985 the car was acquired in poor condition by the present Dutch owner, Hemmo de Groot, it featured the standard MG radiator shape again, and he therefore restored the car in this form, over a seven-year period. However, in 2006 he changed back to the streamlined cowl. The car looks stunning in two-tone blue and has deservedly won a number of concours awards. It has been the subject of several features, notably in *The Automobile* in 2012, and the owner has even set up a website dedicated to this unique car, which he has christened "Symphony".

Then there was TA 0828 of November 1936, which had a special coupé built by Coachcraft for University Motors Ltd in May 1937, with body number 839. It was possibly built for Dockers, the paint manufacturers. Another TA,

Cecil Kimber personally handed over the special TA to Lord Ashley. Nearly 70 years later, the car was photographed at an MG event in Austria. (From growninengland.co.uk/mg-van)

SPECIALS AND SPECIAL-BODIED CARS

chassis number TA 1242, registered MG 5429, was modified by Offord for Anthony Ashley-Cooper, Lord Ashley (eldest son of the Earl of Shaftesbury, 1900-47). It had fuller, skirted front wings, with headlamps partially faired into the wings, and 16-inch wheels. Lord Ashley was photographed with Cecil Kimber when he collected this car at Abingdon. It was photographed in Austria in 2006.

Finally, TA 2852 of October 1938 is believed to have started out with a standard body. It was exported to Denmark where the MG and Morris importer Vilhelm Nellemann arranged to have it re-bodied as a convertible with a streamlined tail by JH Jensen of Højer, one of the leading Danish coachbuilders. At the same time, they bodied a batch of Wolseley chassis.

I saw the car with its Højer body in the early 1970s, in poor unrestored condition, but it was then acquired by an owner who did not like the body and had the car re-bodied with a replica of the standard two-seater body. The car subsequently changed hands again and is now believed to be in Germany. I don't know what happened to the Danish body.

There was one TB-based special. It was commissioned by RMB Duke-Woolley (later a much-decorated RAF Squadron Leader) from Peter Monkhouse of Monaco Motors for the 1939 Tourist Trophy race, which was cancelled when war broke out. It was naturally called The Monaco MG. After the war, Monkhouse and Rivers Fletcher planned to build a small series of similar cars, as reported in *The Motor* of 4 July 1945, but in the December 1945 issue of *Motor Sport* it was announced that these plans had been shelved as MG could not supply new chassis, so I do not think there were any replicas. It was fitted with a narrow open-wheel two-seater body and cycle wings, and the engine was bored out to 1385cc.

The car was registered in Hertfordshire under FJH 3, which is still on the DVLA computer as a red MG registered in August 1939, but actually, the Monaco car has been in Switzerland since the 1980s, when it was superbly restored in a most attractive light blue for Philippe Douchet. It is now owned by Philippe Hann, who has raced it. It is registered in the canton of Vaud under VD 137 657 and appeared at the MG Car Club event at Silverstone in 2006.

The original intention was for the Tickford-bodied TA drophead coupé to have this style of rear end with the petrol tank enclosed. (Photo copyright BMIHT)

Unsurprisingly, the TA with a coachbuilt Danish body has some similarity with German bodies of the same period. (Courtesy Dansk Veteranbil Klub)

The TB Monaco is a delightful-looking little racing car. The French racing blue colour could fool you into believing you were looking at a miniature Delahaye or Talbot-Lago! (Courtesy Stewart Penfound)

The dashboard is dominated by an oversize rev counter.

Phillips obviously used MG 7185 on the road as well as for racing. Here it is casually parked along a busy road, complete with tax disc! (Photo copyright BMIHT)

Race regulations stipulated that any spare parts to be fitted during the race had to be carried on the car, but in a flagrant breach of these Phillips sent the mechanic out on the track with a replacement magneto and instructions that he must not touch the car, but only explain to Dryden how to fit the magneto. The ploy might have succeeded were it not for the fact that Dryden afterwards gave the mechanic a lift back to the pits and was instantly disqualified.

During the winter of 1949-50 Phillips had a new engine built, and entered Le Mans again in 1950 with Eric Winterbottom as co-driver. The car was now fitted with extra lamps and extended front wings, and the race number was 39. This time there were no upsets and they completed 1760 miles at an average of 73mph for a second place in the 1.5-litre class behind a Jowett Jupiter.

It was sold to John Dalton after the 1950 Le Mans race and raced by him during the 1951 season. Cyril Witt raced it at Goodwood in June 1955, so presumably it had at least a five year racing career. It was discovered abandoned by its lady owner in a garage at Marazion, near St Michael's Mount, Penzance, in the early 1960s by an engineering apprentice

SPECIAL TCs

I guess that George Phillips's Le Mans car, chassis number TC 2467, registered MG 7185, is the most important special-bodied TC. Phillips bought the car in standard form from University Motors in 1947 for £500. He was not impressed by its performance and after less than a year decided to fit a lightweight body by Lester. This made the car more competitive and Phillips began to do rather well in racing, starting with a class win and fourth overall in the 1947 Manx Cup race.

He managed to get an entry for the first post-war Le Mans, which was to be held in June 1949. To meet Le Mans regulations a new body was made by North London panel beater Ted Goodwin in 20-gauge aluminium over a lightweight frame. The car passed Le Mans scrutineering and was given race number 43.

Phillips's co-driver at Le Mans in 1949 was "Curly" Dryden and everything went well until the ignition system packed up.

MG 7185 during and after the 1950 Le Mans. In the post-race shot, Phillips at the wheel enjoys a much-needed cigarette, and co-driver Winterbottom waves his cap in celebration.

who lived in Truro. He rolled it over a bank in avoiding an oncoming lorry whilst driving along a country lane in Cornwall, destroying the body. The chassis survived, as did the driver and his two passengers (!) but was abandoned. It is believed to exist "somewhere in the West Country".

For the 1951 Le Mans, Phillips would drive a new MG based on the TD, discussed below. In 2015 Phil Cornut built a replica of the Le Mans TC, on chassis number TC 3798, which had been re-imported from the USA. It was registered FAK 57, and was campaigned by owner Simon Evans at Goodwood and in the Le Mans classic. It was auctioned by Bonhams at Goodwood in 2016 and is believed to have been sold, to an unknown owner.

Several sources agree that the MG Car Company built three vans on the TC chassis, although they cannot have been capable of carrying enough payload to make them really practical – but it was a continuation of the tradition of having an MG works van, which had begun with an M-type. The first TC version was allegedly made in 1947, followed by another two in 1949. They were rebodied with standard TC open two-seater bodywork before being disposed of in the early 1950s, and no photos are known. At least one still exists, TC 8221, registered FJB 313. It was raced by Mike Vincent in the 1960s but is now in Sweden. David Darrell, an MG enthusiast in Dyfed, is building a replica on a 1938 TA chassis. Al Moss, the leading American MG T-series parts supplier, also constructed a TC van, registration number BAK ORDR, which still exists in the USA. Another TC-based "TV work van" has been built in California and is used to advertise the Curbside automotive blog website, number plate EAM 646 or MG TC Van.

The Canelas MG apparently started life as TC 2949, registered in Portugal DB-13-42 and originally owned by José Jorge Canelas, an engineer who hill-climbed the car but wanted to improve its performance. Canelas and a colleague, Antonio Andrade, came up with a very good-looking full-width streamlined two-seater racing sports body which has earned the car its nick-name "the Portuguese Ferrari" – well, it is red… The next step was to take this body and the mechanical components and fit them to an all-new chassis constructed from chrome-molybdenum tubes.

Denis Jenkinson of Motor Sport saw the car in action in Lisbon in June 1955 and gave it an enthusiastic write-up in his "Continental Notes" column; he was impressed by its excellent finish compared to most British specials. The chassis was extremely well designed, while front suspension was now by trailing links and torsion bars courtesy of Porsche. Torsion bars were also used at the rear, although on a live rear axle sourced from an Austin A70. The MG engine was then tuned to stage 2, but this did not give sufficient horsepower and somewhere during the transformation the car acquired a 1500cc engine. The top speed has been claimed to be 195km/h (over 120mph). In 2010, it was part of a special exhibition of Portuguese cars in the Museu do Caramulo in Northern Portugal.

By the time this photo of the Canelas MG was taken at a race in 1954, it is likely that it was only really the MG engine that remained as a token of the car's origin. (From News Exchange*)*

THE LESTER-BODIED MGs

It is interesting that in the early 1950s, British special builders and would-be car makers in search of an engine turned mostly to Ford sidevalve 1172cc or MG XPAG ohv 1250cc engines. I am not sure why these engines were preferred over, for instance, engines from the Austin A40 or the Hillman Minx; maybe the Ford and MG engines were deemed more susceptible to tuning. While Ford engines were easily available secondhand and were cheap to rebuild, MG engines mostly had to be bought new from the company, but Abingdon was quite amenable to helping out other constructors.

Of the new sports car makes which proliferated in post-war Britain, Buckler, Dellow, and Paramount were firmly in the Ford camp, while various cars by Cooper, Kieft, Lister, Tojeiro and TVR were fitted with MG engines, and Lotus alternated between the two makes of engine. All of these MG-engined cars however had chassis specially designed by their makers. The only make that should be considered here in more detail is Lester, since several of Harry Lester's early cars were based on complete MG chassis, and are well described in Stewart Penfound's book *Harry Lester His Cars & The Monkey Stable*.

Lester was an engineer and garage owner at first based at Knebworth until he moved to Thatcham in 1950. Between 1944 and 1946 he built three special cars based on MG P-type chassis and raced the second of them. A few other older MGs of various pre-1936 overhead camshaft models were fitted with Lester bodies including Harry's own next racer, which was based on an MG L-type Magna chassis and which he drove to a win in the 1100cc race at the first Goodwood race meeting in September 1948. At the same event George Philips raced his Lester-bodied TC, MG 7185, and won the 1500cc race; this was of course

Philips's Le Mans car discussed in the preceding section.

When Philips had his car rebodied for Le Mans the Lester body was fitted to a 1938 MG TA, TA 2460, KJH 114, which had been Harry's road car and which he sold to Jim Mayers in 1949. The car was raced quite extensively by Mayers and Dick Threllfall until it was shipped to the USA by Don Marsh in 1954. Marsh changed the front end (not for the better…) before selling the car on to Chuck Dietrich. He had quite a good season in 1955 and the car was then passed on to other owners, who continued to race it until at least 1959. It still exists with the modified front end and has been raced in historic events in the USA.

By now Harry had decided that he wanted a car with independent front suspension, so in 1948-49 he built the first proper Lester-MG, featuring his own chassis constructed from 3-inch diameter tubes, fitted with MG Y-type front suspension, and powered by a TC engine linered down to 62mm bore to fit inside the 1100cc limit. Alternatively, Lester would fit a bored-out and linered 1467cc version of the XPAG engine. This car was the first T51, of which Lester built nine up to 1955 as well as a few of other types. His cars mostly had MG XPAG engines and four of the T51 cars were associated with the Monkey Stable racing team, three team cars and a spare; two of them survive.

TD: THE GERMAN-BODIED CARS

For reasons that are not entirely clear, possibly to do with paying less import duty, the German MG importers, JA Woodhouse of Cologne, imported an estimated 40 TD in chassis form between June and September 1951. They commissioned a small and rather obscure coachbuilder, Fritz Hennefarth of Bad Cannstatt near Stuttgart, to make replicas of the standard TD bodies to fit these chassis. No drawings were available, so Hennefarth had to make do with photos and possibly an MG-bodied car as a pattern.

The bodies were made by hand, using simple tools and formers, and although the result looked quite convincing there were numerous differences from the factory TD. As restorers of surviving examples of these cars were to find out years later, standard TD body parts do not fit.

One giveaway is that the rear wings do not have the central crease, and all the bonnet louvres are the same length. Much of the body hardware and some electrical equipment were sourced in Germany, and some bright trim parts were polished aluminium rather than chrome. Some cars used steel of heavy gauge, which increased the weight to the detriment of the performance of the finished car, while others supposedly used some aluminium panels.

It is believed that about five of these German "look-alikes" still exist, including four in the USA, as several were sold to US servicemen stationed in Germany, and one in The Netherlands. Three of the survivors have consecutive chassis numbers TD 8872, TD 8873, and TD 8874, while the two others are TD 9238 and TD 9240; it seems that chassis bound for Germany were built in batches of five at a time.

However, there were other TDs which had German coachwork very different from the standard. Hennefarth bodied one car in a more modern style, along the lines of the Jaguar XK 120, to an order from the Frankfurt-based MG dealer Odendahl. Unusually this was built on a Mark II chassis, TDC 3671, which, since it dates to October 1950, may well have been the first German-bodied TD. The car was modernised in the 1960s with a front end incorporating an MGA grille, it still exists, and is undergoing restoration.

Four other cars were bodied by the coachbuilder Wendler of Reutlingen. Three of these were commissioned by Heinz Mölders, who had raced a special MG TA before the war and who owned the Motor-Company Baden-Pfalz, MG dealer of Heidelberg. The three Mölders cars shared a similar front end design, with a traditional MG grille angled rearwards. One was a roadster with wing lines again like the XK 120, a one-piece windscreen looking like an Austin-Healey 100, loose side screens and internal door handles.

The other two had similar straight-through "ponton" wing

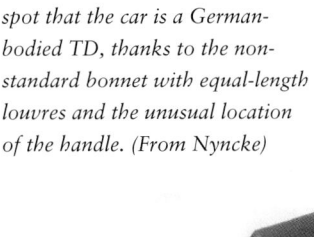

From this angle, it is possible to spot that the car is a German-bodied TD, thanks to the non-standard bonnet with equal-length louvres and the unusual location of the handle. (From Nyncke)

Hennefarth, who had bodied the look-alike TD, also came up with a Jaguar-influenced roadster. The car still exists, with a much modified front end. (From Nyncke)

SPECIALS AND SPECIAL-BODIED CARS

Wendler built at least four different bodies on TD chassis. This was again Jaguar-influenced, but better-looking than the Hennefarth effort. (From Nyncke)

More typical of early 1950s German coachwork, this cabriolet and coupé from Wendler shared the same basic design. (From Nyncke)

lines (to use the common German term for slab-sided styling), like the contemporary German Veritas sports cars – Mölders had raced a Veritas. They featured wind-down side windows in rear-hinged doors with external handles. One was a cabriolet with a split windscreen, the other a fixed-head coupé with a one-piece screen. One of these cars was tested by *Das Auto, Motor und Sport* in February 1952 and was then said to cost DM13,000 (say £1100).

The fourth Wendler car was a private commission by Werner Seyfert of Reichenbach (probably Reichenbach an der Fils in Baden-Württemberg, and nothing to do with Sherlock Holmes). This was again a coupé with a straight-through wing line, but it had a different front end which looked like the Farina-designed Nash-Healey, with headlamps integrated in a low, wide grille. Unusual features included spare wheels mounted inside the front wings, a fuel tank of 110 litres (25 gallons), and a hatch between the boot and interior allowing skis to be stowed away. Mr Seyfert paid no less than DM17,000 (£1450) for his car, which was painted metallic gold.

Weidenhausen of Frankfurt-am-Main built a one-off on a TD Mark II chassis for Emil L von Shwetzer, who ran the American Forces Network, the US Forces radio station. This was a roadster inspired by the Ferrari 166M, with a body made from aluminium, and to get the body and bonnet line lower than a normal TD, a Morris Minor radiator was fitted. However, because of the chassis underneath, the steering wheel

137

The fourth Wendler car had a grille like the contemporary Pininfarina-styled Nash-Healey. The rest of the car was more straightforward. The owner apparently specified a large boot.

Weidenhausen in Frankfurt bodied this car for an American client, somewhat in the style of a Ferrari Barchetta, but with a rather high seating position and windscreen.

Schloemer of Cologne bodied two TD chassis, this cabriolet and a similar coupé. The grille seems to have been cut down from a Morris Minor grille. (From Nyncke)

and the driver were high up in the car, so a high windscreen was necessary – which rather spoilt the overall look. Shwetzer took the car back home to the US where it was reported on by *Autosport Review* in February 1953.

The last German-bodied TDs were a cabriolet and a coupé, and a third car with unknown body type, built by Schlömer in Cologne. Styling was copybook early 1950s German, with a front end inspired by the Porsche 356, but with a semi-circular grille which seemed to have been cut down from a Morris Minor grille.

TD: OTHER EUROPEAN CARS

There were a few TD chassis bodied in other European countries. In Italy, the old-established Milan coachbuilding firm of Castagna, once famous for their Isotta-Fraschini bodies, would close their doors in 1954 – but not before they had bodied at least one MG. Sources do not agree on whether this was a TD or a Y-type, but the few pictures available seem to show a car on a longer wheelbase, so it is probably a Y-type. It is still worth mentioning here, if only to avoid future confusion.

In 1948, the Hollywood-based car dealer Roger Barlow of International Motors hatched a plan to sell Y-types with Italian coachwork by Castagna, Farina, and Zagato. Zagato built a Y-type based coupé, nothing is known about any Farina bodied car, and Castagna built this two-plus-two drophead, in typical late 1940s Italian style. It was red, it had a vertical not-quite MG grille, and ran on what may well be Borrani wire wheels, with the spare wheel rather impractically inset in the top of the boot lid. In 1997 David Knowles stated in *MG: The Untold Story* that he believed it was in the USA.

Motto was one of the smaller fish in the pond of Italian coachbuilders and often acted as subcontractors to the big boys. New York MG racer David Ash had a TD which in 1951 he fitted with a cigar-shaped open-wheel body and raced with some success, including a sixth place overall at Sebring in 1952. Extraordinarily, the car acquired a Mercedes-Benz 170

SPECIALS AND SPECIAL-BODIED CARS

Sempre nuovi successi delle nostre Carrozzerie
Anche la Motto di Torino (Ca-Mo) lavora per gli sportivi americani. Ecco una vettura M. G. speciale carrozzata per gli U.S.A. su telaio normale. Trattasi di una elegante barchetta a due posti, in lega leggera su ossatura in acciaio, del peso complessivo di Kg. 700. L'interno è in pelle blu.

Motto of Turin, also known as Ca-Mo, rebodied a TD for American racer David Ash, in the same style as a body they had built on a Cisitalia chassis.

Gus Ehrmann raced a Motto-bodied TD-engined "Sport Speciale" to eleventh place overall at Sebring in 1954; note the mismatched wheels. (From Knudson)

A modern photo of the Ehrman racer, now with wire wheels all round! (From Moss Motoring)

rear swing axle. However, Ash and New York MG distributor John Inskip commissioned Motto to build a streamlined body on this TD chassis, again specifically for racing. Motto simply produced a clone of a body they had fitted to a Cisitalia. It was followed by another two cars with similar bodywork and MG mechanicals, but with tubular frames made in Italy by Gilco, which must have been lighter. They were badged "MG TD Sport Speciale".

Ash did quite well with Motto cars, including at Watkins Glen and the Giant's Despair hill climb. Gus Ehrman and Fred Allen were fifth in class and eleventh overall in the 1954 Sebring 12-hour race in an MG Motto. The original Motto car was for some time in the Gene Ponder collection, and after a sojourn with dealer Auto Salon Singen in Germany came back to California; it is now red. It is fitted with an MG guarantee plate – presumably a reproduction – giving an engine number of XPAG 29575, unless this is meant to be the car number, but both appear to be 1953 numbers which is unhelpful. At least one of the two cars with the tubular chassis also exists; it is the 1954 Sebring car, now yellow, and was restored by Jason Wenig in Florida in about 2006.

In 1952 American soldier Edward Petot, stationed in Italy, bought a TD, chassis TD 20325, through the Italian importers Fattori & Montani. For reasons unknown he decided to have the car rebodied in the Italian racing car style, and commissioned the little-known coachbuilder Virgilio Schiaretti of Parma to do the work. They came up with a rather good-looking aluminium body with cycle wings at the front, and at the same time the engine was tuned with Weber carburettors, etc; one source says it was supercharged. Other changes were Andrex shock absorbers and Alfin brake drums. Petot took the car back with him to the USA in 1959, where it resurfaced in 1991 and was the subject of an article by Jon Pressnell in *Enjoying MG* in August 2006. More recently it has been displayed in the Lyon Air Museum in California.

Ghia-Aigle of Switzerland bodied at least three TDs, two cabriolets and a coupé. They were presumably all designed by Giovanni Michelotti, who at that time was contracted to design their bodywork. The first cars was a Mark II, chassis number TDC 22878 with right-hand drive. The chassis was built in December 1952. The finished car was exhibited by JH Keller at the 1953 Geneva Motor Show with a price tag of 17,000 Swiss Francs (nearly £1400). Originally with disc wheels, it was later converted to wire wheels. It happily still exists and has appeared at classic car shows in Switzerland.

The next Ghia-Aigle car was chassis number TD 25280

139

The 1953 Ghia-Aigle car was an early design by Giovanni Michelotti. Here it is photographed when new. The lines are very Italian, even with a hint of the tail fins which soon became fashionable. It has the standard TD instruments in a unique dashboard.

This rather poor photo is included to show the first Ghia-Aigle bodied car as it appeared on the Nuffield stand at the 1953 Geneva Motor Show. (From News Exchange*)*

which dates to February 1953, but this seems to have taken longer to finish. It did not appear at the 1954 Geneva Show, but at some regional shows, in St Gallen and in Basel. It was originally metallic blue. This car is said to have been converted to a coupé by another Swiss coachbuilder, Beutler, in about 1962. It was in an auction in Basel in 1980, and still exists, complete with hard top. The third car said to date to 1953 was always a coupé. It had a distinctive front end with large headlamps built into the radiator grille, and smaller lamps in the front wing tips. It had right-hand drive and disc wheels. I

The second Ghia-Aigle car was very similar to the first, but is believed to have been always metallic blue. It was later fitted with a hard top by Swiss coachbuilder Beutler which it still has today. (Courtesy Dr Stefan Dierkes)

Michelotti and Ghia-Aigle then came up with this coupé, which by comparison is rather anodyne. Nevertheless, it won a prize in a Swiss beauty contest for cars.

SPECIALS AND SPECIAL-BODIED CARS

It is believed that it was also Michelotti who designed this coupé for a TD chassis, which was built by Vignale for a Swiss client in Lugano in 1954; the car still exists in this area.

Perl was the Nuffield importer in Vienna. They had previously made a few cars and were competent coachbuilders. They bodied at least three TDs. This is the first attempt, in 1951-52. (From News Exchange)

Apart from importing Nuffield products, Perl also sold the German Champion microcar, which may explain a few things. Their original dodgem-like design was developed into this car, which they tried to sell into the American market.

Finally, by 1954, Perl might have been on to something, with overtones of Lea Francis. This car appears to have a bench seat for three people. (From News Exchange)

The Netherlands saw a few special-bodied TDs. This car was bodied by Verheul, and owner JL Hengst drove it in the 1952 Tulip Rally. The body still exists. (From News Exchange)

think it may have been TD 26939 from April 1953. Nothing further seems to be known.

Vignale built a coupé on a TD chassis, and this body is also said to have been designed by Michelotti. It is therefore not surprising that it has some similarities with the Ghia-Aigle cars. The car was again built on a right-hand drive chassis (so this could have been TD 26939) and was intended for a Swiss customer in Lugano; it still exists, probably in the Swiss province of Ticino. The body was from aluminium. It is now two-tone, red with a black roof and a tan leather interior. It is quite luxuriously fitted out and may be the only MG with a built-in cocktail cabinet.

The Austrian Nuffield importer GH Perl built a body on a left-hand drive TD chassis, probably in 1951. It looked more modern than the standard car but was not very pretty, with a bland oval grille of heavy vertical bars. Perl quickly set about producing an improved design, with a more distinctive radiator grille but sadly not much prettier. The body was made from aluminium and there were wind-down side windows.

A Perl-bodied car was being offered for sale by Bill Frick in Rockville Center, New York, in 1953. According to a report in the December 1953 issue of the American magazine *Autosport Review*, by then Perl had completed a test series of five cars, and were planning for small-scale series production. The third and final design of 1954 was somewhat better-looking and had three-abreast seating; I am not sure where they put the gear lever!

There were at least five special-bodied TDs in The Netherlands. Verheul of Waddinxveen is better known as a coachbuilder of coaches and buses, but they also made a few car bodies. Their streamlined Riley drophead coupé of 1950 is perhaps the most famous, but they also made a body for an MG TD in 1951 or 1952, probably for the owner J L Hengst, who used the car to compete in the Tulip Rally of 1952, where he finished 71st overall and 11th in class. The body of the Hengst car still exists in unrestored form, but the chassis has been fitted with a standard body. Around the same time in 1952 the MG

Meanwhile, Dutch MG dealer Roeloffzen put this unusual hard top on to a standard TD body. There were also a few hard tops in the UK, on both the TC and the TD. (From News Exchange*)*

The most intriguing of the Dutch MG specials is this razor-edge coupé body by Veth of Arnhem. The car still exists and is or will be undergoing restoration.

The Dutch driver FMA Eschauzier had this TD-based car, which looks quite similar to van der Lof's better-known one. He won his class in the sports car race at Zandvoort in 1955. (From News Exchange*).*

dealer Roeloffzen of Enschede put an all-steel hard top on to a standard MG TD.

A more ambitious attempt at creating a closed TD was by R Veth & Sons of Arnhem, an old-established coachbuilder which is still active, now as Veth Automotive, in the field of light commercial vehicles. They seem to have built very few car bodies after World War II. Their TD body was a coupé of almost razor-edge design, and it is not certain whether they built the body when the car was new or some time later. The car appeared at a Dutch car show in 2014, and the owner was then planning to restore it.

A complete contrast was the very stark TD-based racing special built for Andries "Dries" JM van der Lof, a wealthy manufacturer of electric cables of Haaksbergen. He began by racing a TC, but changed to a TD in 1950 and won a race at Zandvoort in June 1950. In that event the car was already modified from standard by his mechanic Sieverink, it had very close-fitting cycle wings and a fairing over the front of the chassis. It was claimed to do 169km/h (105mph) and was registered E 31350. This TD was later fitted with a very low and narrow body with just about enough room for two and the same cycle-type wings. With Martin Odink as co-driver, van der Lof won the 1.5-litre sports car category in the 1952 Tulip Rally, and was third overall. The car still exists in the ownership of the family, now with the number plate BD-59-92.

THE ARNOLT-MG

The romantic version of the Arnolt story goes as follows.

Once upon a time there was an Italian coachbuilder called Bertone. His company was in a bad way and he was at his wits' end to drum up business. Somehow he managed to buy two chassis from one of those small English sports cars. By burning the midnight oil and staving off the creditors, Bertone got two bodies – a coupé and a convertible – built on these chassis which happened to be MG TDs, and he hired a stand at the Turin Motor Show in April 1952 to show them off.

On to Bertone's stand walked a gigantic American in a cowboy outfit. He said he wanted to buy the cars. An astounded Bertone could not believe his luck; the American wanted to buy both cars? No, said the American, who happened to be "Wacky" Arnolt, the ebullient Nuffield distributor from Chicago – he wanted a hundred cars of each type. A deal was struck, and Bertone was back in business.

In actual fact, the two Bertone-bodied cars appeared at the Turin show in April 1952 on the stand of the Nuffield importer, Fattori & Montani of Rome, and were said to have been commissioned by them. One source suggests they were built on the chassis of two wrecked TDs, but they were apparently built on chassis TD 9930 and TD 10058, both of which left the factory as chassis only in September 1951. Incidentally, Bertone themselves showed a wire-wheeled Arnolt coupé on their stand at the 1953 Turin show.

It is believed that the two 1952 show cars were shipped to

SPECIALS AND SPECIAL-BODIED CARS

"Wacky" Arnolt advertised the Bertone-bodied TDs as the "Arnolt Family-and-Sports car". (From Knudson)

the USA and exhibited at the Elkhart Lake SCCA race meeting on 6-7 September 1952. Arnolt persuaded MG at Abingdon to lay on a supply of chassis. From November 1952 to May 1953 a total of 101 chassis were sent to Turin, where they were finished with hand-made coachwork. Including the two 1952 prototypes there were 67 coupés and 36 convertibles. The cars were then shipped to Arnolt in Chicago.

Unfortunately for "Wacky", they proved rather difficult to sell, and he did not shift the last few cars until 1958 or even 1959. The reason for this was that the Arnolt-MG cost $2995 (£1070) for the coupé and $3145 (£1123) for the convertible (with disc wheels, less extras) when it was launched in New York in April 1953, at a time when the standard TD cost $2157 (£770) and a Jaguar XK 120 less than $4000.

The Bertone bodies were made from steel, with doors, bonnet and boot lid in aluminium. They were two-plus-two seaters with a generous boot. The styling was straightforward early 1950s Italian, with a traditional MG radiator grille incorporated. The chassis were supplied from MG with a complete set

The first two Bertone-bodied TDs were commissioned by Italian Nuffield importer Fattori & Montani of Rome and displayed on their stand at the Turin Motor Show in 1952. Incidentally, they also handled Jaguars. (From News Exchange)

Arnolt exhibited a wire-wheeled car at the New York Motor Show in 1953, with both MG and Arnolt badges on display. (From News Exchange)

At the Turin Show in 1953, this car was on the Bertone stand, with apparently a slightly different radiator grille pattern.

143

FACTORY-ORIGINAL MG T-SERIES

These two restored Arnolt cars were at one time part of the famous MG collection owned by Gene Ponder in Texas, until auctioned in the early 2000s.

of instruments which were installed in front of the driver, speedometer and rev counter on each side, with the instrument and switch panel directly above the steering column, mounted upside down! Interestingly enough, the cars were trimmed in Connolly leather and even painted with ICI paints.

Many Arnolt cars were fitted with Borrani or Dunlop wire wheels, and other options included heater, radio, a fresh-air ventilation system, a badge bar, as well as cast aluminium rocker and tappet covers, both made by the Arnolt corporation. One or two of the later cars are now fitted with a 1466cc XPEG (TF 1500) engine. The engine numbers originally fitted by MG can be documented in the TD Guarantee Plate Issue ledger held by the MG Car Club, but it has been speculated that some cars were fitted with XPEG engines by Arnolt prior to being sold.

Chassis intended for Arnolt were supplied from MG in small

PRODUCTION FIGURES: The first and last Arnolts were:

Chassis number	Date of chassis	Arnolt number	Coupé body number	Convertible body number	Paint colour	Trim colour
TD 9930	4 Sep 1951	219	4301*		Red	Beige
TD 10058	7 Sep 1951	218		4401*	Ivory	Brown
TD 19182		220	4302		Maroon	Grey
TD 28023	28 May 1953	317	4367		Sun Bronze	Brown
TD 28024	28 May 1953	318		4434	Larch Green	Beige
TD 28025	28 May 1953	319		4435	Haze Blue	Beige
TD 28026	28 May 1953	320		4436*	Grecian Grey	Brown

*body numbers not confirmed

SPECIALS AND SPECIAL-BODIED CARS

The interior of the Arnolt, here a convertible, was finished to a very high standard, which may have helped to justify the elevated price. Note how the instrument panel is fitted.

batches typically of six chassis with consecutive chassis numbers. They carry a large Arnolt plate under the bonnet, which quotes not only the chassis and engine numbers allocated by MG, but an Arnolt "car number" in a series which runs from 218 to 320, and a four-figure "body serial" which starts with 43 on the coupés and 44 on the convertibles, and go as high as 4367 and 4436 respectively. In addition, the plate carried the paint and trim colours and their ICI and Connolly codes for respectively paint colour and leather.

Around 74 of the 103 Arnolt-MGs are known to survive, and some have been imported to Britain from the late 1980s onwards. A convertible auctioned in the USA in 2010 reached

Under the bonnet of this Arnolt coupé are several interesting extras, including most prominently a supercharger.

KNOWN PAINT COLOURS INCLUDE:	
Colour name	ICI code
Black	253-122
Grecian Grey	222-2141
Haze Blue	222-2168
Ivory	Not known
Larch Green	222-2119
Maroon	Not known
Peacock Blue	222-2013
Post Office Red	253-438
Racing Green	222-2191
Sun Beige	253-186
Sun Bronze	222-2027

$143,000 (say £93,000), which probably gives this car the distinction of being the most expensive Arnolt so far… In 2014 another convertible reached "only" $110,000 (say £67,000) at auction. One car was kept by "Wacky" Arnolt's son until it surfaced on e-bay in 2013 and was sold for $60,500 (nearly £39,000). Much of the information on the Arnolts has come from Terry Sanders, who runs the register for these cars, and I am grateful to Terry for allowing me to reproduce this.

Inskip produced a small leaflet for their four-seater version of the TD.

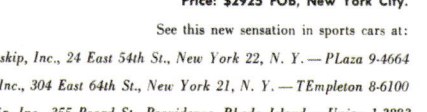

An example of the TD-based four-seater was exhibited on the Inskip stand at the 1953 New York Motor Show. This car has some fancy wheel trims, but no lion mascot.

TD: THE INSKIP AND MOSS CARS

JS Inskip was the MG importer and distributor in New York. The founder, John S Inskip, had originally been in charge of Rolls-Royce's sales office in New York and also ran the Brewster coachbuilding business, which made special-bodied Ford V8s after Rolls-Royce stopped making cars in the USA. When Brewster closed down, Inskip continued under his own name as the Rolls-Royce distributor in New York. In 1948, Inskip took over Motor Sport Inc, originally founded by the Collier brothers, which had imported MGs before and just after the war. Inskip had considerable coachbuilding expertise, and at the New York Motor Show in 1953 launched their version of the MG TD, a lengthened four-seater tourer, perhaps owing to the fact that MG's own YT had just been discontinued.

Dick Knudson, the American MG T-type guru, wrote in 1981 in *M.G.: The Sports Car America Loved First* that there were twelve of these TDs. They all started life as standard cars, but Inskip's coachbuilders cut them in half and added ten inches to the frame and to the body. This created enough room for a rear bench seat in the tonneau with adequate legroom. There were separate bucket seats in front and much wider doors. A chrome flash was added along the side of the bonnet and on to the door. Some had a rather grand lion mascot.

The cars were distinctive and good-looking (at least with the hood down), but they cost $2925 in 1953. They are likely originally to have had disc wheels but two known survivors now have wire wheels. These are TD 23255 EXLNA and TD 26606 EXLNA, the cars seen in photos on many websites since both went through auctions in the early 2000s, with rather varying results.

Moss Motors, originally founded by MG TC owner Al Moss in California in 1948, is one of the leading suppliers of parts for

SPECIALS AND SPECIAL-BODIED CARS

The TD-based pick-up became famous through its association with Al Moss, but here it is in 1954 while still in the original ownership of Richter Motors who converted it. (From News Exchange*)*

The TD-based Le Mans contender was finished to a very high standard. Here, Syd Enever at the wheel demonstrates the high seating positon imposed by the TD chassis. Gathered around him are SV Smith, MG's managing director, unknown, John Thornley of MG, and Vic Oak, Nuffield's technical director. (Photo copyright BMIHT)

MGs and other classic British sports cars, and is equally well established and respected in the UK and Europe. Their famous TD Pick-up was originally commissioned by Roy Richter, a sports car dealer of Bell, California, in 1952, and was put together from two wrecked cars. The frame was lengthened by six inches and a simple steel truck bed was fitted behind the seat. The car was originally painted red.

Al Moss bought it in 1956 and restored it in white, also fitting Borrani wire wheels and a supercharger. He eventually sold the pick-up, which went through several changes of ownership and various modifications before being finally re-purchased by the Moss Motors company. An American enthusiast has constructed a latter-day look-alike (or "tribute"), but this was built on the basis of a 1971 MGB.

A TD FOR LE MANS

George Phillips had managed to impress John Thornley and Syd Enever at Abingdon with his performance at Le Mans in 1949 and 1950 with the TC-based special, and they offered to build a new car for him for the 1951 race. This was based on a TD Mark II chassis, which according to David Knowles in *MG The Untold Story* was TD/C 5336, with engine number XPAG/TD 7710, built around 8 January 1951, although the guarantee plate was only issued on 17 May 1951. Anyway, the project and thus the car were code-named EX.172 on 5 January 1951.

It was fitted with the mildly-tuned Mark II engine and was cloaked in an all-new and very striking aerodynamic body, designed by Enever, quite possibly with an eye on the Gardner record car, EX.135. Since officially the racing ban from 1935 was still in place, work on the car had to be undertaken discreetly, and it was pushed out of the way whenever SV Smith, MG's managing director, paid one of his weekly visits from Cowley. In the end, Enever showed the car both to Smith and to Nuffield's engineering director AV Oak, and obviously got their blessings.

As photographed at Abingdon in 1951, the car appears to have been beautifully finished and was even fitted with hub caps, but these were removed for the race, and extra driving lamps were fitted low down either side of the radiator grille. The main problem with EX.172 was that because of the high and narrow TD chassis, the driver sat perched on top of the chassis side frame member, very high up in the bodywork, with not very much protection against wind and weather from two low aero screens.

It was registered under UMG 400, which was one of the Middlesex registration marks issued through University Motors Ltd, the MG distributor in London, which seems a little odd. If the car was and remained the property of the MG company, one would have expected it to be registered in Berkshire, unless the registration was to camouflage the fact that it was really a works car.

The car was unveiled to the public in *Autosport* on 1 June 1951, not unnaturally in view of the fact the George Phillips had now joined the magazine, which had been launched in August 1950 and where he became chief photographer. The

The interior of UMG 400, with a speedometer possibly from a Y-type saloon. An intriguing detail is the matching rev counter of a style which would otherwise only appear on the TF in 1953. None of the other instruments are of standard MG type. (Photo copyright BMIHT)

When UMG actually got to race at Le Mans, hub caps – and possibly other fripperies – had been dispensed with.

Le Mans race was held on 23-24 June. Phillips's co-driver this time was Alan Rippon.

While EX.172 proved to be good for almost 116mph (186km/h; presumably with a higher final drive ratio than the standard 4.875:1 of the TD Mark II) down the Mulsanne straight, there was apparently a problem with the quality of fuel provided by the Le Mans organisers, which caused pinking. Either due to poor fuel, or because Phillips got a little carried away, is uncertain, but less than a third of the way through the race a valve broke and dropped, holing the piston.

There was some ill-feeling on both sides when Phillips returned to Abingdon; Enever and Thornley thought he had been lead-footed, while he was disgruntled that they could not build an engine just as bullet-proof as the engine he himself had built for the 1950 race. Still, Phillips agreed that the shape of the car was good, and if the driving position could be lowered it might have the makings of a decent car; the rest is history. UMG 400 was photographed at the factory in October 1951 but then disappeared from view. It has been stated that Phillips turned down an offer to buy the car, and although its subsequent fate is not clear it is likely that it was scrapped.

MORE BRITISH TD SPECIALS

T Shipside Limited were Nuffield distributors in Nottingham. In 1950, they built a racing special based on a TD for Bill Shipside's son Ken. This car had a rather different narrowed two-seater body, with an elongated tail and cycle-type wings; it was registered LVO 2, a Nottinghamshire issue of October 1950. It was called "Little John", which was at least better than "Friar Tuck"... This must be the car that Ken raced with some success from 1950 to 1952, with wins or good placings in several club races, mainly at Silverstone and his local track at Gamston Airport.

After its retirement from racing it was rebodied with a fastback coupé body built from aluminium for Ken's father Bill (TW Shipside). It was not a particularly handsome car, even if it has been compared with the Aston Martin DB2 or the Bristol 401; it had rear-hinged doors and there was no external boot access. It was photographed when Mr Shipside visited the Morris factory at Cowley in 1955. It was then claimed to be capable of 105mph (169km/h)!

Some sources have speculated that the coupé was built on a later TF chassis and the registration mark transferred, but the Nuffield Exports magazine *News Exchange* for May 1955 described it as a "TD Special" and referred to Ken Shipside having raced the car. LVO 2 is on the DVLA database as a Blue 1250cc MG registered in February 1951, and apparently the car still exists. One source quotes the engine number as is XPAG/TD 853, which (assuming this is the engine original to the car) would make the car chassis TD 0498 built in January 1950.

Dick Jacobs, well-known racer and MG tuning expert, built

The rather odd-looking coupé which Bill Shipside (seen with the car while on a visit to Cowley) had built on the chassis of son Ken's original racing TD. Not quite Aston Martin shape or Bristol fashion... (From News Exchange; *photos copyright BMIHT)*

a number of special MGs, as described in his book *An MG Experience*. He started in 1949 with a TA-based car, chassis number TA 2161, registered CS 7695, fitted with a lightweight racing body, a blown 1100cc engine based on a Morris Ten unit, and 17in wheels. Jacobs had seven wins with this car over two seasons. This car still exists and is now back on the road after a 50-year lay-up! For 1951, the development department at Abingdon amazingly enough built a very special chassis for Jacobs, with rear suspension similar to the Fiat 1400, combining coil springs with quarter-elliptic springs which functioned as radius arms.

The engine was an XPAG fitted with a supercharger and a Laystall crankshaft which had a shorter stroke of 76mm for 1088cc. A good-looking aluminium racing body was made for the car, which was registered SHK 7. It was not to be as successful as the earlier special, and Jacobs did not get it fully sorted before he was made a generous offer for it. It subsequently went through several hands and is thought to have been in Japan by 2013, when it was allegedly auctioned by the National Tax Authority, according to a post on the internet forum mg-cars.info…

In 1953 Dick's business Mill Garage undertook to build a fibreglass bodied two-seater on a new TD chassis, a car which was registered XNO 2, more or less at the same time that they were building a fibreglass coupé body on the last YB chassis, which was registered XNO 1. The two cars were similar in basic design, but the coupé was arguably better looking, with a more integrated windscreen. Both cars seem to have Morris Minor quarter-lights and door handles, and a one-piece front end hinged at the front to swing up, Triumph Herald style.

Both bodies are believed to have been supplied by Dick Shattock's RGS Automobile Components company, and were similar to other bodies sold by them to various special builders. XNO 2 seems to have disappeared but the Y-type coupé was restored by Stuart Dean in 2006. It is now finished in pastel green rather than the original dark blue, but has lost the XNO 1 registration mark to a Volvo estate. It was unfortunately damaged while racing at the MG Live Silverstone event in 2018.

THE FIBREGLASS BRIGADE

Dick Jacobs was not the only special builder to use the new fibreglass material which had appeared after World War Two. It was rapidly adopted as a cheap and convenient way of making sports car bodywork, starting with the American Glasspar in 1949. The Chevrolet Corvette of 1953 was the first car from a major car maker which used the new material, followed by Jensen in the UK in 1954. Many small specialists both in the USA and the UK made fibreglass sports car bodies to be fitted to a variety of chassis.

Most such bodies in the UK were intended for fitting to old Austin Seven or Ford Eight/Ten chassis, but some were inevitably fitted to MG chassis as well, including as we have seen the RGS bodies used by Jacobs. Some MGs also ended

Dick Jacobs's special MG of 1951 clearly featured front suspension and steering much like the TD, but had an otherwise very special chassis with Fiat-like rear suspension, apparently developed at Abingdon.

up with Rochdale bodies, including a TA registered ENY 242. There were however rather more makers of such special bodies in the USA, and at least one in Australia.

In California, the one-off fibreglass bodied Hawk special based on a TD was a close copy of the Motto (previously discussed) even to the extent of having an identical "MG TD Sport Speciale" badge fitted. The original TD on which the Hawk was based was driven by Cary Grant in the 1952 film *Monkey Business* directed by Howard Hawks, who then gave it to his son David. As David had set his heart on a Ferrari, he was none too impressed, but eventually they settled on a compromise: having a Ferrari-like Barchetta body made for it with the help of Dad's film studio.

The car ended up in Gene Ponder's MG collection, where it was restored to the original Romany Red colour, with tan leather interior and special carpets incorporating the Hawk MG badge. It is fitted with Borrani wire wheels, an after-

In 1953 Jacobs built this car for a customer, on a TD chassis, with a fibreglass body from RGS Atalanta. The clumsy windscreen spoilt the overall appearance. Spot the Morris Minor features!

The Hawk special is a looker – not surprisingly as it was more or less copied from the Motto shown earlier – in the typical Ferrari-inspired Italian style of the early 1950s. However, unlike Modena's or Turin's finest, the body is made from fibreglass. The high-set steering wheel betrays the usual problem with TD-based cars, the high chassis.

market wood-rim steering wheel and a Marshall supercharger. When RM Sotheby's auctioned the Ponder collection in 2007, this car sold for $77,000.

Most of the other fibreglass bodies also seem to have come from small Californian specialists. Devin eventually became a car manufacturer in its own right. Bill Devin started in 1954 by building a series of racing cars, using of all things Panhard-Dyna mechanical components in a special chassis and with fibreglass bodywork. A couple of years later the company launched a roadster bodyshell, using a mould taken from an Italian Scaglietti-bodied Ermini sports car. This looked rather like the body, also by Scaglietti, found on the better-known Ferrari Monza.

The trick about the Devin body was that their mould was made up of several interchangeable parts which could be adjusted or combined to make bodies of different sizes and could thus be adapted to many different chassis, of which MG T-types were only one. The bodies typically sold for $295 and became very popular.

In 1951-52, the architect and designer Vale Wright built a fibreglass body for his MG TC which more or less copied the 1948 Cisitalia Spyder, complete with embryo tailfins. The

MG origins were further camouflaged by the car having 15in wheels. The design was taken up by Consolidated Plastics of Danville, California, who apparently continued making similar bodies until about 1958. It was stated the Wright body could also be fitted to Willys and Kaiser chassis.

Another Cisitalia copyist was the company started up by Bill Burke, Roy Kinch, and Mickey Thompson. This was the same Mickey Thompson who in 1960 drove his Challenger 1 at Bonneville at over 400mph, but as it was a one-way run it did not qualify as a World Land Speed Record. At first in 1952 they traded as Atlas, but they renamed the company Allied in 1953. Until about 1955 Allied offered the Swallow coupé and the Falcon roadster, which could be fitted to 94in wheelbase MG TC or TD chassis, but the Allied bodies were also offered for Ford-derived or special chassis with 100in wheelbase.

These bodies were pretty, which is not surprising since the Swallow was a direct copy of Pininfarina's famous 1949 Cisitalia coupé. Burke had actually taken a mould off one of these cars, and the open Falcon was more or less the same thing with the top taken off. In 1953 Burke drove a Swallow coupé with gull-wing doors at Bonneville at 167mph (269km/h), so one presumes that this car did not use MG mechanicals. One Swallow had a Duesenberg engine, and another Swallow body was fitted to a Lincoln-engined Kurtis Kraft 500 chassis. It is estimated there were about 25 Allied bodies made, selling at $685 for the coupé and $585 for the roadster, including all fixtures and fittings.

In Annandale, NSW, Australia, Nat Buchanan, Jock Morgan, and Bruce Maher built a car in 1956-57 with a fibreglass body on an MG TD chassis fitted with a TF engine over-bored to 1466cc and allegedly giving 80bhp. The body looked rather like an Aston Martin DB3S, with the characteristic scallop cut-outs behind the front wheels – in fact Buchanan is said to have taken a mould off an Aston.

This car was very successful in racing and orders came in for replicas, so they ended up making about 80 to 100 bodies before selling off the moulds in 1959 to J & S Fibreglass, who then made another 40 to 50; some sources suggest J & S took over Buchanan's company. Some of the original Buchanan shells were fitted to chassis from MG Y-types, MGAs, or other makes. Buchanan went on to make the Cobra in 1958, a small sports car based on Standard Ten components, but the ground was cut from under this when the Austin-Healey Sprite arrived in Australia.

MG RACERS IN THE USA

The heyday of MG T-types in racing was the 1948-55 period, especially in the USA. Many cars raced here were extensively modified as regards both mechanical components and bodywork. It was fairly common practice to discard the standard body and substitute a lighter and narrower open-wheel racing type, with cycle wings if any. The TC special built by Al Coppel was typical; he was a prolific and successful

Jack Hagemann built this special-bodied TD for Bill David, who raced at Palm Springs in 1952. (From News Exchange*)*

science fiction writer who also raced an OSCA, and later, once, the Jaguar C-type XKC 017.

Bud Hands's car and Ed Light's so-called "Bogus Lotus", since it looked like an early Lotus, were very similar in principle. Bill David's TD, which raced at Palm Springs in 1952, was rather more sophisticated, a two-seater with a round bullet-shaped nose, proper doors and a faired-in headrest for the driver. In fact it was built by Jack Hagemann, a well-known Californian constructor of custom cars and specials. He built other MG specials for Bob Gillespie, Chic Leson and Joe Playan, as well as specials on chassis of other makes.

Then there were Ken Miles's famous MG Specials. English-born Miles had come out to California in 1952 as service manager for Gough Industries in Los Angeles and International Motors, the MG dealership in Hollywood owned by Roger Barlow. He raced a TD before building his

Ken Miles's first TD-engined special made its debut at Pebble Beach in 1953. Note how low it is compared to the standard TD. That is a BRDC badge on the car. Miles, born in Sutton Coldfield and once apprenticed to Wolseley, was proud of his British origins. (From News Exchange*)*

There is actually a TC under the all-enveloping Diedt body of John Edgar's racing car, which was usually driven by Jack McAfee. (From News Exchange*)*

John von Neumann of Competition Motors in California raced this much-modified TD before switching to Porsches. (From News Exchange*)*

first special MGR1 in 1953. It was remarkably successful, with a claimed 14 wins in SCCA races in one season, and Miles went on to build his famous MGR2 or "Flying Shingle" with a very low aerodynamic body on a specially-built tubular space frame. While it still used an MG engine, transmission, and some other components, it was somewhat removed from being an MG. In spite of the limitations imposed by the engine, albeit now of 1466cc, it proved competitive even against the Porsches.

Both cars still exist, and the Flying Shingle appeared at Pebble Beach Concours in 2006. Ken was one of the drivers for the MGA team at Le Mans in 1955. He later worked with Carroll Shelby and Ford, and was killed while testing the Ford J-car sports racing prototype at Riverside Raceway in August 1966.

Charles W Bowen, who worked for Bell Helicopters at Hurst in Texas, had bought a TC, car number TC 7576, in 1949. By 1954, he had rebuilt this into a special race car, with part aluminium, part fibreglass bodywork, and incorporating scrap helicopter tubing and other parts acquired from his employer. He, and at least once his wife Betty, raced the car mainly in Texas, and also did some rallies or time trials. After Bowen's death the family sold the car. It was for many years owned by Joanne Raymond and later by Dan Leonard, who had it restored.

John von Neumann, who set up the dealership Competition Motors in Hollywood, had raced a TC from 1948, and in 1950 had a TD modified for racing. It had an engine bored out to 1500cc which, together with other modifications, resulted in 90bhp. The chassis was lowered, the bodywork modified by Emil Diedt, and the car was fitted with 16in wire wheels. Neumann first raced the car at Pebble Beach in November 1950 and had a number of class wins through 1951. The car was later owned for a time by Al Moss and still exists. Neumann, who was born in Vienna but came to the USA in 1939, later found greater fame by becoming the first Porsche dealer in California.

John Edgar began in 1951 by having his TC fitted with an Italmeccanica supercharger by Ernie McAfee, but by October of the year the car had been modified with an all-enveloping aerodynamic body, possibly by Diedt. It was usually driven by Jack McAfee (no relation to Ernie), had class wins in Californian races during 1951 and 1952, and together with other Californian racing MGs was featured in the Nuffield Exports magazine *News Exchange* in September 1952. It was destroyed in making the film *On the Beach*, based on Nevil Shute's dystopian novel.

Another approach was to make your MG more powerful, and it was common practice to fit superchargers where allowed by race regulations. Some racers took a more radical approach and fitted completely different engines, even if doing so took them out of the normal racing class for their MGs. In the USA several TCs and TDs were converted to the small Ford V8 60 flathead engine in period. Bill Stroppe, owner of the Automotive Research shop in Long Beach, California, fitted a Ford engine in Bill Cramer's TC and raced it during the 1951 season. That car was driven by Phil Hill and Ritchie Ginther. Bob Holbert similarly fitted a V8 in the TD which he raced in 1953-54. He later switched to racing Porsches.

One TC was fitted with an Offenhauser four-cylinder dohc engine which I imagine was the 97cu.in (1.59 litre) size often used in American Midget racers, not the much larger engines favoured for Indy 500 cars. MG-Offenhausers were raced by Bill Lloyd at Bridgehampton (and elsewhere) in 1952 and by David Michaels at Suffolk County AFB on 9 May 1954. I expect it could have been the same car.

In 1952 Bill Stroppe fitted a Willys engine, modified with twin carburettors, in a TD. This was apparently the 2640cc (161.1cu.in) six-cylinder with F-head (i.e. inlet over exhaust valves). According to the October 1952 issue of *Speed Age*

SPECIALS AND SPECIAL-BODIED CARS

This MG Special raced at the Langa-Langa circuit in Kenya. The driver was Colonel RT Grantham, the year was 1952, and it is presumably a TD. (From News Exchange*)*

Peter Gammon's TC-based car LBP 150 was fitted with this ungainly front end in later ownership, here photographed in 1969, but has since been restored. (Courtesy Roly Alcock)

magazine, the car was owned by Mrs Marion Lowe from Santa Cruz, CA. Stroppe drove the car in the Golden Gate Road Race on 31 May 1952 and finished twelfth. Stroppe is better known for his long-term involvement with Lincoln-Mercury, and for racing off-road vehicles. The car was raced by Mrs Lowe herself on a few occasions in 1953. It was undergoing restoration in 2016, at which time it still had the Willys engine fitted.

... AND IN THE UK

In the UK Peter Gammon was one of the most successful drivers of an MG special with his 1948 TC-based car, chassis TC 9561, registered LBP 150. He scored over 25 firsts in many different races in 1952-53, winning the club trophy awarded by *Motor Sport* in the latter year, and then changed to an MG-engined Lotus Mark VI registered UPE 9. In the 1960s to 1970s his TC special was owned by Peter Chapman, by which time it had had a very ugly front end grafted on to it in place of the nicely rounded nose of the original. It was restored by Dave Saunders in the 1990s with a front end more like the original.

Gammon took the engine from LBP 150 and fitted it to UPE 9 for racing, but although UPE 9 still exists, it no longer has the MG TC engine. Apart from the Gammon car, many others of the 110 Lotus Mark VI cars are believed to have had MG engines, as did a few later cars, until the company changed over to Coventry Climax engines from say 1955.

Nothing much seems to be known about the Copgrove special, which from the registration mark KLY 923 appears to be a late TC, registered in London in 1949 or early 1950, although it has been described as a 1945 car, rebuilt at Henley-on-Thames in 1949, possibly by a garage called Copgrove. It is believed to have a 1500cc engine, while the chassis appears to have been lowered, the body is special, and the car sports cycle wings. The dashboard carries a Goodwood racing badge from 1966. In 1994 the car was owned by Leah Cole of Scottsdale, Arizona, and was featured in the Moss Motoring newsletter published by the Moss Group.

Finally, a trio of Irish MG specials. The first was probably the 1949 TC owned by Dr Henry Tinsley of Belfast. In 1950 he had his car fitted with a new lightweight racing body, while the engine was reduced to 1100cc, apparently using a Morris Ten block, and subjected to the usual tuning measures. However when in 1951 the owner acquired a Jaguar XK 120, he put the MG up for sale. Joe Flynn of Dublin raced a TC which looked fairly standard but had been stripped of wings and was fitted with a supercharger; he had wins at Curragh and in the 1952 Ulster Trophy Formula Libre race.

At least once, in the Dungarvan hill-climb in May 1953, Flynn raced against Torrie Large's rebodied single-seater TD; they were respectively second and third in the 1250cc scratch race. Large's car looked quite professional, in the mould of contemporary Formula 1 GP cars, but it does not appear to have been particularly successful in racing.

TF: THE GHIA-MONVISO EVEREST

Some historians now believe that the TF supposedly bodied by Ghia was in fact bodied by Monviso, a coachbuilder that was merged with Ghia in 1955, so it all depends on exactly when the car was (re-)bodied. It was called the "Everest" and carries Everest name plates on each front wing.

It is car number HDB46 5014, which was issued in April 1954, and which (from the car number prefix) apparently left Abingdon as a complete car with left-hand drive, for some reason to North American Specification, and painted grey; the

There is some discussion about whether this car was built by Ghia, or by Monviso as a sub-contractor. It is one of very few special cars on the TF chassis. It was another Michelotti design, and was built for a French company.

speedometer may well be in miles-per-hour, although from the few poor photos I have seen the dials do not appear to be the original TF instruments.

Nothing much seems to be known of the early history of the car. It is believed to have been one of four cars built by Ghia-Monviso to designs of Giovanni Michelotti for a Paris-based company, SAPCAR, together with two Panhards and a modified Renault 4CV. SAPCAR is poorly documented but the letters may stand for Société Anonyme de Paris pour Carrosseries Automobiles ...something. A badge on the car shows the SAPCAR legend above the crest of Paris.

One source claims it was built for Prince Moulay Hassan (later King Hassan II) of Morocco, who is supposed to have given it to a French actress, Etchika Choureau, with whom he had a relationship in the period 1956-61. The Prince was actually in exile in Madagascar from January 1954 to November 1955. The car took part in the Concours d'Élégance at Enghien-les-Bains near Paris on 18 June 1955, when it carried a French number plate 1152 WWO (effectively a dealer or trade plate) and was photographed with another actress, Jacqueline Pierreux.

It was advertised by a Swiss classic car dealer in Geneva in 2007, when it was said to have covered 6300 miles from new, to have been in a museum collection for many years, and to be registered in France. It was said to be original, and while it was finished in a light metallic green (not unlike the MG EX.181 record car), the interior combined dark blue upholstery and trim with bright red carpets. One comment on the French MG Forum website suggests that in 2007 the car was sold to a buyer in Ireland.

Apart from the Everest, according to the Abingdon production statistics there were two TFs supplied in chassis form for the home market in 1954. The production records show that HK1 5271 built in May 1954 was a chassis-only delivery but nothing appears to be known about its bodywork or subsequent fate, and it does not appear to have survived. Then there was 6470 built in July 1954. The production record ledger describe this car as "chassis only", but the guarantee plate issue ledger gives the car number as HDA16 6470, a fully completed RHD car in black, and it does exist as such to this day. I have not found any other car in the records which appears to have been a chassis-only delivery.

BUYING GUIDE

There is usually a good selection of T-types available on the market at any given time. In Britain, the TC was originally sold in the greatest number – more than the TD and TF combined – but since the 1980s when the import wave began the number of TDs and TFs has grown as cars have been repatriated from the USA. There are quite a few TAs in the UK, but this model is rare in other countries, and the TB is a rarity anywhere. I recently discovered that there is a TA in a Chinese museum, but this is a recent import from the USA.

In the USA the TD predominates, the TC and the TF are relatively common, and pre-war models are very scarce. In other countries the numbers of preserved cars are much smaller and most are post-war models.

Since the 1980s there has been a growing tendency for classic cars of the commercially marketable kind (and any T-type is certainly that) to change hands through dealers or at auctions. This perhaps applies especially in those now frequent cases where a car is sold from one country to another. In the 1960s they used to be shipped out of Britain either to the USA or to Europe, but with ups and downs in the exchange rate many have come back across the Atlantic. Many cars from the USA have found new homes in Britain, in Europe – convenient because American TDs and TFs have left-hand drive – and even in Australia, where however they have to be converted to right-hand drive.

As regards private sales, many cars now make an appearance on e-bay and other websites which offer classic cars for sale, and in the many classic car magazines, but it is still worth keeping an eye open for cars advertised in the publications of the MG clubs in the UK, or whichever other country you are in.

With T-types ranging in age from over 60 years for the youngest TF to more than 80 for the oldest TA, it would be too much to expect to find the well-maintained low-mileage all-original one-owner car. Apart from that, few T-types were owned by careful old ladies (although some may have been by vicars!) from new. Any car now coming on to the market is likely to have had some restoration work carried out at some stage. A few cars still seem to turn up in unrestored condition, which is a nice way of saying that they are wrecks.

The most important things to look for are a sound chassis – not rusted, bent or cracked – and an engine which can be rebuilt. If a running engine shows less than 40psi oil pressure when hot, a rebuild is likely to be needed. Almost anything else is available from the T-type spares suppliers. Complete new bodies are available, built-up or in kit form, and virtually any other part can be bought, renovated or remanufactured. Among the major parts which are not available are chassis frames and cylinder blocks.

There is not actually an acute shortage of engines, except for the not very robust MPJG engines fitted originally to the TA models (many of which have been fitted with XPAG engines from later cars). Some specialists at one time bought engines from the Wolseley 4/44 saloon, which used a single-carburettor version of the TD/TF engine and of which 30,000 were made from 1953 to 1956. The cylinder block and crankshaft from the 4/44 can, with a few modifications, be worked into rebuilt XP-engines to MG specification. Still, I guess that the supply of Wolseley engines must by now have dried up, and there are only a few hundred of these cars in existence anyway, which I hope will be preserved.

Any T-type is extremely simple in design and construction. I do not mean that they are crude or unsophisticated – they were in fact very well made – but in common with most MGs built at Abingdon they were largely assembled cars, made up of components and sub-assemblies from many sources and put together in frankly primitive conditions. Therefore the cars had to be simple and, to be honest, they were always built to a price. But this all works to the advantage of the present-day owner or restorer of a T-type; I can think of few other classic sports cars which are as suitable for the enthusiastic amateur restorer working in the garage at home. And because of steadily increasing value, a T-type MG is now a car – unlike plenty of others – which at the end of a restoration project may be worth the time and money that have been spent.

For those enthusiasts who simply want to enjoy the car without having to worry about restoring it, there are perfectly useable cars available. And if work is needed, there are MG specialists or general classic car restorers prepared to undertake it. If possible, try to shop around, or get recommendations from fellow club members.

Not very many T-type owners are now likely to rely solely on the car for their everyday motoring needs – a T-type is for high days and holidays. For limited usage, there is not a great deal to choose between different models. You would not expect to be able to compete with modern cars on performance – the quickest T-type, the TF 1500, has a top speed of perhaps 85mph and will get from 0 to 60mph in

BUYING GUIDE

just over 16 seconds – but you will be able to keep up with modern traffic in most non-motorway conditions. The cars steer and brake well enough, even by modern standards, and your fuel consumption should be on the right side of 30mpg (9 litres per 100km). From the usability point of view, the TD and TF probably have the edge, with more comfortable suspension and roomier cockpits.

Some modifications to original specification are commonplace and are sensible for cars in regular use, to give increased safety, reliability or simply more relaxed driving. Most cars will by now have had their engines adapted to tolerate unleaded fuel. Current catalogues from parts specialists typically include halogen headlamp conversions, alternators, electronic ignition systems, stainless steel exhausts, brake improvements including servos, five-speed gearboxes, higher final drives, modern shock absorbers, electric cooling fans, oil coolers – as well as classic favourites such as aero screens, walnut veneer dashboards and superchargers!

It is up to the individual owner to choose from this cornucopia. For the purist, it is possible to stick with replacement parts to largely original specification. For the T-type owner who wants to go racing, you need to think in terms of smaller wheels, a roll cage and safety harnesses, apart from engine tuning.

It is probably a futile exercise to try to quote actual values of cars, but it seems that since the 1980s good T-types have multiplied a few times in value, and T-types are at the time of writing typically on the market in the bracket between £20,000 and £30,000. The classic car market took a downturn in the early 1990s, but ever since good cars seem to have been going up and up. An interesting development in recent years has been that cars in original condition, even if scruffy and known as "oily rags", have begun to narrow the gap in price to those which have been restored or perhaps sometimes over-restored. Of the different models, it seems that a TF, particularly a TF 1500, is still worth more than a TC or TD, although not perhaps by quite the same margin as used to be the case. Even so, the T-types (and other MGs) remain more affordable than some of their contemporaries.

In the UK, legislation in recent years has perhaps made it more attractive to own and run a classic car, with concessions such as age-related registrations, and exemptions for road tax and even the MoT test for older cars. All the MG T-types benefit from these measures, but owners and restorers would do well to bear in mind that vehicles which are not subject to the MoT test, still have to be in roadworthy condition. Similarly, legislators in many other countries have become increasingly aware of the cultural significance of historic vehicles, and have often introduced some form of concessions which help owners continue to use and enjoy their cars. However, one wonders what will happen over the next 30 or so years; we are told that the British and other Governments intend to ban the sale of new petrol and Diesel-engined vehicles within this time span, and this may have knock-on effects also on the practicality of using historic vehicles.

Nowadays there is an immense amount of material on MGs in general and on T-types in particular on many websites, from clubs, private enthusiasts, parts specialists etc. so you are not likely to be short of leads to further information. Admittedly, some web-based information may disappear from time to time, or go out of date. You can easily access much information simply by googling, and websites of course have links leading to further information.

Rather than list websites or the many commercial parts suppliers, it is sensible here at least to list the major UK clubs, which all have their own premises, and the most important American club catering for these cars, with their contact details:

THE MG CAR CLUB was the first MG club, originally founded in 1930, and has numerous local centres in the UK and abroad, as well as registers for all the different models, including the T-register. The club publishes a monthly magazine, Safety Fast!, and many other useful publications. The main annual rally, MG Live, is traditionally held at Silverstone in June. The club holds the original guarantee plate issue ledgers for all the T-types. The T-register has made these available from the club website – all you need to do is type in the chassis number, and you will get then original engine number and the date the guarantee plate was issued, but not much else.
Kimber House, 12 Cemetery Road, Abingdon,
Oxfordshire OX14 1AS
Tel 01235 555552
Website www.mgcc.co.uk

THE MG OWNERS' CLUB, first founded in 1973, quickly established itself as the largest MG club, and indeed claims to be the largest one-marque club in the world. They publish the monthly magazine Enjoying MG and offer a wide range of practical services to members, including spares. The club states that it has an emphasis on models from the 1950s onwards, but T-type owners will still find much of interest to them.
Octagon House, 1 Over Road, Swavesey,
Cambridge, CB24 4QZ
Tel 01954 231125
Website www.mgownersclub.co.uk

THE MG OCTAGON CAR CLUB will be of particular interest to many T-type owners, since this club, founded in 1969, caters exclusively for pre-1956 MGs and this is reflected in the contents of their *Bulletin*, which appears eleven times a year, and the range of spare parts offered.
Sparkenhoe Business Centre, Southfield Road, Hinckley,
Leicestershire, LE10 1UB
Tel 01455 611746 or 01455 617961 (NB: check website for opening hours)
Website www.mgoctagoncarclub.com

THE NEW ENGLAND MG T-REGISTER does exactly what it says on the tin, even if it now covers all of the USA, not to say North America, while members in all other parts of the world are equally welcome. Founded in 1964, it publishes the magazine Sacred Octagon. Its bi-annual rallies are the "Gatherings of the Faithful", and it has held over 100 of them.
PO Box 1028, Ridgefield, CT, 06877-9028, USA
Website www.nemgtr.org

For further information and email contact addresses, please visit the main club websites. The three British clubs listed will usually all be present at the major classic car shows in the UK, in particular the spring and autumn shows at the National Exhibition Centre, Birmingham.

There are many websites dedicated to MG T-type cars. One which deserves mention is ttypes.org, the website of **The MG T Society**, a UK-based organisation which offers a bimonthly technical publication, **Totally T-Type**, which can be read on-line or downloaded free in pdf form. They also run a T-type database on the website with the ambitious aim of creating a comprehensive online record of the 52,647 T-types made; they were up to over 6000 by mid-2018, and all T-type owners are encouraged to add details and photos of their cars.

Apart from the club magazines, *MG Enthusiast* magazine has been published in the UK since the 1980s and is now produced by Kelsey Publishing. It is available from good newsagents, or on subscription, but can also be obtained in digital form. Clearly this magazine covers all MGs from the 1920s and right up to date, but there will often be articles on T-types.

There is no such thing as a dedicated MG Museum anywhere in the world, and many fine private collections once much admired have been reduced or split up. Still, there is an excellent selection of historic MG cars, of many models from "Old Number One" onwards, in The British Motor Museum (formerly the Heritage Motor Centre) run by the British Motor Industry Heritage Trust at Gaydon, including the important archive which holds major collections of MG material, such as company business records, vehicle production ledgers (from TF onwards), the original Morris Motors and MG photographic archive, and MG literature. There is also a growing archive held by the **MG Car Club** at Abingdon.
British Motor Museum, Banbury Road, Gaydon, Warwick
CV35 0BJ
Tel 01926 641188
Website www.britishmotormuseum.co.uk